READING **BRENDAN**
BEHAN

READING **BRENDAN**
BEHAN

Edited by John McCourt

CORK **c**
u UNIVERSITY
p PRESS

First published in 2019 by
Cork University Press
Youngline Industrial Estate
Pouladuff Road
Togher
Cork T12 HT6V
Ireland

ISBN-978-1-78205-337-8
Printed by Hussar Books in Poland
Typeset by Alison Burns at Studio 10 Design, Cork
Photograph of Brendan Behan © Getty Images

CONTENTS

ABBREVIATIONS

Primary

Confessions   Brendan Behan, *Confessions of an Irish Rebel* (London: Arena, 1990)

CP   Brendan Behan, *The Complete Plays*, Introduced by Alan Simpson (London: Methuen, 2000)

PPI   Brendan Behan, *Poems and a Play in Irish* ed. Proinsias Ní Dhorchaí with an Introduction by Declan Kiberd (Dublin: Gallery Press, 1981)

BB   Brendan Behan, *Borstal Boy* (London: Arrow, 1990)

BBI   Brendan Behan, *Brendan Behan's Island: An Irish sketch-book* with drawings by Paul Hogarth (London: Hutchinson, 1962)

Wake   Brendan Behan, *After the Wake* ed. Peter Fallon (Dublin: O'Brien Press, 1981)

Letters   Brendan Behan, *The Letters of Brendan Behan*, ed. E.H. Mikhail (London: Macmillan, 1992)

Secondary

Brannigan   John Brannigan, *Brendan Behan: Cultural nationalism and the revisionist writer* (Dublin: Four Courts Press, 2014)

CL   Myles na gCopaleen, *Cruiskeen Lawn* column, *Irish Times*

Kearney   Colbert Kearney, *The Writings of Brendan Behan* (Dublin: Gill & Macmillan, 1977)

O'Connor   Ulick O'Connor, *Brendan Behan* (London: Abacus, 1993)

O'Sullivan   Michael O'Sullivan, *Brendan Behan: A life* (Dublin: Blackwater Press, 1997)

NOTES ON CONTRIBUTORS

JOHN BRANNIGAN is Professor of English in University College Dublin. He is the author of *Brendan Behan: Cultural Nationalism and the Revisionist Writer* (2002) and more recently *Archipelagic Modernism: Literature in the Irish and British Isles, 1890-1970* (2015).

MICHAEL G. CRONIN is Lecturer in English at Maynooth University, where he directs the MA in Literatures of Engagement. He is the author of *Impure Thoughts: Sexuality, Catholicism and Literature in Twentieth-Century Ireland* (2012), along with essays on twentieth-century and contemporary Irish fiction and on gender/sexuality politics in Irish culture. His current project is provisionally entitled 'Revolutionary Bodies: Homoeroticism and the political imagination in Irish writing'.

MARIA DiBATTISTA teaches literature and film at Princeton University. Her books include *Imagining Virginia Woolf: An Experiment in Critical Biography* (2008), *Novel Characters: A Genealogy* (2010) and, with co-editor Emily Wittman, two volumes of essays on life-writing: *Cambridge Companion to Autobiography* and *Modernism and Autobiography* (2014). Her latest work, co-authored with Deborah Nord, is *At Home in the World: Women Writers and Public Life, from Austen to the Present*.

PAUL FAGAN is the co-head of the Vienna Centre for Irish Studies and co-founder of the Vienna Irish Studies and Cultural Theories Summer School. He has lectured in modernism, Irish literature, and cultural studies at the Universities of Vienna, Salzburg, and Tromsø. He is co-founder and president of the International Flann O'Brien Society, as well as co-founder and series editor of *The Parish Review: Journal of Flann O'Brien Studies*. Fagan co-edited *Flann O'Brien: Contesting Legacies* with Ruben Borg and Werner Huber, which was listed on the *Irish Times*'s top ten non-fiction books of 2014, and *Flann O'Brien: Problems with Authority* with Borg and John McCourt. His work has been published in *James Joyce Quarterly*, *European Joyce Studies*, *Joyce Studies in Italy*, *Partial Answers*, and *Irish Studies in Europe*, and collections from Syracuse University Press, Palgrave Macmillan, Manchester University Press, Cork University Press, Dalkey Archive Press, and Brill/Rodopi. He is currently working on the edited volumes *Flann O'Brien: Gallows Humour* (with Borg), *Flann O'Brien: Acting Out* (with Dieter Fuchs), and *Irish Modernisms: Gaps, Conjectures, Possibilities* (with John Greaney and Tamara Radak) and is completing a monograph on the Irish literary hoax.

DEREK HAND is a Senior Lecturer and Head of the new School of English in Dublin City University. He is interested in Irish writing in general and has published articles on W.B. Yeats, Elizabeth Bowen, Colum McCann, Molly Keane, Benedict Kiely, Mary Lavin and William Trevor, and on contemporary Irish fiction. He has lectured on Irish writing in the USA, Portugal, Sweden, Singapore, Brazil, Italy, Malaysia and France. The Liffey Press published his book *John Banville: Exploring Fictions* in 2002. He edited a special edition of the *Irish University Review* on John Banville in 2006 and co-edited a special edition of the *Irish University Review* on Benedict Kiely in 2008. He was awarded an IRC Government of Ireland Research Fellowship for 2008–9. His *A History of the Irish Novel: 1665 to the Present* was published by Cambridge University Press in 2011 and has recently come out in paperback. He has co-edited a collection of essays on John McGahern entitled *Assessing a Literary Legacy: Essays on John McGahern* (2019).

MÍCHEÁL MAC CRAITH is a Franciscan priest who spent thirty-four years teaching in the Department of Modern Irish in NUI, Galway. He held the established Chair of Modern Irish from 1997 to 2011. On his retirement he spent six years as guardian of Collegio S. Isidoro in Rome. His interests include contemporary literature in the Irish language, seventeenth-century literature and the Irish diaspora in the early modern period. He has written extensively in these areas. He now lives in the Franciscan House of Studies, Killiney.

JOHN McCOURT is Professor of English literature at the University of Macerata. He is a specialist in Joyce Studies and in nineteenth- and twentieth-century Irish literature. The co-founder of the Trieste Joyce School (1997), he is widely published and best known for *James Joyce: A passionate exile* (2000) and *The Years of Bloom: Joyce in Trieste 1904-1920* (2000). His most recent book is *Writing the Frontier: Anthony Trollope between Britain and Ireland* (2015). He co-edited *Flann O'Brien: Problems with Authority* with Ruben Borg and Paul Fagan for Cork University Press in 2017.

DEIRDRE McMAHON is an Irish Research Council doctoral scholar with the School of English, Drama and Film at University College Dublin. Her PhD thesis title is 'Brendan Behan and European Modernism: A critical reassessment of modernist aesthetics in the writings of Brendan Behan, 1942–64'. The thesis is supervised by Professor John Brannigan. McMahon holds a BA in English, and an MA in Anglo-Irish literature and drama from University College Dublin.

RIÓNA NÍ FHRIGHIL lectures in contemporary Irish-language literature in NUI Galway. She is author of *Briathra, Béithe agus Banfhilí* (2008), a comparative study of the poetry of Nuala Ní Dhomhnaill and Eavan Boland. She compiled a multi-author collection of essays on critical theory and contemporary poetry in Irish called *Filíocht Chomhaimseartha na Gaeilge* (2010). She is also co-editor of the peer-reviewed journal *Léann*. Ríóna was the principal Irish-language researcher on the AHRC-funded project 'The Representation of Jews in Irish Literature'. In 2018 she was awarded substantial research funding under the prestigious Irish Research Council Laureate Award scheme and is Principal Investigator of the project 'Human Rights and Modern Irish Poetry'. She is also co-director of the multidisciplinary project *Aistriú: crossing territories, languages and artforms* which is funded as part of Galway's European Capital of Culture programme (2020).

CLÍONA NÍ RÍORDÁIN is Professor of English at the University Sorbonne Nouvelle-Paris 3, where she teaches Irish literature and translation studies and convenes the master's programme in Irish Studies. She holds degrees from the National University of Ireland and from the universities of Lyons and Paris. Her research interests lie in contemporary Irish poetry, and sociolinguistics. She directs the Irish Studies research group, ERIN. Her most recent publication is the bilingual anthology *Jeune Poésie d'Irlande* (2015), co-edited and translated with Paul Bensimon. At present she is working on a new monograph which explores French influences on the work of the poet Ciaran Carson.

MICHAEL PIERSE is Senior Lecturer in Irish Literature in the School of Arts, English and Languages at Queen's University Belfast. His research explores Irish working-class life and culture, particularly literature, and associated issues of cultural value and community co-creation. Over recent years this research has expanded into new multi-disciplinary themes and international contexts, including the study of festivals and theatre-as-research practices. Pierse has contributed to a range of national and international publications, is author of *Writing Ireland's Working-Class: Dublin after O'Casey* (2011), editor of *A History of Irish Working-Class Writing* (2017), and co-editor of *Rethinking the Irish Diaspora: After the Gathering* (2018) and *Féile Voices at 30* (2018). Current/recent research projects include: a digital humanities crowd-sourced history of the west Belfast festival Féile an Phobail (http://www.feilebelfasthistory.com/); a study of creativity on the margins, including a participatory theatre project (www.creativeinterruptions.com) and a scoping study of untapped archives of northern Irish working-class history and culture (https://pure.qub.ac.uk/portal/en/persons/michael-pierse(f5c650e3-b7a1-492f-b2e2-3744379a6075).html).

READING BRENDAN BEHAN: INTRODUCTION

JOHN McCOURT

In December 2017, what Christie's auctioneers described as 'The literary and personal archive of Brendan Behan' was sold in London, almost unnoticed, for the relatively modest sum of £200,000. Containing 1,500 pages of unseen materials that were held initially by Behan's widow, Beatrice, this is a hugely significant collection that includes, among many other items, an early draft of *Borstal Boy* written in Mountjoy Prison and two further annotated typescripts of the novel. The National Library of Ireland chose not to buy these precious documents, which were sold without earning as much as a mention in Irish newspapers. They were purchased by the Princeton University library where they will be given a safe home and be made accessible to scholars.

Just three years earlier, in 2014, a number of notable events were held to mark the fiftieth anniversary of Behan's death. They included a successful production of *Borstal Boy* at Dublin's Gaiety Theatre; an international conference in Rome, jointly organised and hosted by Barry McCrea of the University of Notre Dame and by the undersigned, then of Università Roma Tre; a primetime showing on RTÉ of Stephen Douds' sensitive and insightful documentary 'Brendan Behan – The Roaring Boy', directed by Maurice Sweeney and presented by Adrian Dunbar; the publication of a special Behan issue of the *Irish University Review*, edited by John Brannigan. Despite the success of each of these ventures, the fiftieth anniversary celebrations and the lack of Irish institutional interest in the Behan archive contrast shockingly with the impact in Ireland and internationally of Behan's death in 1964. His funeral was, famously, one of the largest and most heartfelt that Dublin had ever seen: the city's streets were lined with mourners as thousands of people paid their respects to a celebrated fellow Dubliner who had died far too young, his life cut tragically short at forty-one, because of a fatal combination of neglect, alcoholism and diabetes.

While retaining a place of genuine affection in popular memory, the relatively limited academic and popular celebrations of Behan on the fiftieth anniversary of his death and the somewhat uneven interest his writings have attracted in the years that followed suggest a literary legacy that is not entirely secure. Were it not for John Brannigan's groundbreaking *Brendan Behan: Cultural nationalism and the revisionist writer*, originally published in 2002 and reprinted in 2014, the first twenty years of this century would have yielded no substantial monograph on the author, a sign that, for all his name recognition, Behan's place within the academy remains shaky.

Behan is remembered too often as a hell-raiser rather than as a highly accomplished and successful – if always complex and controversial – bilingual dramatist, novelist and poet. This volume seeks to build on important earlier studies by Ulick O'Connor and Colbert Kearney, among others, as well as on Brannigan's more recent monograph, and hopes to add renewed critical weight to their collective contention that Behan's works deserve a more prominent place in the pantheon of twentieth-century Irish literature and in the canon of European late modernism.

This collection situates Behan as a singular artist who found himself in mid-century among a small coterie of Irish writers attempting to deal with the dull, even dour, aftermath of the previous, more heroic age of Irish twentieth-century history. This was a narrow, inward-looking age of disappointment and anti-climax that failed to deliver on the promise of the early decades of the century; as Behan has the lag Dunlavin put it in *The Quare Fellow*: 'the Free State didn't change anything more than the badges in the warders' caps' (*CP*, 59). This volume associates Behan with his great Dublin predecessors Joyce and O'Casey, who, like him, made ample use of the city's popular culture in their works, but, also links him with near contemporaries, such as Máirtín Ó Cadhain and Flann O'Brien. It also pays prominent attention to his formative time across the water, to his links with English theatre directors such as Joan

Littlewood, as well as to his engagement with politics and popular culture on both sides of the Irish Sea. These variegated connections make Behan a unique, if initially unlikely, bridge between the two countries and cultures.

Perhaps partly because his early political beliefs were so forcefully challenged in Britain, there was an inevitability about his feeling at sea in mid-century Dublin, despite his belonging to a colourful, lively but very small bohemian circle. He was uncomfortable among the majority of his literary peers and for the most part alienated from the rural aesthetic that reigned supreme in Irish letters in these years, as he explained to a correspondent in 1951:

> Cultural activity in present-day Dublin is largely agricultural. They write mostly about their hungry bogs and the great scarcity of crumpet. I am a city rat. Joyce is dead and O'Casey is in Devon. The people writing here now have as much interest for me as an epic poet in Finnish or a Lapland novelist.[1]

Against this background, Behan found himself attempting, almost single-handedly, to give voice to the Dublin working class and to Dublin republicanism but also straining to represent a working class that transcended nationalism, and finally to write within the umbrella of a modernist or late modernist European aesthetic. His modernist credentials were bolstered through his spells in Paris, where he forged literary friendships with Samuel Beckett, Albert Camus, Jean-Paul Sartre and Simone de Beauvoir, among others.

There is little doubt that Behan's resistance to any neat pigeonholing, his capacity to transcend boundaries and limits, hindered rather than helped the long-term cause of his own writing. His at times outrageous lifestyle may have fuelled his immediate celebrity but it too distracted and detracted from the building of a more durable legacy. Behan left behind him a trail of reputations that dwarfed his literary output and he was often seen as a jack of too many trades, not all of them profitable, popular or even reputable. Thus, with monotonous regularity, we have Behan the boozer; the dyed-in-the-wool Dubliner; the character; the chancer; the house-painter; the 'drinker with a writing problem'[2]; the untimely and sporadically repentant IRA terrorist; the loud-mouthed Irish republican; the stage-Irishman; the singer; the entertainer; the raconteur; the internal exile; the brawler and lout. All of the labels listed point to the complexity and humanity of the man but they also obscure much of the humour, humanity, insight, artistic inventiveness, polemics and politics of his more successful writings.

To be sure, the elements that rendered him an outsider in Ireland – his working-class background and socialist beliefs, his bisexuality, his involvement in acts of republican terrorism at a time when it was neither profitable nor popular, and his disdain for what Brannigan calls 'institutionalized and sanitized nationalism' (*Brannigan*, 87) – all contributed to obstructing a more nuanced critical appraisal of his writings. Equally challenging to the mainstream was his desire to put groundbreaking (in terms of both content and form) avant-garde theatre on the Irish stage at a time when it was largely dominated by conventional social realism. All these elements worked against his acceptance in the theatrical, cultural, political and academic mainstream.

And yet, as John Jordan succinctly put it when taking issue with those who tried to wish away Behan's controversial sides, he was the sum of all of his parts and they all have to be kept in mind when reading his work:

> If Brendan had not been an alcoholic, if he had not been sexually bent, if he had not been a jailbird, if he had not been a republican, and so on, he would have been a great writer. A great writer of what? I suggest that he was not a great writer, but only a very good one, with glaring faults. But the work of any writer is what it is because of the nature of the man. Dismiss Behan completely, rather than dream up an hypothesis.[3]

Augustine Martin approached the problem differently when he wrote in 1963 (the year before Behan died) about the manner in which Behan's personality obstructed critical appreciation:

> Brendan Behan does not invite critical comment on his work. The whole character of the man discourages it. The public image that he has created is so tremendously alive and exuberant that one is inclined to regard the writing as a mere casual offshoot of his rollicking personality. As if, in fact, the work was there as an excuse to display the man. Again one feels a little silly in treating his work with more attention and respect than he allows it himself.[4]

In claiming that Behan's character discouraged critical comment on his work, Martin was perhaps underestimating Behan's own respect for his craft and in any case the critic today works at a safer distance from what was, at the time, an almost overwhelming myth. Now it is easier to put the cult of Behan's personality in its place but also to acknowledge that Behan was not the best judge of his own work. He was, rather, a writer often rattled by his creative insecurity and fragility. As he told Iain Hamilton, who had commissioned *Borstal Boy* for Hutchinson: 'We have no proper view of our own work – we think we're James Joyce one minute and plain gobshites the next' (*Letters*, 147). It is the task of the reader and the critic to assert the primacy of the text, to establish a 'proper view' or, better, proper views. This would be rather less difficult if we had all of Behan's works to hand as he intended them. Nothing close to a definitive or a complete edition of his dramatic works is available and probably none is possible given the large gap between what was initially written and what was eventually performed for the stage. For all the notable service that Alan Simpson did Behan, first as director, and later as the co-author or at least as the editor-assembler of the unfinished *Richard's Cork Leg*, his Methuen edition of *The Complete Plays* does not adequately represent its author today. It is an incomplete and rather poorly produced reprint of a 1978 edition containing no critical apparatus, no appendix of difficult (often Hiberno-English) terms, and no index. Furthermore, it offers no real account of how, for example, the text of *Richard's Cork Leg* came to assume the form that it did. We only have Simpson's word that this version represents what Behan would have wanted. Michael Pierse makes effective use of earlier drafts of the play in these pages (and further work will surely be done in this area given that the materials acquired by Princeton include sixteen pages of autograph notes and drafts for the play as well as typescripts of several scenes dictated by Behan). In a similar key in this volume, Deirdre McMahon argues convincingly that Behan's pre-production script of *The Quare Fellow* is 'more progressive' than the final printed version with which we are familiar.

Given the emergence of new manuscript material, it would seem inevitable that further genetic work will take place in the short term, but equally it seems probable that research is also needed to disentangle what we might call Behan's collaborative impulse: the manner in which he allowed his plays to be shaped and finessed by both directors and actors alike, something that is a more standard theatre practice today. Behan's method was not simply a matter of not caring or not being available during rehearsals, it was also evidence of a belief in the collaborative nature of theatre and of how much those who actually gave voice and form to his works on stage could bring to the final artistic product. Yet, the gap between the literary text and the performance text is one that is very difficult for the critic to deal with and of course the 'exact' performance text can never be replicated as it was first presented. In a real sense, Behan's written texts as we have them are more like partial transcripts than fully rendered scripts. As Joan Littlewood commented in a radio interview with regard to *The Hostage*: 'The thing about "The Hostage" was that it changed each night as Brendan put in the news of the day [...]. We played "The Hostage" each night, differently, for what it was worth, each night and didn't particularly bother about what was written down and the tragic thing was that somebody [...] wrote down a very bad travesty of what was very difficult to preserve.'[5]

What remains an incontrovertible fact is that audiences continue to flock to Behan's plays and to plays about him, such as Janet Behan's *Brendan at the Chelsea*, starring Adrian Dunbar as Behan, which had its first production at the Lyric Theatre in Belfast in 2011 before playing in Dublin, London and New York. Equally popular are adaptations of his works, such as Peter Sheridan's successful 2017 stage version of 'The Confirmation Suit' starring Gary Cooke, or *Borstal Boy*. In all of these productions the persona or personality of Behan hovers over and around the drama on stage continuing to belatedly hog the limelight. This constant return of or to the author risks overwhelming the autonomous work that is being performed and seems to bolster Derek Hand's claim in the opening essay in this volume that the 'work has never truly been able to stand on its own: it has always been closely bound by the life of the author'.

While there was much to admire in the popular *Borstal Boy* revival at the Gaiety, audiences tend to forget that this work is an adaptation, albeit a highly successful one by Frank McMahon, of Behan's autobiographical novel of the same name. McMahon's *Borstal Boy*, originally commissioned and then directed by Tomás Mac Anna, became the longest-running play in the history of the Abbey Theatre when it was staged there in 1967 and it went on to win the 1970 Tony Award for Best Play after a long run at the Lyceum Theatre in New York. This adaptation readily equates the protagonist of the drama with Behan himself, thus mixing fiction and fact and, as a result, doing neither the original fiction nor its real-life author full justice. There is also much of McMahon in the work, not least in the decision to put two Behans on stage and to make use of a device that owed much to Brian Friel's staging of Gar Public and Gar Private in his great 1964 success *Philadelphia Here I Come!* In McMahon's version, the older Behan is a sort of Behan Private, looking back not in anger but with irony, and commenting on his own younger self. This mechanism worked extremely well in the Gaiety production, in which the older Behan was played with great empathy and restraint by Gary Lydon, an actor who bears an uncanny resemblance to the writer. Peter Coonan's younger Brendan was arguably less convincing, as was the black and white contrast offered between the idealistic republican youth and the more mature and successful writer who has come to understand that there is more to life than politics and has moved beyond his republican beliefs. This is a convenient over-simplification of Behan's own political convictions. In a sense, however, it is fitting in a stage version that turns a very serious (and entertaining) novel into a very entertaining but perhaps not sufficiently serious play, at times dumbing down the controversial elements of Behan's writing. This is not to slight McMahon's accomplished adaptation but to say that there is more to Behan's original work than what we see on stage (and certainly far more than would have been permissible on a Dublin stage back in the sixties). In the end, the stage *Borstal Boy* is – almost by necessity – a sort of *Borstal Boy* 'lite', which did not and indeed could not fully convey the harsh realities of what was, for Behan, the undoubtedly rich but complex learning experience at Liverpool's Walton Prison and Hollesley Bay. It is high time for a genuinely new *Borstal Boy* production, because there is much in the novel that can speak to the Ireland of today (including its homoerotic elements, brilliantly explored by Michael G. Cronin in this volume).

It is high time also to give Behan's broader theatre canon the airing it deserves. Why, we might well ask, apart from the obvious commercial reasons of cast size and costs, have Behan's major plays *The Quare Fellow* and *The Hostage*, not to mention his excellent and original Irish-language version of the latter, *An Giall*, not become more regularly produced classics of Irish theatre? Abbey productions of *The Quare Fellow*, which premiered magnificently in Alan Simpson and Carolyn Swift's tiny but precious Pike Theatre (an institution the importance of which to Irish and European theatre is incisively illustrated in Deirdre McMahon's essay), were staged in 1956, 1960, 1969 and

1984 – the most recent staging already more than thirty years ago. Since then, the play has been neglected. Why this has happened is not clear, given the almost universal critical appreciation his work initially received. Kenneth Tynan proclaimed that Behan was fulfilling the Irish duty to 'save the English theatre from inarticulate glumness', that the play was a 'supreme dramatic achievement'.[6] Irving Wardle was equally enthusiastic:

> Easily the finest play to come out of Ireland since Seán O'Casey's *The Plough and the Stars*, it has a prodigious richness of language, and an undiscriminating range of human sympathy that extends to the Mountjoy warders as well as to the prisoners; and by ignoring petty targets it rises to a passionately humane attack on the degradation of the prison system itself.[7]

The Hostage has not fared any better. It has not been produced at the Abbey since 1996 and, before that, enjoyed just two productions there, in 1970 and 1981. It was also successfully produced by The Druid Theatre Company in 1987.[8]

The concern, however, of this volume, is not to take issue with the relative paucity of Irish productions of Behan's great plays but rather to study the full span of his writings in both Irish and English. There is space to look not only at his plays, but also to examine his shorter fiction and his poetry with a view to reinvigorating debate about them. Although *Borstal Boy* sometimes plays second fiddle in critical appraisals of Behan to his well-known plays *The Quare Fellow* and *The Hostage*, in this volume it occupies a central place and is shown to function as the core of Behan's entire output. Derek Hand's article, 'Brendan Behan's *Borstal Boy*: The public persona and the delicate art of deceit', sets out the Irish contexts in which Behan wrote but also suggests, problematically, that the chief Irish context for the reception of his works in the country was Behan himself. It seems that little has changed in that regard since the late 1950s and that the Behan persona continues to risk overwhelming an adequate analysis of his works. At the same time, Hand outlines how Behan's works engage in a conscious social commentary of working-class life in Dublin, of the routine of prison life and of the realities of IRA activities, and he situates him, somewhat surprisingly, not with the usual suspects – Patrick Kavanagh and Flann O'Brien – but alongside writers such as O'Connor and Ó Faoláin (who was editor of *The Bell* when Behan's early draft of *Borstal Boy* first appeared there). All of these writers, Behan included, were faced with the difficulty of identifying the proper role for the post-independence Irish writer in a country where clerical and political policing and rigid censorship laws allowed little room for artistic manoeuvre. For writers working in the 1940s and '50s, too many subjects remained off limits and conformist Ireland offered little material to work with. Censors and many readers were unwilling to tolerate subjects that threatened the conservative status quo.

All of this makes the eruption of *Borstal Boy* into print all the more extraordinary, even if it was promptly prohibited and became part of what Behan humorously called 'the best banned in the land' (*O'Sullivan*, 243). Hand argues that Behan's text should be read, straightforwardly enough, as an autobiographical novel in which the author is rehearsing the acquisition of identity. He points to Behan's careful craftsmanship and his attention to structure, even if the author writes as he might speak, his text exhibiting the transformation of the oral anecdote into the realm of literary art. In Hand's reading, Behan's novel shows that 'abstract ideology cannot withstand the pressures of individual acts of kindness'. Thus Brendan is reformed, his ideas of nationality challenged, and his anti-British sentiments softened. Furthermore, he can return home and Ireland can perhaps become for him a location for art and possibility.

Through Brendan, Behan articulates a partial or a tentative reversal of the conclusion of the Irish *Bildungsroman* par excellence, Joyce's *A Portrait of the Artist as a Young Man*, which of course ends with the necessary promise of departure and exile. But it might be argued that Behan also offers a riposte to the generation of O'Connor and Ó Faoláin, who remained in Ireland even if they felt constrained by it. The close of *Borstal Boy* – closely read by several of the critics in this volume – the ambiguous 'It must' response to the question/affirmation which is turned from the original Irish into the English: 'It must be wonderful to be free' (*BB*, 372), suggests the problematic hurdles that lie ahead for Brendan and that lay ahead for Behan, who would seek an alternative path to the definitive exile chosen by Joyce and Beckett and to the internal exile in which figures like Flann O'Brien and Patrick Kavanagh found themselves. Behan's choice would be to make his way as an author in Ireland but also to intermittently take refuge abroad, most prominently in Paris.

The fictional Brendan returns to Ireland armed with experience and with an education and his time is justly seen by Maria DiBattista in her 'Lessons of Detention' as having been hugely formative. She also focuses on *Borstal Boy*, connecting it with what she describes as its 'parental text, Oscar Wilde's *De Profundis*'. She argues in favour of reading *Borstal Boy* as a novel rather than as a memoir or as an autobiography. Detaching the work from the lived experience that helped to generate it is a way of granting it a literary autonomy of its own as part of the Irish tradition of the novel, which places the individual at the centre and privileges the form of the *Bildungsroman* as a way to counter centuries of Irish misrepresentation.

In 'Bohemian Behan: Late modernism, sexual politics and the "Great Awakening" of Brendan Behan', John Brannigan explores Behan's involvement with Irish republicanism and looks at the key roles played by Seán Furlong and Fred May in encouraging Behan to move away from violent republicanism. He too argues for the importance of Behan's unorthodox but efficacious education at Mountjoy and the Curragh and shows how he acquired a command of both the Irish language and Irish writing while incarcerated, thanks to his fellow inmate and Irish language scholar Seán Ó Briain and, later, Máirtín Ó Cadhain, both of whom played an instrumental role in introducing him to works such as Brian Merriman's *Cúirt An Mheán Oíche*, Tomás Ó Criomhthain's *An t-Oileánach*, and the stories of Pádraic Ó Conaire.

After his time in jail, Behan delved into the Bohemian social and cultural circles of both Dublin and Paris in the 1940s; and both impacted decisively on his developing aesthetics. Brannigan shows how Behan's work connects and bears affinities with, among others, that of Joyce, Beckett and Genet. Behan's writings in the late 1940s and early '50s engage in a restless search for appropriate forms for radical and revolutionary cultural politics in the wake of the Second World War. Brannigan refuses to read Behan simply in the light of the Irish situation, preferring instead to draw analogies between his aesthetic and political positions and those of Sartre and Camus and arguing in favour of recovering a French Behan.

Deirdre McMahon expands on this reading and argues strongly in favour of seeing Behan as a modernist writer, exploring similarities between Behan's formal strategies in *Borstal Boy* and those used by Beckett in his novel *Molloy*. She also looks at the significance of Dublin's Pike Theatre as an Irish centre for late modernism (not least through its introduction of *The Quare Fellow* onto the Irish stage). McMahon argues that it would be wrong to take Behan's multifaceted use of form and genre as a sign of indiscipline, and claims instead that Behan repeatedly and deliberately subverts conventions for political purposes. Adopting a strategy that has parallels with *Molloy*, the retrospective nature of *Borstal Boy* allows Behan to create a de-territorialised space in the liminal prison setting. Here he can negotiate an identity that is otherwise beyond the codes and conventions of Irish nationalism. McMahon also argues that Behan presents a vision of a more pluralistic and inclusive society, which includes a redefinition of gender identity beyond the hetero-normative. McMahon explores the irony that Behan not only uses a British prison setting to counter narrow ideologies within Irish nationalism, but that he does so using a very pointedly European modernist form.

Michael G. Cronin also reads Behan's time in prison as vitally formative. In his view, in *Borstal Boy* the reader discovers that incarceration is not necessarily only about punishment. In a rather Wildean paradox, the space of imprisonment becomes, in Behan's novel, a space of unexpected freedom. In Cronin's reading, *Borstal Boy* offers a glimpse of the possibility of homoerotic desire. The novel situates young Brendan's physical desire for his fellow prisoner, Charlie, within a dense web of emotional and affective relations with the other boys. The initial acknowledgement and the later expression of a sexual need paves the way for a whole gamut of unmet emotional yearnings and desires that might, almost bizarrely, be more forcefully policed outside of prison than they are within.

Ríona Ní Fhrighil attests to the importance of Behan's poetry in the Irish language, showing how the author reimagined older Gaelic poetic forms in order to better explore contemporary themes and to develop a modern lyric mode in Irish. She refutes the assumption that Behan's Irish-language poetry represents a merely transitory phase in his creative development or that it was principally motivated by politics. She comments on Behan's only overtly republican poem, 'The Return of McCaughey' ('Filleadh Mhic Eachaidh'), an elegy to the IRA leader Seán McCaughey who died on hunger strike in Portlaoise Prison in 1946 and sees it, following Kearney, as a partial re-elaboration of Liam Dall Ó hIfearnáin's 1760 poem 'A Phádraig na nÁrann'. Ní Fhrighil argues winningly, and to some extent following Barry McCrea, for the bilingual nature of Behan's imagination that never expressed itself exclusively or fully in either English or Irish.

Clíona Ní Ríordáin and Mícheál Mac Craith also both focus on Behan's bilingualism and in particular on his most important Irish-language play, *An Giall*. Ní Ríordáin addresses the issue of whether *The Hostage* should be considered as a translation, an adaptation or as a recreation of *An Giall*. She focuses on the self-translational element in the passage of the text from its first embodiment as a work in Irish for Dublin's Damer Theatre, before its recomposition in English as a profoundly different text for production at London's Theatre Royal. Comparing Behan's versions to similar self-translations carried out by Beckett, Nabokov, and Elie Wiesel, among others, she argues against attempting to give precedence to one text or the other or to one language over the other while also pointing out that it is correct to view *The Hostage* as a co-authored text in itself, rather than as an 'othered' version of *An Giall*.

Having outlined some of the criticism that focused on attempting to impose a hierarchical rating for *An Giall* versus *The Hostage*, Mícheál Mac Craith seeks to move beyond such sterile argument (while still putting the case for a new English translation of *An Giall*).[9] He doubts the usefulness of returning to the regularly trotted out claim that Frank O'Connor's short story 'Guests of the Nation' (1931) may be the source of Behan's play and provides an eloquent example of the benefits of expanding the contexts in which Behan can be read by focusing on the similarities between Behan's play and Elie Wiesel's *Dawn*. What emerges from interventions such as Mac Craith's is that Behan's relevance and resonance can be better appreciated by taking him out of an exclusively Irish literary and political setting and setting him loose in the bigger fields of European and world letters to which he aspired to belong.

My own essay, entitled '"Not Exactly Patterned in the Same Mould": Behan's Joyce', explores the powerful influence of James Joyce, both as a chronicler of Dublin and as an Irish modernist, on Behan. It shows how carefully and sympathetically the younger writer read Joyce's works and focuses on Behan's incisive but somewhat rambling 1962 New York talk on Joyce. Behan's lecture assesses the importance of Joyce as a rare precursor who wrote about Dublin and it is testimony to the extent to which Behan engaged with his older counterpart and followed with both surprise and interest Joyce's growing international acclaim.

Paul Fagan explores the interrelated fates of Brian O'Nolan and Brendan Behan and examines Behan's treatment at the hands of the writer who is increasingly seen as the final member of a great Irish modernist trinity, with Joyce and Beckett. Most of O'Nolan's articles about Behan tend to be written under his Myles na gCopaleen pseudonym in his long-running *Irish Times* column *Cruiskeen Lawn*. Not surprisingly, the column, written by the self-proclaimed 'most important and influential man in the town next to Brendan Behan',[10] provides an ambivalent but always witty take on the 'intimate and awkward', close but competitive, personal and literary relationship between Myles and Brendan. Myles' view is shown to have been jaundiced at times, perhaps by his discomfort at Behan's rapidly rising fame, which contrasted with his own deepening disappointment and frustration. Myles is also seen regularly attempting to prise Behan back from the claws of the European avant-garde with Beckett representing the Irish tip of the continental modernist iceberg.

Michael Pierse, in his 'Behan's Graveyard of Radical Possibility: *Richard's Cork Leg* and the (Irish-) American dream', focuses on Behan's last, posthumous and perhaps most problematic work. Although the play enjoyed some initial commercial success, it has, with some justification, endured a problematic critical reception. Pierse does not dispute the criticism that has come its way but notes that, despite its obvious faults, *Richard's Cork Leg* also offers glimpses of Behan at his best. He claims that Behan was tantalisingly close to creating something that might have reached the heights of *The Quare Fellow* or *The Hostage* and that extant fragments of the play held at the National Library of Ireland suggest possibilities for a more successful future production.[11] Behan's focus on the 'graveyard', which signals the conjunction of a narrow-minded Irish nationalism (as represented by the Blueshirts of the play) and a reifying American consumerism (as represented by Forest Lawn's commercialisation of death), is both paradoxical and illuminating. If Irish nationalism is shown to be keen to refashion its radical past to suit a stiflingly conformist present, American consumerism is seen to be busy promoting the apparently liberating yet ultimately illusory optimism of the American Dream, which, like Forest Lawn's 'happy Eternal life' (*CP*, 261), suggests an idea of heaven purchasable in hard cash. In Pierse's view, Behan's depictions of how both the Irish and American cultures 'sell' empty illusions – in this case, death – ultimately reveal a barren vision of life, in which the disenfranchised remain disenfranchised and even silenced.

Collectively, these essays by a diverse international group of leading literary scholars and critics shed much new light on the relatively small but profoundly significant body of writings by Brendan Behan. While engaging in much close reading, the essays also interconnect and engage with many fields of criticism, among them cultural studies, theatre studies, translation and comparative studies, post-colonial theory, queer theory and reception studies. It is hoped that they will collectively invigorate scholarly interest in Behan's writings in Irish and English and renew critical appraisal of one of Ireland's funniest, trickiest and, at the same time, most serious experimental writers.

1

BRENDAN BEHAN'S *BORSTAL BOY*: THE PUBLIC PERSONA AND THE DELICATE ART OF DECEIT

DEREK HAND

Brendan Behan's writing and career, as one of the first generation to inherit the post-independence space within Ireland, encapsulates the contradictions and the tensions inherent within a state emerging into the possibilities of the post-Second World War international scene. As a poet, playwright, short-story writer, novelist and memoirist, moving uneasily between the English and the Irish languages, he looks backward to traditional forms while simultaneously looking forward into uncharted territory. His literary output registers this in-between position, with references to ballads, poetry and well-told and honed stories, while formally oscillating between the (seemingly) haphazardly improvised nature of the plays and the more highly wrought work on display in short stories like 'The Confirmation Suit' and a novel such as *Borstal Boy* (1958). His writing situates itself on the line between artifice and anecdote, between the realm of literary gravity and the immediacy of the bar room quip. Indeed, the 'talk books' that make up the tail end of his career in many ways materially embody and manifest that anxious space. Of course, what is also confusing for the reader is how this work has never truly been able to stand on its own; it has always been closely bound by the life of the author. Behan's own life on the streets of Dublin's northside, his republican politics and his prison experiences are the source of much of the material for his writing. There is nothing unusual in this; that same autobiographical impulse underpins a great deal of Irish prose writing in the twentieth century, from James Joyce to John McGahern and Edna O'Brien. Unlike those writers, however, Behan is a figure – somewhat similarly to Oscar Wilde before him – who moved consciously between the life and the work, between the genius of creating a persona and the talent of his writing. Thus the boundary between what is inside and outside the text is blurred and made indistinct as art and life become interchangeable. In Behan's case the art has been overshadowed by the persona to the extent that one of the main difficulties for the literary critic in coming to his work has been to try and view the art precisely as art and not merely as an extension of his personality.

From the moment of its publication in 1958 readers of Brendan Behan's *Borstal Boy* have dealt with the problem of adequately locating the work within his *oeuvre*. Contemporary reviews suggest a reception of a book that already possessed a context in which it could be read and understood – that of Behan himself:

> I can't think of anyone I would rather share a cell with than Brendan Behan in spite of the noise. Lively, generous, imaginative, and consistently cheerful, I would expect him to give out a sustained glow of euphoria like a sun-ray lamp of emotions.[1]

It can be forgotten how, by the time of this book's publication, Behan was a hugely successful and famous writer in Ireland and abroad, especially in Britain. *The Quare Fellow* had made his name and his reputation in theatre and now *Borstal Boy*, as another prison story, confirmed that reputation in prose. Reviews mostly read the book as straightforward autobiography, detailing Behan's time in a British borstal after being arrested on an IRA mission to bomb the Liverpool docks in 1939. One way of viewing *Borstal Boy* is as something of an addendum, or supplement, to *The Quare Fellow*, giving background to Behan's knowledge of prison life and furthering his critique of the institutionalisation of punishment in the twentieth century. When we consider *Borstal Boy* and *The Quare Fellow* as embedded in the 1950s culture out of which they emerged, what we discern is that an element of their appeal lies in their conscious positioning as social commentary, and Behan's status as articulate, perhaps even reformed, insider can only add to this attraction. His, then, is a rendering of that world, replete with the whiff of sulphur coming from the descriptions of the routine of everyday prison life and the frisson of the authentic in the deployment of working-class slang and prison argot. *Borstal Boy* thus fits in with the trend in the 1950s and '60s for the realism of the 'kitchen sink drama' which, in this instance, even with the absence of the sink, presents a gritty, realistic world in the company of petty thieves and ne'er-do-wells.

In Ireland this role of social commentator is given another added twist because of Behan's republicanism and his imprisonment for IRA activities. An early draft of *Borstal Boy* was published in 1942 in the literary magazine *The Bell*, as 'I Became a Borstal Boy',[2] and was a contribution to that journal's mission to bring voices not being heard in post-independence Ireland to notice. When published, Behan himself was in prison again, this time in Ireland for IRA activities and membership. Thus for *The Bell* IRA republicanism in the 1940s is one more ideology and identity – along with 'Gentile or Jew, Protestant or Catholic, priest or layman, Big House or Small House'[3] – that is, part of the intellectual and cultural mix open to scrutiny, comment and critique. Ironically, on the publication of *Borstal Boy* in 1958, dealing with events of nearly twenty years previously, Behan and 'Brendan's'[4] story of historical IRA activities was once again thoroughly newsworthy, as the IRA was involved in a campaign of bombing border areas (1956–62). This Irish context meant that Behan's autobiographical novel could be read within the Irish nationalist tradition of prison literature and, as the *Irish Times* reviewer noted, that Behan himself could engage in his work in an extended critique of that same nationalist political tradition that put him in prison in the first place.[5] What in Britain is a gritty realistic story, with a modicum of comedy, becomes a potentially tragic dialogue about identity and politics in Ireland. Absent from this early Irish response, though, is an acknowledgement of the subtleties and the nuances of Brendan's politics in the text. Indeed, that lack persists into much of the subsequent literary criticism of the novel.

What is also mostly missing from the critical evaluation is any attempt to place and consider Behan's *Borstal Boy* in relation to Irish writing of that period, save for the usual focus on the personalities of Behan in relation to writers like Patrick Kavanagh and Flann O'Brien. Beginning to contextualise the text in this way can open some productive avenues for understanding the nature of Behan's autobiographical novel. An astute contemporary review by novelist and short-story writer Frank O'Connor recognises the dangers inherent in confusing Behan with Brendan, and the danger of the work and the life becoming muddled:

> Behan is not the only young Irish writer who has been forced into violent exhibitions of nonconformity, and I am afraid that his mannerisms may grow in him and overlay the quality in him that makes *Borstal Boy* important.[6]

At an unconscious level, perhaps, O'Connor is giving voice here to the dilemma of the post-independence Irish writer, himself included, of what exactly the role of the artist ought to be in this New Ireland. It would appear that to write is not enough and to create lasting art is nothing without an attendant public function that promotes the art and is in critical conversation with it. For Behan's generation and indeed for the generation of writers led by O'Connor and Ó Faoláin (who was editor of *The Bell* when Behan's early draft of *Borstal Boy* first appeared there), the difficulty lay in finding a proper and a productive connection with one's readership/audience. After the glories achieved by writers such as W.B. Yeats, James Joyce and Seán O'Casey, not only had the generation who came after them to contend with the anxieties of literary influence but they also had to re-imagine their relationship with the community, and with the idea of the nation. While the national question still remained to trouble the artist as it always had, it perhaps was no longer as easy, or even desirable, to attach oneself to the notion of nation in the ways in which the literary revivalists had earlier done. At the end of his life Yeats could declare that 'I am no Nationalist, except in Ireland for passing reasons; State and Nation are the work of intellect.'[7] Being close to death Yeats is orienting himself towards the future, a future that he will not inhabit himself. He is signalling to those who will come after him that the role of the artist in Irish life is about to change or has to change.

It is this altered landscape that writers like O'Connor and Ó Faoláin inhabited in the 1940s. Their reaction to it would influence Irish cultural life for the next generation and it can be argued that they set out the issues and concerns that those who came after them would have to deal with. They saw their role as one of critiquing post-independence Irish society, of opening up the world of the post-revolutionary period to scrutiny. Thus they both moved between the realm of the aesthetic and that of social commentary and felt compelled to wed their aesthetic theories to a wider critique of Irish society and the stagnation of Ireland when compared to the modernity of, as they saw it, everywhere else. It can be argued that their quarrel is not with any aesthetic notion of what the written word can or cannot do; rather theirs is a quarrel with Ireland itself and with its lack of societal depth and normality. O'Connor's 1942 essay 'The Future of Irish Literature' suggests a bleak future for Irish writing because the writer is being denied the opportunity to compose a necessary and 'fundamental quarrel with his material'.[8] The certainty of the past, even in its uncertainty, offered Yeats and his Revivalist contemporaries the opportunity of a conflict to work with and work against. For O'Connor there is no such conflict and the cultural apparatus of the state, particularly censorship, makes the writer irrelevant and invisible. He ends by saying that the Irish writer 'must be prepared to come into the open'.[9] Later in 1949, Seán Ó Faoláin similarly complained that everyday Irish life was a debilitatingly unexciting one for the Irish fiction writer:

> Our sins are tawdry, our virtues childlike, our revolts desultory and brief, our submissions formal and frequent. In Ireland a policeman's lot is a supremely happy one. God smiles, the priest beams, and the novelist groans.[10]

For Ó Faoláin it appears that Ireland offers the would-be novelist no suitable material to work with, or to stand in opposition to; that the Irish world is far too fixed and far too rigidly conformist.

Ó Faoláin's comments and his various activities at this time – journalist, critic, man of letters – suggest a variety of roles he might choose to play. Here, for instance, his argument is not with the novel form itself, its aesthetic possibilities or impossibilities in an Irish setting; rather his criticism is with Irish reality and its supposed lack of development into modernity. He is acting the part of social critic, of public commentator, rather than simply artist.[11] One consequence is that the major shift in Irish writing – and it still remains prevalent today – is towards acts of revelation and exposure. Indeed, his involvement in *The Bell*, the monthly literary and cultural journal published between 1940 and 1954, is an extension of the public role of the liberal intellectual, bringing a searing light into the dark recesses of Irish life and culture. Thus realism became the dominant aesthetic mode best suited to exposure in Irish writing. Some literary critics have a problem with realism/naturalism being so central to Irish twentieth-century writing,[12] but they singularly fail to acknowledge this basic desire to tell stories that had not been told before, to get at the real beneath the veneer of official Ireland. What is also missed by these critics is how these writers reflected the palpable shifts in wider culture by moving their focus away from the travails of the nation – as evidenced in the historical fictions of this period – towards the sovereignty of the individual. And yet, this moment is also marked by a profound tension between the demands, and indeed the rights, of the individual in the context of a wider society. All commentators acknowledge that this era is one of social revolution, when governments and policy-makers began to enact changes in the way in which different sections of society should be treated. This is a time when people believed that there was such a thing as society and that its betterment was an achievable end.[13] The effect on the novel is that rather than dealing with a singular hidden Ireland, its proper focus is now multiplied and it is hidden Irelands and individuals, who escape traditional labels and stereotyping, that are now the proper object of the novel, or ought to be.

The literary space afforded a writer like Brendan Behan in the 1940s and '50s is quite narrow and proscribed. The possibility of the grand gesture or the grand thought which had seemed appropriate, perhaps even an obligation, for Yeats and his generation was now no longer possible in either art or life. Now Ireland's reality seems to be such a mean and backward one that any lingering energies or radical potential generated in the immediate aftermath of independence is utterly dissipated. Perhaps it is this constricted space that leads to the extravagant and larger-than-life nature of Behan's public persona, along with those of Kavanagh and Flann O'Brien. In Behan's case this is fuelled not so much by alcohol but by a savage indignation at being seriously pigeonholed by the likes of O'Connor and Ó Faoláin and thereby destined to be profoundly misunderstood in the one place where he wants desperately to be understood: his home place. While the 'broth of a boy' image is the one most remembered today, it is not the only role that Behan adopted. His literary roles are many and varied. Moving between the Irish and the English languages, he is a poet in the Irish language, a playwright, a novelist and a short-story writer. It could be said, too, that at one level all these roles cause him no anxiety in that he excels at all of them.

Borstal Boy, as a *Bildungsroman*, is of course a story of development, of be-coming. If, as has been argued, the story of the individual becomes paramount in the literature of twentieth-century Ireland then it ought to follow that the only story to tell is the story of the birth or development of that singular self. All fiction, from *Don Quixote* onwards, flirts with the boundaries between the real and the invented, and in twentieth-century Ireland the novel form increasingly becomes closely linked to realism and its variants. Ireland is not a place of fictional invention, the made-up plot appears impossible and only the stuff of life itself will have the tone of authenticity that might hold a reader's attention; anything else will look like an imposed or convenient compromise. It suggests, though, that the story of the self is the only important story to be told and perhaps, indeed, the *only* story that it is possible to tell. Autobiog-raphy was one means by which the earlier revivalist generation could come to know themselves, precisely as themselves,[14] and this is accentuated in the pro-liferation of personalised fiction as noted in the prose work of contemporaries of Behan's such as John McGahern, Edna O'Brien and Patrick Kavanagh.

In *Borstal Boy* then, as an autobiographical novel, it can be argued that Behan is simply rehearsing the acquisition of identity. When considered in this way it can be seen how structured the work actually is. All readers can be bewitched by the bravura linguistic performance of 'Brendan' in the book: Behan writes as he might speak. That playfulness with the oral realm encap-sulates all the anxieties and energies between the personality and the art of Behan. The text possesses the vitality of the anecdote and its immediacy, and yet that oral world is translated into the realm of writing and literary art. The constructedness of the text can be overlooked, although early critics such as Colbert Kearney and Corey Phelps[15] are at pains to demonstrate the labour and the artifice of the finished work, arguing convincingly how Behan altered various versions and drafts from 1942 onwards before finally publishing the work in 1958. Richard Brown also suggests that there is a very clear tripartite structure to the novel; everything happens three times in different ways in order to show the reader the development of Brendan's relationship to his Irish politics.[16] This *Bildungsroman* occurs neither in the domestic space nor on the streets of a city – the usual locations for growth and discovery – but in the confines of the prison space it envelops the spheres of both the public and private, so that Brendan's personal development is constantly being tested in his relationship not only to himself but to others. Edward Said famously argued that the colonial space is always encountered institutionally in the guise, for instance, of the school.[17] The prison, as the manifestation of state law and the site of punishment and correction, is a place that allows for the colonial experience to come to the fore. In spite of the location, Brendan, on the surface at least, following the template of a traditional *Bildungsroman*, does come to learn the classic liberal lessons of the world. After being caught on a bombing mission for the IRA in Liverpool, the teenager spends time in three types of penal institution, finally ending up in a borstal for young offenders. The journey he undertakes is one from incarceration to freedom, registered not only in the spaces he inhabits, from cell to open farm prison, but also in his burgeoning social interaction with other prisoners.

Cultural critic and journalist Fintan O'Toole has recently read Behan's *Borstal Boy* as a classic *Bildungsroman* in that he suggests that what Brendan learns within the British penal system is the humanity not only of the individual British person, but also the liberal humanity inherent within the modern British state:

> These were not holiday camps, but they were reasonably enlightened institutions with an emphasis on rehabilitation – a good deal safer and more decent than their industrial-school equivalents back home in dear old Ireland. And this is the great drama of *Borstal Boy*. It captures the mind of a child terrorist trying to cope with the shock of kindness. The evil enemy refuses to behave with appropriate cruelty.[18]

Despite O'Toole spectacularly confusing the myth of the man with the artist, as so many had done before him, there is undoubtedly a truth to this interpretation. The key to it is in understanding the essential emphasis on the 'liberal' which O'Toole makes in his argument. O'Toole suggests that in the modern moment the *only* lessons to be learned are liberal ones; no other ideas or ideologies are permitted. Thus, issues of nationality or exposing the power plays inherent in colonialism are to be left behind as the future of a common and shared humanity are embraced. The *Bildungsroman* genre amplifies this, as it has always been primarily a genre that allows for the bourgeois individual to emerge into view and take his or her place in the modern world. Education is the key to the *Bildungsroman* and so characters become refined in their manners and their morals. Brendan's terrorism, in O'Toole's estimation, is undone when he learns that the ideas that underpinned his actions are out-moded and, ultimately, if we take the argument to its logical conclusion, not genteel enough. Brendan's republican ideals are tested as he is forced to question his actions and their worth. Abstract ideology cannot withstand the pressures of individual acts of kindness, and the enlightenment of a borstal penal system that embraces the possibility of reform. His hatred is conse-quently neutered and dissipates. This reading is staggering in its simplicity and the ways in which it reinscribes the hoariest of stereotypes about Ireland and Irishness. It is only Brendan who must learn in this scenario; he must learn about kindness and come to recognise that the real revelation is that there is common cause between Britain and Ireland, indeed between Ireland and the world. Questions of nationality fall away when each of his prison mates can be said to be 'chums':

> I had the same rearing as most of them, Dublin, Liverpool, Manchester, Glasgow, London. All our mothers had done the pawn – pledging on Monday, releasing on Saturday. We all knew the chip shop and the picture house and the four-penny rush of a Saturday afternoon, and the summer swimming in the canal and being chased along the railways by the cops. (*BB*, 232)

Amid the world of prison (even in the edenic borstal) and its reality of con-finement and punishment, there exists a notion of a paradise where difference melts away. This vision of shared cause and common humanity is also present in *The Quare Fellow*, where prisoners and guards are bound to each other in more ways than they would care to admit as each plays their allotted role in the master–slave dichotomy. But, as in that play where boundaries crumble when an Irish-speaking prisoner and guard from the same townland in Kerry share a clandestine conversation, *Borstal Boy* does more than simply register a utopian sense of universal brotherhood.

If it is accepted that Brendan's politics are put under pressure as he learns about the reality of the lives of those people that he would happily have blown to bits on the Liverpool docks, it is also fair to argue that something radical still remains. He *does* learn something in prison, though not simply the liberal lessons of life. *Borstal Boy* is a mish-mash of varying styles and registers: song, poem, personal anecdote, history and literary criticism of sorts. All vie for attention, if not exactly dominance in the narrative. Behan wants to acknowledge the various influences on his version of his youthful self and does so brilliantly. However, Brendan does not abandon any of his historical narratives, or indeed any of these other discourses, or his understanding that presents Ireland's story of oppression and liberation. Some of these snippets might be exaggerated and/or false, but as with the Citizen in Joyce's *Ulysses*, some of it is still of value. None are erased and all remain valid. What actually occurs is that Brendan's ideas modify and transform in the face of his experiences. So, difference might fade away, but the desire for justice and equality emerges as paramount. The common cause that Brendan articulates signals the death of a narrow Irish nationalism that will be exchanged for a republican socialism:

'But I heard you giving out about what the English did on the Irish, and on the Scots, and on the Indians and the blacks out in Africa.'
'That's only the British Empire – that's a system.' (*BB*, 301)

What we witness in *Borstal Boy* is Behan reconnecting with the socialist roots of Irish republicanism, clearly recognising that the future – or the 1960s at least – would move to the left politically and culturally in the West. This is one reason for Behan's popularity on the international scene; he was saying something that people wanted to hear and which chimed with their own politics. In this interpretation Behan is not the only one to be educated; everyone must, or least ought to, learn something. All the inmates – especially those that Brendan is closest to – and some of the warders and the governor, are forced to accept that Brendan is a human being too, replete with all the unresolved contradictions that any human being might possess.

One important way of beginning to understand the nature of Behan's achievement in *Borstal Boy* is to see his creation 'Brendan' attempting to orientate himself towards a future. It can be asserted then that because of this struggle, Behan is a truly post-colonial writer, he inhabits the post-independence space and is concerned with what shape or form that independence might take. As noted above this does not necessarily signal that Brendan must abandon wholesale the narratives of Irish history that he holds dear, those tales of dominance and resistance that take on an added resonance in the confines of a prison cell. What is remarkable is how 'history' for Brendan is not distant or disconnected. His family was involved in the military struggle for independence and Brendan is so bound to their stories that he can 'remember' what he could not have experienced. Many of the famous names of the recent Irish struggle are humanised in Brendan's narrative: Michael Collins gave his mother 'a five-pound note on O'Connell Bridge, a few months before I was born, when my father was locked up by his government' (*BB*, 97), and

> My mother worked in Maud Gonne's house on St. Stephen's Green and my uncle was in the I.R.B. with Yeats, and many is the winter's evening I spent after tea, telling her stories I'd heard from father and mother and uncles about Yeats, Stephens and his lovely red-haired wife, and Maud Gonne, and A.E. (*BB*, 359).

History is a vibrant thing, coming alive in the telling. This linking of historical figures to specific locations creates a geographic map of his Dublin and Ireland that is both public and personal; linking them to his family constructs an Irish historical narrative that has *him* in it. In many ways, what the reader is witness to is a mania for the local. Nothing has any meaning if not connected to the personal; even writers like W.B. Yeats, Seán O'Casey and Richard Brinsley Sheridan possess significance because of their having been known and close in a personal way:

> I could put in a bit about James Joyce because, in one short week as a dairy boy, at the age of ten, I delivered milk to his sister in Mountjoy Square. (*BB*, 268)

What Brendan moves away from is a simple nationalist narrative, recognising the complexity of Ireland as a place and a people:

> I was no country Paddy from the middle of the Bog of Allen to be frightened to death by a lot of Liverpool seldom-fed bastards, nor was I one of your wrap-the-green-flag-round-me junior Civil Servants that came into the I.R.A. from the Gaelic League … No, be Jesus, I was from Russell Street, North Circular Road, Dublin, from the Northside where, be Jesus, the … whole of this pack of Limeys would be scruff-hounds would be et, and bet, threw up again – et without salt. (*BB*, 78)

The real beginning of post-colonial resistance is in acknowledging that the grand narratives of history are personal, or ought to be. Here Brendan is seen performing that manoeuvre again and again as he writes and rewrites *his* version of Irish history.

The dilemma for Behan, as it is for 'Brendan', is how to overcome the perils of nostalgia with this backward look. Here the public persona of 'Brendan Behan' looms large. Very rapidly, it could be argued, in Behan's own lifetime and most definitely after his death, this persona of the 'broth of a boy' solidified into one of the nostalgic glances at 'the rare ould times'. Even before the publication of *Borstal Boy*, Behan is a character in other people's books. He appears in J.P. Donleavy's *The Ginger Man* (1955) as one among many outrageously larger-than-life characters. It is a nostalgic image of a carefree Ireland, bohemian because of its marginality to the real currents of modernity flowing elsewhere. This image of Behan is already dated and of the past, even as it is being created. It would be taken up by others, like Anthony Cronin in his novel *The Life of Riley* (1964) and the memoir *Dead as Doornails* (1976), developing the image of the hard-drinking male artist as signifier of 1950s Dublin. More recently, in John Banville's Benjamin Black novels the thinly disguised Behan becomes a shorthand gesture to all that 1950s' Irish world of drink, smoke and grey jollity. So, in his own lifetime and soon after his death Behan becomes a symbol of the past, acting as a kind of warning, a spectral presence for future writers of how not to live. In that way, his mythological presence is a clear indicator, a line, which denotes what is past and what is present, what is backward and what is future oriented. Behan knew this himself and, at one level, all his work operates in a realm of instant nostalgia. Even *Borstal Boy*, with all its references to local colour, acknowledges that that world is changing if not vanished altogether. Thus the air of thick sentiment and wistful nostalgia is never too far away.

Yet *Borstal Boy*, which obviously flirts with the past, dramatises a shift and move towards the future. This is achieved in a number of ways. Part of the dynamic of the novel is its challenge to the stereotyping not only of the Irish, but also of the English. The revelation of a common bond suggests as much; beneath the surface tics and characteristics of national difference is similarity and shared experience. Still, that reading only goes so far and it too needs to be challenged. While Brendan learns valuable liberal lessons, his 'chums' and the warders in one major respect fail to do so. From beginning to end

Brendan is never called anything but 'Paddy': the generic Irishman. Doubtless he is accepted as an equal member of the group of young men but that act of naming, that failure to use his given name, points to an irrevocable distance and barrier between them.[19] An essential individuality and personhood is denied him. Brendan's own narrative, his own act of storytelling, of history-making, of anecdote and song, work against such narrow labelling; he is not just one thing – he is not simply a 'Paddy' – he is many things, and his access to and deployment of various voices and styles articulates that multiplicity.

The complexities of Irish identity are presented to the reader in the ways in which Brendan comes across so many Irish people in England, from policemen to warders to fellow prisoners. First- and second-generation Irish are to be found everywhere:

'I suppose it was your ancestors were Irish.'
'My mother was Irish – she was an O'Carroll from Longford.'
'A lot of people I've met inside seem to be of Irish descent, sir.'
'It doesn't seem to interest you very much,' said he.
'Well, to tell you the truth, sir, it doesn't. When I was in Walton a lot of the screws were of Irish descent … and to prove that they were as British as anyone else they were worse to me than anyone else.' (*BB*, 288)

As with the sergeant that Brendan meets when he is arrested, who possesses 'a heavy Munster accent, with an English one mixed into it' and who had 'probably … helped to murder people with the Black and Tans during the Trouble, and was afraid to stop in his own country or go near it since' (*BB*, 17), there is a suggestion that some have made political choices in terms of allegiances and loyalties. Nothing is a straightforward given, all roles and identities are possible. Clearly Ireland, and Irish people, are complicated and cannot be reduced to a single type.

It is no surprise that there is an emphasis on language in the novel. Behan's verbal flamboyance is recreated everywhere in Brendan's narrative. He is not only presented as articulate and fluent but also as being aware of accents and speech patterns as an indication of identity and belonging. There is constant reference to Cockney, Welsh and Scottish accents, as well as Irish accents. Indeed, one of the things that young Brendan must learn is the argot of prison life: of being a 'china' and a 'chum' and the currency of 'snout' and the authority of the 'screws'. There is an interesting moment when Brendan's Irishness comes to the fore: "For the love of Jasus," said I, lapsing into the speech of my homeland' (*BB*, 189).

There is a gap between Brendan's interior monologue and narrative role and the Brendan in the world of the novel; one Brendan – the narrator – can revel linguistically in Irishisms and Hiberno-English turns of phrase, and the other must speak like everyone else. This is quite a remarkable moment because it suggests that in the realm of the novel Brendan is constantly and consciously, like some of the other Irish characters, masking his Irishness. In one way it signifies that his 'liberal education' is hard won and it comes at a loss, the submerging of his own identity. Read in this manner, *Borstal Boy* is not so much a narrative of revelation but a narrative of concealment. The real Brendan is never on display because he can *never* be on display. As an IRA man he refuses to join with another prisoner who wants to protest about the execution of IRA men. His republican socialist values are never fully expressed nor, obviously, is that other hidden homosexual self, which has emerged more clearly among readers and critics in recent times. Brendan is seen undertaking a variety of roles throughout the novel. At the beginning he works on his 'speech from the dock', knowing that it will play well to his comrades at home. Later he forces himself to fight some of the other prisoners, knowing that such a display of physicality and violence will be helpful in raising his profile among the inmates, keeping him safe in the future (*BB*, 88). At one stage he declares:

> What I told was ninety per cent lies, and that's being more than fair to myself, for I was an able liar ... (*BB*, 342)

Then later says that 'Liars need good memories, and I have one' (*BB*, 349). As a strategy of survival in this harsh environment lying is essential. Again and again we witness Brendan being untruthful, often artfully so. In his interrogation, when asked to name the partitioned six counties of the North of Ireland, he purposely leaves out County Tyrone (*BB*, 3). He cleverly wants to give his interrogator a moment of triumph and does so. With another prisoner, whose name was 'Donohue', Brendan tells us that:

> I said that by a coincidence that was my mother's name. It was not her name, but civility costs nothing. (*BB*, 29)

There is no real reason for this lie, it does not aid his need for survival or further his ingratiation with the other prisoners or the warders. It is casual and throwaway; he does it because he can. Later, one of Brendan's chums, Joe, comes into the borstal chapel singing a song as Brendan and another prisoner, Tom, are painting the ceiling. Tom is not happy with Joe's comic rendering in such a sacred place:

> 'Disgusting bastard,' said Tom, looking down from the plank, 'no respect for nothing.' I laughed down at Joe but put on a disapproving look when I turned to Tom on the plank. (*BB*, 307)

This is a less than flattering image of Brendan who, two-faced, can be seemingly friends with both. In the end he does not stay loyal to his friend in this situation and is called out on it and must manufacture another story for Joe to explain his actions: 'I think my story convinced him' (*BB*, 337).

Not reading *Borstal Boy* as a traditional *Bildungsroman* concerned with the moral growth and development of a youth, has profound consequences for our understanding of Behan's text. Brendan's story has little to do with a journey towards the discovery of an authentic selfhood – moral, national or individual. The reader cannot believe in one version of Brendan over any other, as one should not privilege any one interpretation of *Borstal Boy* over any other. Brendan, ultimately, cannot be pigeonholed or typecast; he is many things to many people and, to an extent at least, is in control of the various roles and personae he presents to the world. This totally improvised and pragmatic Brendan is utterly liberated; he does not simply give up Irish republicanism to become liberal because he has been shown kindness, as that would be swapping one restrictive role for another. Brendan, instead, is the continually self-making man of modernity and the future is the location where this making will be played out.

It is the future, rather than the past, which the novel orientates itself towards by its close. After his experiences of the wider world, of different people from different places, of having his cultural horizons exposed to new ideas, he is sent home to Dublin having served his time. It is a reversal of what had become the formulaic route for the Irish hero of fiction, which was a move away from Ireland and the homeplace into exile. In Joyce's *Portrait*, George Moore's *The Lake*, Elizabeth Bowen's *The Last September*, Patrick

Kavanagh's *Tarry Flynn*, it is exile and the story of leaving that brings the story to its end. Exile or escape from backwardness is the only possible way to enter into modernity. It is also important that in each of the novels mentioned it is central that escape might lead to artistic expression; to be an artist in Ireland one must endure being left behind. Behan, however, dramatically reverses that notion and rather than departure at the close, the reader is offered a sublime moment of return:

> There they were, as if I'd never left them; in their sweet and stately order round the Bay - Bray Head, the Sugarloaf, the Two Rock, the Three Rock, Kippure, the king of them all, rising his threatening head behind and over their shoulders till they sloped down to the city ... I had them all counted, present and correct and the chimneys of the Pigeon House, and the framing circle of the road along the edge of the Bay, Dun Laoghaire, Blackrock, Sandymount Tower, Ringsend and the city; then the other half circle, Fairview, Marino, Clontarf, Raheny, Kilbarrack, Baldoyle, to the height of Howth Head.
>
> I couldn't really see Kilbarrack or Baldoyle, but it was only that I knew they were there. (*BB*, 371)

Truly an act of imaginative repossession is performed here; even the places he cannot see become part of his topographical reclamation. An immigration officer then greets him:

> He looked very serious, and tenderly enquired, 'Caithfidh go bhfuil sé go hiontach bheith saor.'
> 'Caithfidh go bhfuil.'
> 'It must be wonderful to be free.'
> 'It must,' said I, walked down the gangway, past a detective, and got on the train for Dublin. (*BB*, 371–2)

While some might quibble at the need for translation at all, at least Behan acknowledges his dual inheritance *and* the autonomy it might afford him. In this final moment Brendan tells us, and performs for us, how Ireland can again be a location for art and possibility. No longer do energies have to be diverted into an act or art of exile; better to put those potential exertions into an art that might possess a European or universal sensibility because it is centred in Ireland, not in spite of it. Here, however, the realms of the public persona and the character within the art collide. The presence of the Irish detective at the end of the gangplank suggests that despite the 'liberal' lessons he has been exposed to in the borstal system, young Brendan is still viewed as a potential threat in Ireland. Indeed, Behan the author would be arrested again only a year later for shooting at a garda at a republican commemoration of Wolfe Tone. Still, this upbeat ending enacts that moment of self-realisation, the realisation that he is free to create a worthy self. It is not the escape of exile that is being embraced but the escape that such self-creation allows, and he will revel in it. Reading that moment back into the body of the text means that we can witness how all that role-playing leads up to this point.

The problem for Brendan Behan, however, was that he was unable to keep his art and his life distinct and that this emphasis on identity and selfhood and creation spilled over into the public arena as he became a representative figure in the public eye. Oscar Wilde famously quipped: 'I had put all my genius into my life; I put only my talent into my works'; Behan, it could be argued, actually put his genius into both. In a lengthy interview from 1961 Behan returns again and again to *Borstal Boy*, not its plot or character, but the actual writing of it.[20] It is as if he is concerned only with the act of creation itself, with the processes of that creation, not with what was created. Behan's dilemma is that his modernist creation became a postmodern nightmare, in that he lost control of that image of himself, even in his own lifetime. His fate was to be no longer the author of his own story, as he became a bit player in everyone else's.

Borstal Boy can be read as articulating the nature of self-formation and self-creation in 1950s and '60s Ireland, and against the legacy of a very critical artistic stance on Irish culture in relation to modernity, Behan celebrates the Irish space as one of possibility and potential.

2
LESSONS OF DETENTION
MARIA DiBATTISTA

Reading Brendan Behan's *Borstal Boy*, it is hard to visualise the brash insurgent fully equipped with the 'Sinn Féin's conjuror's outfit' (*BB*, 1) as a stammerer. There is hardly a trace of 'the lad with the nervous stammer' (*O'Sullivan*, 211) in Behan's unsparing, fluent account of the harrowing, if sometimes grimly comic, ordeals he endured during his various terms and places of confinement. From the moment he is abruptly apprehended *in medias res* – Behan literally seems to have been in the middle of making a bomb when, as he recalls, 'Friday, in the evening, the landlady shouted up the stairs' – *Borstal Boy* moves relentlessly and garrulously onwards in defiance of the adversaries Behan had pledged himself to demoralise and destroy. He does not hesitate, much less stumble, in recounting the sights, sounds, *smells* (especially the smells, which might make anyone gag) and describing the unexpectedly varied company of warders ('screws'), fellow prisoners, and the 'chinas' (pals) that made up his life in detention. If one were to judge by the fluent narrative manner of *Borstal Boy* one might be excused for thinking that Behan was so perfected in his knowledge of the penal system and of his forced development within it that he could retrace his rite of passage from a Dublin to a borstal boy without a single verbal misstep.

In this respect, *Borstal Boy* is the story of an education administered within the confines of what Oscar Wilde, in his own prison chronicle *De Profundis*, called 'that terrible school' where one learns 'the meaning of sorrow and its beauty'.[1] *De Profundis* hovers over *Borstal Boy* like a fretting parent text, but like the obstreperous child he apparently was, Behan refuses to make sorrow and its beauty the immediate subject of his own story. The 'unconscious iconoclasm' that the IRA activist Bob Bradshaw detected in hearing the ten-year-old Behan stammer out a speech about 'O'Casey, Shaw and Wilde, with quotations from their selected works' (*O'Sullivan*, 20) also courses beneath the fervid cultural nationalism declaimed in *Borstal Boy*. The lessons of detention that he commits to memory, indeed that he memorialises in *Borstal Boy*, are less exalted, although finally as spiritually sobering as those Wilde learned during his tormented days in Reading Gaol.

The first and fundamental lesson Behan learns in detention is mandated instruction in his own creatureliness. Given his teachers and the 'schoolrooms' where Behan's education takes place, this is necessarily a lesson in bodily ab-jection, a lesson reinforced by the all-pervading, sickening smell of jailhouse shit and soap against which there is no effective barrier or available palliative. His first night at the Criminal Investigation Department headquarters is suf-ficient to give the young Behan a new knowledge of what the body is, what it can suffer and what it alone knows. Finding himself beset by anxiety about whether he will be sentenced as an adult or juvenile offender, Behan decides to 'put my mind on other things' and enjoy the one bodily pleasure 'at least and at last permissible to a man in my position' (*BB*, 8). Behan falls asleep, 'more pleasantly tired', he drolly reports, from his masturbatory diversion than he had hoped to be. But morning restores him to his senses, in every possible meaning of that term:

> Waking, I felt the hardness of my resting-place. I didn't wonder where I was. I knew that all right. I looked up at the grey light, through the barred windows, and remembered it better. A blunt and numbing pain it was to wake up in a cell for the first time. (*BB*, 8)

What the incarcerated body feels and repeatedly declares is its own 'defenceless misery' (*BB*, 22), a knowledge that it iterates indifferently and in the most pitiless terms. To judge from *Borstal Boy*, the abject body speaks in a hard-boiled idiom picked up from the streets, American detective novels or film noir, and refined, if that is not too polite a term, by blunt and numbing pain: 'I didn't wonder where I was. I knew that all right.' This is how you talk to yourself when confronted with things as they bitterly are and might never be otherwise. A world-weary Sam Spade or Philip Marlowe could not have said it better.[2]

It does not take long for Behan to learn other harsh lessons in bodily abjection. There is, for example, the searing humiliation of his first body search. His hair is combed for any cigarette butts that might be secreted there – a trick he has not had time to learn – and his anal cavity probed with a pencil torch, an indignity he had read about but never actually understood. This distinction between mental knowledge and physical experience will become one of the more important lessons learned in detention: 'I had heard of this personal search in Fenian times, in a book by Tom Clarke, when he got fifteen years for the bombing campaign of the eighties, but I did not know what it meant' (*BB*, 42). Prison is the place of appalling realisations, the terrible school where Behan, a great if somewhat naïve reader, learns the literal, agonisingly physical meaning of brutal experiences that had only existed for him as words on a page.

The second lesson of detention teaches Behan about states of moral, rather than physical, abjection. Behan's tutorial in subjugation is overseen by a Mr Whitbread, one of the few thoroughly despicable figures in *Borstal Boy*, a warder viciously eager to impress the prisoners under his watch with a proper sense of his power over them. Behan recalls his meeting with this sadistic interrogator as a particularly mortifying one. When called upon to identify himself, Behan stammers out his name; the Behan he can manage, the Brendan is what bedevils his tongue. Whitbread shouts in his face, mocks him as 'an old Irish rebel' and then, seeing him distracted by the laughter raised at his expense, orders him to look at him directly in the face. Behan, trying to summon his moral courage, not to mention his voice, inwardly invokes and attempts to mimic the posture of one of the legendary defenders of Éire:

Young Cuchulainn, after the battle of the ford of Ferdia, on guard the gap of Ulster, with his enemies ringed round him, held his back to a tree and, supported by it, called on the gods of death and grandeur to hold him up till his last blood flowed.

I looked at Mr. Whitbread. 'I am looking at you,' I said. (*BB*, 34)

His body might have taught Behan where he was, but it has nothing to say about who he is or how he should conduct himself. Nor can it be trusted to stand on its own. Only the heroic codes and legends of Irish political myth promise to support and sustain him in his hour of trial. Yet the heroic model fails him, as it is bound to do in a domain where literalism reigns. There is no tree to support his back and the gods of death and grandeur that held up Cuchulainn until his body shed its last drop of heroic blood have long ago deserted the earth. Left to his own devices, Behan can only look at his tormentor and assure him that he is doing just that (and no more); hardly the heroic riposte that might have earned him a place, even if only a footnote, in the annals of Irish rebellion.

This encounter quickly and predictably deteriorates into ignominy. Behan is repeatedly struck in the face by Whitbread's henchman until his 'sight was a vision of red and white and pity-coloured flashes' (*BB*, 35). Beaten into submission, he drops the pose of heroic defiance and blurts out: 'I, sir, please, sir, I am looking at you, I mean, I am looking at Mr Whitbread, sir' (*BB*, 35). Whitbread, satisfied that 'you have learnt that lesson', decides he needs another: 'remember this', he advises him, 'we've only three sorts of tobacco 'ere. Three Nuns – none today, none tomorrow, and none the day after' (*BB*, 35). Despite its reputed source, Behan appreciated this bad pun and used it again in *The Quare Fellow*, only this time the 'funny remark' belongs to the prisoner Dunlavin (*CP*, 50). In *Borstal Boy* the dark joke is meant to mislead as well as humiliate the new boy on the block. As Behan soon discovers, tobacco is in fact the currency of prison life. In Borstal it even helps identify the different ranks of the prison congregations, which are seated 'according to the amount of tobacco allowed the different sections' (*BB*, 169). Later Behan relates that 'The smoking was the big part of the day' (*BB*, 98), not *a* big part of the day but *the* big part of the day. In fact so many butt-ends and smokes are exchanged and savoured that one can emerge from reading *Borstal Boy* gasping for air.

The third lesson Behan learns in detention, which follows upon even as it spiritualises his harsh course in bodily and moral abjection, entails a new apprehension of time. This is hardly surprising, given how slowly time must pass for those enduring seemingly endless and usually empty days, months and years of unvarying routine. 'The clock was not made that would pass the time between now and Monday' (*BB*, 7), Behan laments after being locked up only ten minutes. The very pealing of the church bells suggests to the newly imprisoned Behan a conspiracy for 'mak[ing] misery mark time' (*BB*, 7). Nonetheless, misery's way of marking time gives *Borstal Boy* its disconsolate but sturdy structure. Behan's obsessive timekeeping is most pronounced in the first part of *Borstal Boy*, where nearly every chapter opens with a notation of the time of day or prison schedule. These notations are not neutral, but portentous, foretelling, or perhaps merely hoping for, some drama to come. 'Friday, in the evening' (*BB*, 1), the phrase that opens the memoir, signals an abrupt plunge into a new order of existence. 'Not that we were not reminded of Sunday in another way' (*BB*, 21) begins the chapter that follows, and then, in order:

> Mornings, we were wakened at six and slopped out, throwing the contents of the chamber-pot into the bucket brought round by a prisoner appointed to that position (*BB*, 45).
> After breakfast on Sunday… (*BB*, 53)

These opening sentences eventually form a sort of time code tracking Behan's gradual induction into the routines and regimens of prison life.

Within this dreary round of days, Behan finds not just solace, but active interest in reading, so much so that he ruefully hails the advent of a new book to read as a 'kind of pay-day to look forward to' (*BB*, 69). That day arrives and is commemorated in the chapter that begins: 'One of the books was *Under the Greenwood Tree* by Thomas Hardy, and the other was the life of General Booth, the founder of the Salvation Army' (*BB*, 70).

Although the titles at first perplex him, these two books are singled out because they introduce Behan to the prospect of a life that could be very different from the one he has always known or hopes to have. The book on Booth and the Salvation Army alerts Behan to the tradition of conversion narratives, although the deliverance Behan seeks is unlikely to come through the spiritual solicitude of his Protestant jailers. The Hardy novel offers an equally unlikely alternative to his past and present life; it invites Behan's imagination to wander in the green – and fragrant! – fields of the pastoral, a realm that, rather surprisingly, seems to appeal strongly to his sceptical, combative and sardonic temperament. Behan will later quote long passages from Elizabeth Gaskell's *Cranford*, seemingly to heighten the contrast between the polite quarrels and trivial misunderstandings that embroil the sedate village of Cranford and his own rough, often brutal society of warders and inmates. Yet these pastoral novels of country life represent possibilities that, as we shall see, Behan adapts to his own spiritual needs and moral outlook when he is released from detention.

With new objects and habits of reading come a renewed attention to the act, means, occasion and purpose of writing. 'Now I began to get letters from Ireland wishing me "a happy Christmas"' (*BB*, 103), he begins the chapter that will recount his own progress from avid reader of other lives to ardent writer of his own story. That word 'now' sounds a hopeful portent and suggests that Behan is reconnecting to his old life, with its own ritual partitions of the year that not only mark, but also sacralise time. The letters not only boost his morale, but embolden him to write in his own voice in his own defence. Indeed, the last chapter of the first section of *Borstal Boy* opens with something like the announcement of his writerly vocation: 'I got paper for the purpose of preparing my defence and wrote on it' (*BB*, 124). This simple, almost stupefyingly literal sentence announces a complex inner transformation: Behan, now animated by a sense of purposefulness that prison routine had eviscerated, reaffirms in and through writing his identity and agency as an Irish rebel, taking his rightful and honourable place in the ranks of those countrymen who, like him, have testified

> to the unyielding determination of the Irish people to regain every inch of our national territory and to give expression to the noble aspirations for which so much Irish blood has been shed, so many brave and manly hearts have been broken, and for which so many of my comrades are now lying in your jails. (*BB*, 124)

Time here takes the grand form of a tradition of national aspiration in which Behan 'now'—that fateful word that opens the chapter – participates and perpetuates through his writing.

This moment of articulate defence also marks a decisive turn in Behan's relationship with Irish history. There was something almost platonic about the way the callow young boy remanded to Borstal proclaimed the sacred lore he seemed to have entered the world knowing. But prison has educated as well as steeled him in the dark, complicated and treachery-filled course of Irish rebellion. This becomes evident in his histrionic confrontation with the priest Father Lane. Trying to intimidate Behan into renouncing his IRA ties and abjure his republican sympathies, Father Lane chastises him: 'Haven't you any manners, Behan?' In response Behan answers firmly that 'The IRA is not a murder gang, Father' (*BB*, 64) but also shows his manners through formulaic courtesy: 'With no disrespect to you, Father' (*BB*, 65), only to render the entire question of 'manners' moot as he launches into a sustained and eloquent denunciation of the church's treachery. The betrayals are legion and horrific. Behan takes more than two pages to itemise them in all their squalid and damning detail. He begins by pointing out that 'A synod of Irish bishops held at Drumceatt in 1172 decided that any Irishman that refused to acknowledge the King of England was ex-communicated' and then describes the church's inhumanity during the Famine:

> 'Didn't they condemn the men of Forty-eight and tell the people to give up their crops and die of hunger in the ditches at home, with the grass-juice running green from the dead mouth of a mother clutching a live infant–!'

He finally concludes: 'Wasn't my own father excommunicated and him in Kilmainham Prison in 'Twenty-two?' (*BB*, 66). The history of Irish rebellion supports Behan in a way the legend of Cuchulainn never did or even could; it provides him with a sense of common purpose and inducts him into a heroic lineage of Irish patriots extending from those excommunicated by twelfth-century Irish bishops to those excommunicated in 1922, including his own father.

Complementing and ultimately supplanting Behan's heroic evocation of the tradition of Irish rebellion is another, less flamboyant nationalist rhetoric and a different apprehension of time as the medium of change and apocalyptic transformation. This sense of time is obliquely introduced in the epigraph taken from Virginia Woolf's *Orlando*, in what surely qualifies as the most idiosyncratic literary homage to Woolf's fantastical biography. Behan's epigraph isolates the climactic moment in Woolf's account of the Great Frost of 1608 when the Thames, frozen solid for months, suddenly thaws, throwing everything into 'riot and confusion':

> One crew of young watermen or postboys [...] roared and shouted the lewdest tavern songs, as if in bravado and were dashed against a tree and

sunk with blasphemies on their lips. An old nobleman – for such his furred gown and golden chain of office proclaimed him – went down not far from where Orlando stood, calling vengeance upon the Irish rebels, who, he credited with his last breath, had plotted this devilry […].[3]

The grave spectacle of creatures overwhelmed by terror as they sink to their death in 'the appalling race of waters' is undercut by Woolf's robust parody, which verges on and finally succumbs to caricature. The comic desperation of blasphemous postboys and vengeful nobles anticipates not just the matter – the calamitous relations between Ireland and England – but the manner – the comic bravado—of the memoir that follows. The most curious, yet largely unremarked, manifestation of Behan's literary bravado is his decision to acknowledge his debt to two *English women*, both suspect, even anathema categories for an Irish writer schooled in IRA culture. Behan's iconoclasm, whether unconscious or not, is never more appealing than in his intimating that the genteel comedy of Gaskell's *Cranford* and the impertinent satire of Woolf's *Orlando* inspired his own original, subtle and affecting mingling of comedy and pathos. He may have been alerted to the ways pathos can co-exist with sardonic humour by a few well-considered and less heartless lines from *Orlando* that immediately precede and in a way prepare for the grimly comic scene of young watermen and postboys, roaring and shouting vulgar tavern songs as they sink to their watery graves: 'But what was the most awful and inspiring of terror was the sight of the human creatures who had been trapped in the night and now paced their twisting and precarious islands in the utmost agony of spirit.'[4] That Behan did not cite these words, in which pity and awe are commingled, seems not so much an oversight or a deliberate elision as a calculated move to cover his own emotional tracks. Quoting these lines might have struck him as too indiscreet, so tempting it would then be to associate 'human creatures … trapped in the night and now pac[ing] their twisting and precarious islands in the utmost agony of spirit' with the moral terror and spiritual isolation that Behan, trapped in the long nights and dark days of detention, experienced in the islanded cells of English prisons.

This *kairotic* sense of time as an opportunity or necessity for spiritual reck-oning is registered in an extraordinary passage in which Behan, who will later condemn the church and gladly accept its decree of excommunication as a badge of honour, reflects that he is glad he has not lost the faith. For what the faith gives him is a sense of time sacralised by human ritual and redeemed by divine ordinance. It is one of the few passages of defiant rejoicing that is not parochial and partisan, but ecumenical. It expresses a joy that comes out of a newly learned understanding of what the word 'catholic' originally meant, still promises and might portend:

> now I was glad that in this well-washed smelly English hell-hole of old Victorian cruelty, I had the Faith to fall back on. Every Sunday and holiday, be at one with hundreds of millions of Catholics, at the sacrifice of the Mass, to worship the God of our ancestors, and pray to Our Lady, the delight of the Gael, the consolation of mankind, the mother of God and of man, the pride of poets and artists, Dante, Villon, Eoghan Ruadh O Sullivan, in warmer, more humorous parts of the world than this nineteenth-century English lavatory, in Florence, in France, in Kerry, where the arbutus grows and the fuchsia glows on the dusty hedges in the soft light of the summer evening. *'Deorini De'* – 'The Tears of God' – they called the fuchsia in Kerry, where it ran wild as a weed. *'Lachryma Christi'* – 'The Tears of Christ' – was a Latin phrase, but in future I would give Him less reason for tears, and maybe out of being here I would get back into a state of grace and stop in it – well, not stop out of it for long intervals – and out of evil, being here, good would come. (*BB*, 54)

I would not care to pronounce on how much irony infuses this extraordinary passage, with its emotionally raw but also highly polished mix of vernacular, liturgical pastoral and high Miltonic rhetoric, but I would unhesitatingly venture not as much as we might think. Irony can muffle, but it cannot mute this *cri de coeur*, one that places *Borstal Boy* securely within the tradition of captivity narratives that figure redemption as a new relation to time.

With this new apprehension of time comes a new sense of narrative, or rather an old sense of narrative, perhaps the oldest narrative of mankind, the story of time as the medium of change and redemption. Behan's faith is what gives him hope that he may yet enter a state of grace and that, moreover, he might remain there – here the note of realism intrudes – with only occasional forays into dereliction and devilry.

Time, which in his first night of detention was marked by the 'cold and lonely' peals of the church bell sounding 'the dreariest noise that ever defiled the ear of man' (*BB*, 7), is infused with grace in another way and in another mode in the penultimate chapter of *Borstal Boy* when Behan seems to bless his fellow prisoners after a frolic in the sea: 'The whole field was tired and silent, and their faces round their bushes, in the soft and gathering dark, reposed and innocent' (*BB*, 341). The soft and gathering dusk encloses the scene in the hush of pastoral repose, which descends on the faces of his fellow prisoners, indeed descends on the narrative, like a reprieve and a benediction.

Such moments suggest that Behan has made the harsh lessons of detention the basis of a new vision of reality and of himself within it. Whether or not he attains to the state of grace he aspires to and whether, having done so, he will remain there is a question the memoir declines to answer. Yet we can still gauge how thoroughly he has been educated and re-formed by his time in detention by comparing his experience to Wilde's, even if we must, of course, allow for the obvious differences in the places and reasons for their incarceration. Wilde concludes *De Profundis* with this bleak moral accounting:

> What lies before me is my past. I have got to make myself look on that with different eyes, to make the world look on it with different eyes, to make God look on it with different eyes. This I cannot do by ignoring it, or slighting it, or praising it, or denying it. It is only to be done fully by accepting it as an inevitable part of the evolution of my life and character: by bowing my head to everything that I have suffered.
>
> How far I am away from the true temper of soul, this letter in its changing uncertain moods, its scorn and bitterness, its aspirations and its failures to realise those aspirations, shows quite clearly; but do not forget in what a terrible school I am setting at my task, and incomplete, imperfect as I am, my friends have still much to gain. They came to me to learn the pleasure of life and the pleasure of art. Perhaps I am chosen to teach them something much more wonderful, the meaning of sorrow and its beauty.[5]

'Before me is my past …': this is the bleak horizon that Wilde contemplates as he plunges back into a life where beauty, if it is to be glimpsed and savoured at all, will only wear the aspect of sorrow.

Behan ends *Borstal Boy* by claiming, in effect, that for him, too, the past is before him. Of course he means something very different by this. For Behan's past returns to him not in the form of a reproach but as a reinstatement. He experiences a feeling of precious time regained upon returning to Dublin and discovering, with a relief approaching joy, that the land he had left has not changed:

> There they were, as if I'd never left them; in their sweet and stately order round the Bay – Bray Head, the Sugar Loaf, the Two Rock, the Three Rock, Kippure, the king of them all rising his threatening head behind and over their shoulders till they sloped down to the city. (*BB*, 371)

As if to assure himself that the remembered vista and the present reality before him are one and the same, Behan counts the spires of the churches, the chimneys of the Pigeon House and the framing circles of the roads around the bay. But if his past is before him, so too is his future, as he is made aware when he hands his expulsion order to the immigration officer who welcomes him with 'his long educated countryman's sad face, like a teacher' (*BB*, 371). A new teacher, then, and a new course of instruction awaits. Like all good teachers, the man speeds him on his way – in Irish – with a grave and tender solicitude:

> 'Céad míle fáilte sa bhaile romhat.'
> A hundred thousand welcomes home to you.

He then adds words of both wonder and encouragement:

> 'Caithfidh go bhfuil sé go hiontach bheith saor.'
> 'It must be wonderful to be free.' (*BB*, 371–2)

'It must,' Behan replies as he descends the gangway, passes a policeman and boards a train to Dublin. This last exchange may serve as a sign, if we need one, that Behan has been well schooled in those categorical, but stubbornly equivocal, imperatives that posit freedom as both an obligation and a possibility. The very openness of this ending may either hearten or alarm us with its suggestion that in freedom there will be still more lessons to be learned.

3

BOHEMIAN BEHAN: LATE MODERNISM, SEXUAL POLITICS, AND THE 'GREAT AWAKENING' OF BRENDAN BEHAN

JOHN BRANNIGAN

In July 1960, when Brendan Behan was enjoying still the fruits of his international fame, he took the time to welcome the re-publication of Flann O'Brien's *At Swim-Two-Birds*, and recalled the unusual circumstances in which the novel, when it was first published in 1939, formed part of his literary education:

> The first time I saw a copy of *At Swim-Two-Birds* was at Killiney Castle, which was at that time occupied by the IRA, then engaged in a campaign of bomb explosions and fire-raising in England. In the intervals of reading about BT2, the formula for blowing holes with gelignite in masonry bridges, and the manufacture from potassium chlorate and paraffin wax of the explosive known as 'Paxo', I listened to Peadar O'Flaherty (the Lord have mercy on him) read out bits of *At Swim-Two-Birds*, which he didn't always do too coherently owing to bursting out laughing when it proved too much for him.[1]

At Swim-Two-Birds – that masterpiece of late modernism, of ludic and satirical humour, which parodies the folkloric predilections of the Irish revival and follows a labyrinthine and burlesque structure – was not a popular success. In fact, it was a very niche interest in 1939, and only gathered a cult following among writers in the post-war decades.[2] So Behan and his IRA comrades were not only in a very small cadre of republican revolutionaries, increasingly isolated and thwarted in their desperate bombing campaign in Britain, but they were also in a very small minority in terms of their literary and cultural interests. The intersection of the two is a complex matter: of course, not all IRA volunteers were enjoying avant-garde burlesque novels and, likewise, it is hard to see the connection politically between O'Brien's daytime desk job as a civil servant known as Brian O'Nolan and his apparent literary appeal to gelignite revolutionaries. Yet, however complex and contradictory, the link between revolutionary art and politics conveyed in this scene described by Behan is reminiscent of the same concoction that animated the bohemian and avant-garde movements into existence at the end of the nineteenth century.

In popular conception, the bohemian is not easily associated with the working-class culture from which Behan emerged; in Walter Benjamin's characterisation of one of the most distinctive examples of the bohemian figure, the flâneur, he is associated with a leisured intelligentsia, tied specifically to the rise in the nineteenth century of bourgeois commodity markets and culture.[3] His economic position is, at worst, uncertain, as indeed is his political function. It is not clear at all, for Benjamin, whether the flâneur is merely the product of a bourgeois commodification of art, or an agent capable of critiquing capitalist culture. Yet, in the modernist period, as conventionally periodised from the 1890s to the 1930s, the bohemian artist becomes more clearly linked to revolutionary politics, and the subversive intent of his art is usually articulated within a framework of manifestos and affiliations that are explicitly revolutionary. Peter Brooker defines the bohemian in the modernist period as 'a conspicuous example of the modern artist; committed in gesture, polemic, poem and painting to the subversive force of an aestheticizing temperament in the face of a resilient conformism and bare-faced commodity culture'.[4] By the 1930s, however, modernism could no longer be coherently explained in relation to revolutionary politics; the revolutionary possibilities of the beginning of the century had hardened into new conformities and orthodoxies more rigid than before, and 'high' modernism had become associated in some cases – most notably T.S. Eliot, Ezra Pound and W.B. Yeats – with reactionary right-wing politics. For Tyrus Miller what emerges in the wake of high modernism is an art and literature of dissolution, exhaustion and scepticism; late modernism, he argues, 'weakens the relatively strong symbolic forms still evident in high modernist texts' and 'reopens the modernist enclosure of form onto the work's social and political environs, facilitating its more direct, polemical engagement with topical and popular discourses'.[5] Thus, we find Louis MacNeice, W.H. Auden, George Orwell, Djuna Barnes, Mina Loy, Samuel Beckett, Elizabeth Bowen and many others according to Miller's characterisation of late modernism, unravelling the ends of modernism and, in some cases, beginning to recover the socialist orientations of modernist forms. This is where I think we are beginning to place Brendan Behan and, indeed, to see him as particularly well placed to carry on some of the bohemian legacies of a fusion of art and politics in the late modernist period.

THE 'GREAT AWAKENING'

By 1939, however, when Behan's training in making bombs was somewhat more advanced than his training in the art of literature, the causes and principles to which both revolutionary politics and revolutionary art might be dedicated were increasingly uncertain. Behan's literary guide in Killiney Castle, Peadar O'Flaherty, depicted as being almost overcome with laughter when reading Flann O'Brien's ludic masterpiece, was also architect of the IRA bombing campaign in Britain, and chiefly responsible for training young men to manufacture and plant explosives. The campaign, which had commenced with a declaration of republican sovereignty in January 1939, was intended to force Britain into ceding Northern Ireland through a series of indiscriminate bombings of targets in English cities, but historians have argued that the campaign was neither sufficiently resourced, nor sufficiently conceived intellectually or strategically, to have the slightest chance of success.[6] O'Flaherty was also reputed to be a fascist sympathiser and was second-in-command to Seán Russell, the IRA chief-of-staff who spent the summer of 1940 as an honoured guest of the Third Reich, and whose plans for collaborating in the German invasion of Britain and Ireland were thwarted when he died from a perforated ulcer on the U-boat that was bringing him back to Ireland.[7] The bombing campaign for which Behan was being trained and in which he would play such a brief and mercifully ineffective part was timed to capitalise on the pressures mounting on Britain as a result of the impending European war, but when that war broke, the IRA became increasingly complicit with Nazi Germany.

For the IRA leaders, many of whom had taken part in the Easter Rising of 1916, collusion with Germany in a war against Britain was not new, nor was it necessarily indicative of political approval for fascism (although in some cases there was very strong evidence of Nazi sympathies). For Brendan Behan, who was born in 1923, the commitment to revolutionary politics was steeped in the drama of 1916, surrounded as he was in his youth by men and women who never ceased to speak and sing of the Rising:

> When I was nine years old I could have given you a complete account of what happened from Mount Street Bridge out to the Battle of Ashbourne, where I was giving Tom Ashe and Dick Mulcahy a hand. I could tell you how Seán Russell and I stopped them at Fairview, and could have given you a fuller description of Easter, 1916 than many an older man. You see, they were mostly confined to one garrison – I had fought at them all.[8]

Perhaps Behan found in Killiney Castle something of the same intoxicating conflation of militarism and theatricality which had inspired devotion in the men and women of 1916, although it was perhaps inevitably the affective power of representations of the Rising which he recalls more vividly:

> 'To take as a headquarters the most prominent target in the whole city', said a man in a middle-aged growl, 'what ridiculous strategy'.
>
> Old George Roberts took the tumbler from his little full lips and stroked on his beard. 'But what taste – what impeccable taste', said he.
>
> Me life on you, said I: for I knew what he meant. Hadn't I stood in the Queen's Theatre, with the frenzied Saturday night crowd, for the 'Transformation Scene: Burning GPO', while the very amplifiers carrying Pearse's oration over the grave of Rossa were deafened in a mad roar of cheering that went on till the darkness came down and we had till the end of the next act to compose our features and look at our neighbours without embarrassment?[9]

This sense of being trapped in the imaginative fervour of a revolution which had conspicuously failed to effect any meaningful social change for the mass of Irish people is a recurrent theme in Behan's writings and indeed in Irish late modernism in general. So too is the increasing emptiness of the rhetoric of that revolutionary struggle, particularly when pitted against its apparent futility in a world engaged in wars of global extent and significance. *Borstal Boy* is arguably Behan's most eloquent and public testimony of that feeling, with its acknowledgements of the jail journals of prominent Fenians and republicans in its early pages and the absurdly theatrical stand for the rights of an Irish Small Farmers and Workers Republic, giving way in that narrative to a scepticism about revolutionary rhetoric. *Borstal Boy* does not show any signs of abandoning Behan's commitments to real freedoms – freedoms from poverty, repression and drudgery – but it does achieve a more expansive understanding of what those freedoms entail than he had encountered in the republicanism of his youth. The first short story he published as an adult, 'I Become a Borstal Boy', which appeared in *The Bell* in June 1942 shortly after Behan was imprisoned in Dublin for shooting at two detectives, shows us a young Behan still determined to cloak himself in the theatrical gestures of the IRA of his youth. On hearing the news of the hanging of two men who were convicted of murder for the Coventry bomb, Behan rallies the Irishmen imprisoned with him in Walton Jail to honour their sacrifice as martyrs by reciting the *De Profundis*. This is a markedly different account from the one he later gave in *Borstal Boy* and the change in Behan's perceptions happens in the early 1940s in prison.

His disillusionment with IRA rhetoric and actions of the late 1930s is clear from his correspondence from Mountjoy Prison in 1942, where he was beginning to serve his sentence of fourteen years' penal servitude. Some of Behan's letter and of the reply from his step-brother, Seán Furlong, is captured (literally) in intercepted correspondence in Home Office files, which contain intelligence reports and evidence gathered by Special Branch and MI5:

> It's the futility of it all that's getting me down. Personally I think the Irish people are just about browned off with all this bloody game of private armies (that won't even perform the primordial functions of armies). Seán, I am firmly convinced that Republicanism (God Almighty it's not even Republicanism with the half of them) of this particular brand is defunct. ...

The lads here are good, sincere and honest, most of them anyway. But there [is] as bad a split here as in the Curragh. I support the O/C and Council more or less against the majority of my countrymen (who are a poor lot anyway – most of them came into this thing about 1940). ... The last straw – a B___ (politically I mean, otherwise nice lad) from Tyrone after being on parole is brought back here – is an ex-member of Duffy's Brigade in Spain. ... There are a good number here who think Yo-Yo Duffy is O.K. and that he and us are pretty much on the same track. I can't see any sense in stopping here – I wish I could see you. I'm in favour of signing out ... give me your advice on the matter.[10]

Seán Furlong was then living in Cumbria, where he worked on the construction of the Royal Ordnance Factory in Sellafield, and was known to British Intelligence as a socialist activist and trades union organiser. In MI5 notes on the file containing the letter, Behan is himself described as an 'extreme Left Wing agitator' and he makes regular appearances in surveillance files throughout the 1950s, not for his republican sympathies, but for his contacts with activists in the communist and socialist movements. Behan's letter was intercepted only because Seán Furlong had enclosed it in a letter he was sending to Fred May, the Irish composer and then musical director of the Abbey Theatre.

Furlong was soliciting Fred May's help to campaign for Behan to be released from prison on condition that he repudiated membership of the IRA (hence Behan's reference in the letter quoted above to 'signing out'). In particular, Seán was pressing May to use his influence with his friend, the Attorney General, Kevin Haugh. To read the correspondence alone, it would appear that Fred May was a family friend, who called with some frequency upon Kathleen and Stephen Behan, who visited Brendan regularly in prison accompanied by family members and whom Seán commends for his 'great human interest in Brendan'.[11] As Michael O'Sullivan established in his biography, Behan and Fred May were lovers, the older composer having befriended Behan when he was fifteen, visited him frequently in prison in the 1940s and renewed a sexual relationship with him upon his release in 1946 (*O'Sullivan*, 91ff, 112, 116–17, 136, 139). O'Sullivan describes May as a 'character in the same pattern' as Micheál Mac Liammóir, who 'with his exquisite manners, finely-tailored clothes and habitual white cotton gloves, could not have failed to make a striking spectacle against the grim background of prison visiting facilities'.[12]

It took considerable devotion and audacity on May's part to campaign for Behan to have opportunities for parole, special visits, and a reduction of his sentence. Behan also wrote to the prison authorities to allow for open visits with May, although there are also some indications that Behan was occasionally overwhelmed and frustrated by May's attentiveness.[13] May was also somewhat brazen in what he was requesting on behalf of a prisoner who might well have been executed for the severity of his crimes. He requested, for example, that the prison governor of Mountjoy allow Behan to attend the final Oireachtas concert performance of his *Scherzo for Orchestra* on 1 November 1942, a mere six months into Behan's fourteen-year sentence. May was at the height of his all-too-brief career as a composer, however, and enjoying a rare spell of attention. His attempts to alleviate Behan's imprisonment coincided with the performance of one of his key works, *Songs from Prison*, which was broadcast on BBC Radio on 14 December 1942. In *Songs from Prison*, May sets the poems of Ernst Toller to music and conveys the emotional depths of a political prisoner who finds solace and hope in the sounds and sights of a swallow's nest outside the bars of his cell window.[14] It is an expressionistic composition, which carries in its baritone vocals the pervasive sense of oppression and yearning for hope, reflecting its wartime context. Toller had been imprisoned as a left-wing radical after the First World War in Munich and forced into exile by the Nazi regime in 1933. Philip Graydon notes that with its allusion to the persecution of Jewish and left-wing intellectuals the composition was deemed to be too compromising for Irish neutrality and was therefore prohibited from broadcast on Radio Éireann.[15] This might well have confirmed in May's mind the analogy, which Harry White believes is possible to discern in *Songs from Prison*, between the philistinism of German fascism and the 'creative torpor, the dead weight of tradition' which stifled artistic composition in mid-century Ireland.[16] Mark Fitzgerald goes further to argue that the work's 'general themes of imprisonment, isolation, brutality, intolerance and the belief in the possibility of a better existence in some utopian spring can all be linked directly to the position of May as a homosexual in Ireland in the 1930s and 1940s where liberty of thought and liberty of action were both forbidden'.[17]

The correspondence between the composition and performance of *Songs from Prison* in 1941 and 1942, and May's affections for Behan, the political prisoner he was striving to see and help, are intriguing, as Mark Fitzgerald has suggested, although he also observes that there is no evidence to suggest anything other than coincidence.[18] It indicates, however, something of the shared political sensibilities of the circles in which May and Behan had come together, besides their other shared passions. Toller inspired much homage among left-wing intellectuals after his apparent suicide in New York in 1939, including the poem written in his honour by W.H. Auden, in which his death is understood as a portent of the shadow of war and tyranny which 'hangs over the earth of the living'.[19] May's attempts to mitigate Behan's prison conditions and sentence were rooted not just in love and friendship, but in a profound sense that Behan had been misled in his involvement in a misguided campaign; he co-ordinated his efforts with Seán Furlong to persuade Behan 'to sign a document dissociating himself from any illegal activities in the future, and to sign it without further delay. After all, he has, or should have, most of life before him – why should he waste or jeopardize any more of it?'[20] Seán Furlong made this point more forcefully to Behan in relation to the reactionary politics of the IRA campaign:

> Well Brendan I was really delighted with your letter. It brought out everything in you. It was the Brendan of pre '39 days. The man I looked up to during Hitler's war in Spain. Remember Brendan the line you're about to adopt won't be palatable to a lot. But as you say yourself a lot of those people don't really matter. The unfortunate thing about them is that they are politically ignorant. They are the fatal Idealists. They would sacrifice the USSR for a British defeat, gloat over the defeat of Spanish progress for a so-called Catholic Victory. These people are reactionaries and as such are no good, nay a burden on the Irish working class. [...] I am sure you will succeed in this your 'Great Awakening'. I like yourself must admit that there's still some stout and noble hearts with you and you may be sure that they will come out thro' the clouds that shroud them.[21]

Seán was calling Brendan back to the socialist principles of his upbringing; indeed a good portion of Behan's literary education as a teenager came through the books which his step-brothers, Seán and Rory, had brought into their house from their subscription to the Left Book Club published by Victor Gollancz, including books by George Orwell, Leonard Woolf, Clifford Odets, Ellen Wilkinson and Arthur Koestler. He was also reminding Brendan of his attempts at the age of fourteen to join Frank Ryan's International Brigade, which was recruiting Irish republicans to fight fascism in Spain and, after he was refused because of his age, his work in Dublin to support Ryan's Brigade (*O'Sullivan*, 33).

It is perhaps difficult to fathom how a young socialist republican, determined to fight fascism in Spain in 1937, would just two years later be imprisoned for his involvement in an IRA sabotage campaign that was colluding with Nazi Germany. By the latter half of 1939, it was possibly too late for Brendan to extricate himself from an IRA campaign against Britain which had begun in January, but which after the outbreak of the Second World War was inevitably and dangerously allied to Nazism. The source of Behan's disillusionment with revolutionary politics was not just the moribund and conservative Irish state which had come into existence after 1922, but the incredibly rapid way in which global politics had manoeuvred a supposedly left-wing revolutionary movement into this increasingly compromised and dangerous alliance with fascism. As the correspondence between Brendan and Seán reveals, both were acutely conscious of how reactionary the IRA had become, with a significant number of Russell's staff supporting General O'Duffy ('Yo-Yo' Duffy as Behan refers to him), the former Blueshirt leader who had organised an Irish Brigade to fight for Franco in Spain and offered to organise an Irish Brigade to fight on the eastern front for Hitler. This, I believe, is the source not just of his disillusionment, but also the recognition evident in his later writings that Irish revolutionary politics had to be calibrated to the events and orientations of other revolutionary movements around the globe. Acting supposedly in Ireland's national cause alone proved a slippery course.

It is clear from the correspondence between Seán Furlong, Fred May and Brendan Behan that there was a concerted campaign to persuade Behan to turn away from his loyalty to the IRA, which had ceased to be the socialist republican movement it had been just a few years earlier. It is clear also that Fred May was helping not just with Behan's political persuasions, but also with his turn towards a literary vocation. Brendan wrote to May for help in getting his manuscripts out of prison, for although the governor permitted Behan to write and send out his manuscripts to potential publishers, they had to pass through the Department of Justice for approval and permission to publish was refused in October 1942.[22] An early draft of *The Landlady*, Behan's first attempt to write a play, was inscribed 'For Fred May', either in dedication to him, or addressed to him for his advice and assistance.[23] Brendan also

requested that Fred May send him Maupassant's stories in French;[24] he
professed to be learning French from his former explosives trainer Peadar
O'Flaherty, who had been imprisoned during the 1939 campaign. Although
he admitted that he was not 'doing much good at it', on account of laziness,[25]
the request to May to send Maupassant indicates his literary motivations for
learning French. Indeed, his literary apprenticeship is a common theme of the
correspondence and recollections that we have as records of his prison experiences. Among his other republican mentors in prison were Seán Ó Briain,
an Irish-language scholar who taught the young Behan the Irish language
and who imparted to him a love of Gaelic classic literature, such as Brian
Merriman's *Cúirt An Mheán Oíche*, Tomás Ó Criomhthain's *An t-Oileánach*,
and the stories of Pádraic Ó Conaire.[26] When Behan was moved to the
Curragh detention camp in 1944, he was fortunate to have among his fellow inmates perhaps the most accomplished Gaelic novelist of his generation,
Máirtín Ó Cadhain, who guided and encouraged Behan in his literary education (*O'Sullivan*, 115). Outside of prison both Peadar O'Donnell and Seán
Ó Faoláin, editors of *The Bell*, took a close interest in Behan's development as a
writer in prison, and advised him on drafts of his work.[27] None of this literary
education is recorded in that most unreliable of Behan's books, *Confessions of
an Irish Rebel*, in which his time in Mountjoy, Arbour Hill and the Curragh
passes quickly singing rebel songs and playing handball (*Confessions*, 47–81).

BEHAN IN BOHEMIA

That prison provided Behan with an education in modern languages and
literatures almost equal to the Irish universities to which he would certainly
have been denied access is an obvious conclusion to draw from the evidence
of his correspondence and the recollections of his fellow inmates. However,
what is more remarkable about the education and support which Behan
received in prison is the extent to which it was self-directed and oriented
towards a bohemian tradition of aesthetics and politics. Behan's predilections
for Merriman, Ó Criomhthain and Ó Conaire in Irish drew upon a dissident,
libertarian tradition, quite distinct from the sanctioned, puritan version of
Gaelic Ireland peddled in schools. According to Ó Briain, 'he went far deeper
into the subject than his gaiety would suggest, and he loved to talk and learn

about life on the Blaskets, Dun Chaoin, and Ballyferriter'.[28] His own poems in Irish, which were mostly written in prison and in Paris in the late 1940s, draw upon his bohemian orientations. 'Jackeen ag Caoineadh na mBlascaod', for example, positions the poet as an outsider, at once besotted with and mournful for the passing of these islands 'ar imeall/ An domhain' (on the edge of the world), which he had only glimpsed in the writings of Ó Criomhthain and Muiris Ó Súilleabháin.[29] Like Synge in *The Aran Islands*, Yeats in his account of visiting Aran, or E.M. Forster in his preface to the English translation of Ó Súilleabháin's *Fiche Bliain ag Fás* (*Twenty Years-a-Growing*), Behan admired the remaining Irish-speaking communities of the Atlantic coastline as places apart from modernity, and which embodied freedom from the prevailing social and moral codes of modernity. According to his own affectionate accounts of staying on Aran, he revelled in these freedoms enjoyed by the islanders, and perhaps with a typical snub to Dublin society, claimed that it was only on Aran that he was 'damned nearly civilised'.[30]

In the poems he wrote in Paris, too, Behan identifies himself with dissidence and the intellectual and sexual freedoms of expatriate life. In his poem for Oscar Wilde, for example, he laments the deserted, wasting body of the poet, dying alone in the Latin Quarter, but celebrates his life as one of joyful sinning ways, in which he had it 'every way':

> Dá aoibhne bealach an pheacaigh
> is mairg bás gan bheannacht;
> mo ghraidhin thú, a Oscair,
> bhí sé agat gach bealach! (*PPI*, 20)

The reasons why Behan wrote this poem in Irish, and in Paris, are perhaps more obvious when we look at how it was translated, or 'done into English', by Donagh MacDonagh, in its first publication in Ireland, in the *Irish Times* in 1952:

> Though sin is a broad and pleasant pathway
> It is well to be blessed on your dying day.
> Oscar, my lad,
> You had it both ways.[31]

The translation stresses a tone almost of rebuke, chastising Oscar for the sinful ways which have left him without a death-bed blessing, a tone heightened by the way in which 'my lad' can be read as a term of both paternal affection and parental censure. 'My lad' fails to capture the loving, cherishing sense of 'mo ghraidhin', however, in which it is clear that Behan identifies wholly with Wilde and with his joyful 'ways'. Behan also plays upon a sexual pun in the word 'bealach', which does mean 'pathway' or 'ways', as it has been translated, but also looks and sounds proximate to 'béal', meaning mouth or opening, and 'béalach', meaning loose-tongued, or loquacious. Wilde had been a hero for Behan since his time in borstal, where he first read Frank Harris' biography (*BB*, 244). The moment of discovering Harris' biography is associated for Behan with a young man whose 'cigarette holder and [...] civilian silk tie of rose colour' already marks him out among the borstal inmates for his sexual and class identity, and it is this boy, the nephew of a famous but unnamed English novelist, who tells Behan 'exactly' what Wilde was imprisoned for, and commends him to read Harris' book. The epigraph of Harris' biography alone articulates a persistent theme of Behan's writings: 'The crucifixion of the guilty is still more awe-inspiring than the crucifixion of the innocent; what do we men know of innocence?'[32]

Behan's similarities to Wilde and his empathy for Wilde's last days would certainly have been part of the reason why he gravitated towards Paris in the late 1940s. The literary cachet of James Joyce in Paris was another reason and, as Behan makes clear in his poem 'Buíochas le Joyce', meant that Irish writers in Paris such as Samuel Beckett, Brian Coffey, Thomas MacGreevy and Behan had a literary legacy on which to trade: 'Molaim gach comhartha dár chuiris ar phár / Is mise san Fhrainc ag ól Pernod dá bharr' (I extol every mark you put on paper / and as a result here I am in France drinking Pernod at the bar). As Thomas O'Grady has argued, Behan's poem is much more than an acknowledgement of Joyce's international reputation, or an expression of the anxiety of influence. Rather, it is a complex engagement with ideas of poetic form, language, tone and tradition, in which Behan's careful location of the poem in the Rue Saint André des Arts sets the scene for questions about the very role and place of 'des arts'.[33] Paris might be regarded as a diversion for Behan, as a means of escaping Ireland without breaking his deportation order in Britain, or committing himself to a more permanent exile in America. Yet Paris was the perfect place in post-war Europe for Behan to ask the questions that emerged in his early writings, about guilt and punishment, about sexuality, and about the relationship between art and politics.

In Paris, Behan was not merely walking in the shadows of Oscar Wilde and James Joyce. He was also walking with Albert Camus, sitting alongside Jean-Paul Sartre and Simone de Beauvoir in the Café de Flore and the Café les Deux Magots, and listening to the works of Jean Genet being read aloud. As Stephen Watt has shown, although Behan and Genet never met, the two writers shared many thematic preoccupations and formal characteristics.[34] The extent of Behan's understanding of the philosophical bases of existentialism is not best demonstrated in his poem of that title. 'L'Existentialisme' seems to play with the conceits of the movement, although perhaps it captures a sense he shared with Camus and Sartre of the post-war turmoil in which neither art nor philosophy had secure foundations: 'Maitheas, níl a dhath, / ná ciall, ná pian, fiú amháin, / ná an fhírinne i m'abairt, / ná ina mhalairt' (Goodness, not a semblance, / nor sense, nor pain, even, / nor the truth in my sayings, / nor in their opposites).[35] Colbert Kearney reads the poem as Behan's 'verse doodle' which, if taken seriously, may be read as a signal of his intention to abandon the futility of poetry in Irish, and abandon the self-appointed task of being the 'watchman' keeping guard for the language revival (Kearney, 60–1). Yet, this is to localise Behan's profound doubts about the role of art and politics away from the intellectual uncertainties of post-war Paris itself. For Hannah Arendt, the popularity of existentialism after the war lay precisely in the 'spiritual bankruptcy of the left and the sterility of the old revolutionary élite', and the 'feeling that the responsibility for political action is too heavy to assume until new foundations, ethical as well as political, are laid down'.[36] It would be a stretch to argue that Behan might be considered an existentialist (and, in any case, even Camus and Sartre shrugged off this label), but both *The Quare Fellow* and *The Hostage* certainly bear examination as dramatic demonstrations of Sartre's critique of *l'esprit de sérieux*. Neither virtue nor sin exist outside of social codes and constructs in both plays and the tragic elements of both derive from the actions of those characters who act according to a predetermined faith. Behan did not learn this philosophical lesson from reading *Being and Nothingness*, of course; his own awakening to the shifting moral bearings of the IRA and the hypocrisies of sexual morality he witnessed in the Dublin of his upbringing were more direct and effective sources. Yet he arrived at similar conclusions to Sartre and Camus about the nature of freedom and virtue, the pretence of religious and political morality, and the absurdities of human society; these were the subjects of his art.

Accordingly, it was in Paris that Behan could feel sufficiently free to develop the forms of his art. Paris was the city in which Behan wrote much of *Borstal Boy* and probably the bulk of *The Quare Fellow* also. The two short stories he published in the literary magazine *Points* – based in Paris and edited by Peggy Guggenheim's son, Sindbad Vail – reveal the extent to which he had become a more committed and daring writer than was evident from his earlier writings, such as *The Landlady* or 'I Become a Borstal Boy'. 'After the Wake', which was published in *Points* in January 1951, is a neatly crafted narrative of homoerotic seduction, in which the narrator tells the story of his campaign to persuade a young male neighbour, whose wife dies during an operation for cancer, of how natural and right it would be for the two men to share a bed after her death.[37] The story concludes with the narrator undressing the young man, and preparing to slip into bed beside him:

> I first loosened his collar to relieve the flush on his smooth cheeks, took off his shoes and socks and pants and shirt, from the supply muscled thighs, the stomach flat as an altar boy's and noted the golden smoothness of the blond hair on every part of his firm white flesh.[38]

It is mildly intriguing to wonder what response Behan might have received had he submitted this story to *The Bell*. He did not, of course; *Points* was one of several little magazines publishing late modernist work in Paris in the immediate post-war years that enjoyed the intellectual and cultural freedom to publish work that could be open and exploratory about sexuality, about drugs, about morality. In 'After the Wake', however, Behan is not just availing of an opportunity to be more explicit about homoerotic desire than he could in Ireland. The story is a much more calculated exploration of sexual morality and its social bases. It begins with the thought that, had the young wife known of what the narrator had in mind for her husband, 'she'd feel angry, not so much jealous as disgusted, certainly surprised'.[39] The narrator invites us to share two insights simultaneously: that there is nothing more natural than homosexual love between men, and that there is nothing more unexpected than homosexual love between men. His campaign of seduction succeeds, even though he is surrounded by priests, old women and even the man's mother, because the sexual innocence of his relationship with the young man is presumed throughout. The story is one of considerable moral ambiguity; the narrator is a predator who ruthlessly exploits the innocence of others for his own sexual gain, but as the narrator's desire inhabits the story entirely there is no counter-vailing moral perspective invoked against him. The imagined disgust of the man's dead wife, if only she could know from beyond the grave, is no moral judgement on his actions, since the dead are understood to be no bar to the will of the living. Writing against the criminalisation and demonisation of homosexuality in his own country, Behan found an outlet in Paris for explor-ing the idea that sexuality and morality are social conventions and that virtue lay in the fulfilment of desire.

If 'After the Wake' can be seen as an exceptional story in Behan's oeuvre, the next story he published in *Points* has a central place in the small canon of his best works. 'Bridewell Revisited' is a version of the opening of *Borstal Boy*, which is already very close to the published novel. The pose of the defiant republican rebel is exposed as a performance in the first few pages. Published in *Points* in the winter of 1951, 'Bridewell Revisited' is already a world away from the republican melodrama pastiche of 'I Become a Borstal Boy'.[40] Indeed, in contradistinction from the model of political idealism and honourable sacrifice, which Behan upholds in his story in *The Bell*, this later version of his borstal boy experiences offers a rather more wry and subversive narrative:

> Oh, Cathlin ni Houlihan, your way is a thorny way. Much you knew about it, Yeats, yourself and Maud Gonne, bent over a turf fire reading Ronsard.
>
> A horny way, you mean. Wonder if Emmet did it in prison, or de Valera? Who'd have thought the old man had so much blood in him?
>
> And, tingling all over, pleasantly tired from the exercise, I fell asleep.[41]

In the version of this scene in *Borstal Boy*, he is considerably more circumspect, even discreet:

> I put my mind on other things. It was at least and at last permissible to a man in my position.
>
> Then I settled myself more comfortably and wondered if anyone else had done it in the same position. I didn't like to mention them by name, even in my mind. Some of them had left the cell for the rope or the firing squad. More pleasantly tired, from the exercise, I fell asleep. (*BB*, 16)

The freedom to explore a more irreverent perspective on both republican tradition and his literary precursors was clearly enabled for Behan by publishing in a little magazine in Paris. This does not just entail discretion about what to include and what to omit from his account. After all, even in *Points* expletives had to be obscured with dashes to appease US censors, who could seize and impound copies of the magazine sent from Paris to the vital list of US subscribers. The significance of 'Bridewell Revisited' also lies in how the story of Behan's incarceration is framed. The story ends with a scene which differs hardly at all from the versions published in *Borstal Boy*, in which Behan sings a love song in Irish to Charlie Millwall, the English sailor who shows him kindness and affection in Walton Jail. The scene concludes with the image of both boys whispering good night to each other through the spy-hole of their cell doors.[42] It is a touchingly romantic scene and in concluding the story with it, Behan suggests a narrative trajectory which takes us from his arrest as a failed IRA bomber to his redemption through homoerotic love for an English sailor. It is the same trajectory that we can trace in *Borstal Boy*, but it is made more explicit structurally in *Points*.

Behan went to Paris in September 1948 and stayed in St Germain des Prés among artists, intellectuals and students, and he made lengthy visits for months at a time to Paris over the next five years. 'Everyone admires Paris for the artists,' wrote Behan, 'I equally loved Paris for the barricades.'[43] Yet Paris was not just the city in which he brought together art and politics. Although he published little in Paris, what he did publish displays a more expansive and expressive sense of sexual identity than anything he was able to publish or perform in Ireland, or England. It is undoubtedly the case that the social and intellectual circles in which he moved in St Germain des Prés afforded him the freedom to explore a more irreverent and expressive mode of writing than was previously possible. There is also, however, the more tantalising prospect that Paris was not just stimulating as a city of exile, but as a home, in which he found he shared much in common with the most prominent French writers in the city at that time – Camus, Sartre and Genet – and indeed much in common with other writers enjoying Paris as exiles, such as Alexander Trocchi, James Baldwin and Samuel Beckett.

BEHAN AND LATE MODERNISM

Anthony Roche made a groundbreaking and convincing case many years ago for seeing Behan and Beckett as preoccupied with similar thematic and formal problems, partly based on the production of their first major plays in Ireland in the Pike Theatre in Dublin in 1954–5.[44] To some extent, Roche was re-situating Beckett within an Irish context to counter the tendency of theatre critics to see his work as closely allied to Sartre.[45] Yet, there may be grounds for reversing the analogy: we might wonder about comparisons between Behan and Sartre, whose *Men Without Shadows* was performed at the Pike Theatre in an unusual and contrasting double bill with Behan's stage adaptation of his radio play *The Big House* in April 1958. It could not have been performed in the same programme as *The Quare Fellow* or *The Hostage*, but while there are considerable differences in tone between Sartre and Behan, as indeed there are differences in tone between Beckett and Behan, there are certainly similarities between Sartre and Behan in their treatments of the themes of innocence, authority and morality. The differences in tone were perhaps less evident in the Pike productions of Sartre and Behan than they might appear now from reading the plays. Alan Simpson recorded how in one of the most gruesome scenes in *Men Without Shadows*, the actor playing Henri struggled to suppress his giggles during the desperate act of killing his young Resistance accomplice, François, when the schoolboy actor mischievously winked at him.[46] The Pike developed something of a reputation for affective theatre around both playwrights; it was reported that female members of the audience for *Men Without Shadows* fainted during the torture scenes (there had been riots when the play was performed in Paris), and some of Behan's former prison mates declared their feelings of discomfort during the opening night of *The Quare Fellow* on finding themselves inside claustrophobic prison walls again.[47] Plays by Sartre, Ionesco and Camus were produced with some frequency in the mid-1950s at both the Pike Theatre and the Studio Theatre Club in Upper Mount Street. Simpson records that it was on the occasion of the Pike producing the first English-language version of Sartre's *Nekrassov* that Behan, flush with the success of *The Quare Fellow* in London, donated substantially to theatre funds.[48] That much of this interest in performing existentialist plays from Paris in Dublin theatres followed in the wake of the success of Behan as well as Beckett might indicate that there is as much to recover of a French Behan as there has been in recent scholarship of an Irish Beckett.[49]

If in 1939 in Killiney Castle, listening to the words of Flann O'Brien's *At Swim-Two-Birds* while hunched over his trainee bomb-maker's kit, Brendan Behan was becoming dimly conscious of the absurdity of his profound estrangement from the major currents of events flowing across Europe, by the mid-1950s he was part of a generation of Irish artists and writers who were bringing the reviving intellectual energies of Europe to Dublin. When he heeded the calls of those who loved him to turn away from a political movement that had lost touch with its own ethical springs, his literary apprenticeship in a succession of prisons and in the bohemian enclaves of Dublin and Paris would bear fruit, albeit tragically short-lived, in the success he enjoyed around the world with *The Quare Fellow*, *The Hostage* and *Borstal Boy*. What he shared aesthetically with the other post-war writers whom he encountered in Paris – Beckett, Camus, Trocchi, Sartre and Baldwin, among many others – is not easy to summarise or label.[50] Theodor Adorno perhaps captured a shared feeling of this generation best in the opening lines of *Aesthetic Theory*, when he wrote: 'It is self-evident that nothing concerning art is self-evident anymore, not its inner life, not its relation to the world, not even its right to exist.'[51] It is a line that might have appeared mock-seriously in *At Swim-Two-Birds*, but it reflects the restless spirit of late modernist writers such as Behan, struggling to imagine humanity anew – in its bareness, in its capaciousness – in an age characterised by its brutal inhumanity.

4

BRENDAN BEHAN:
MODERNIST WRITER

DEIRDRE McMAHON

That Brendan Behan was working in a modernist tradition should be obvious. It can be seen in the minimalism of his early poem 'Uaigneas'; the challenge to heteronormativity in 'After the Wake'; the expressionism and absurdism of *The Quare Fellow*; the sophisticated aesthetics of *An Giall* and its unruly offspring *The Hostage*; and in *Borstal Boy*, the autobiographical novel which troubles orthodox views of identity and achieves subjective autonomy through psychological exploration. In light of current critical assessments of Irish modernism, Behan's work seems more and more evidently comparable to the modernist work of Moore, Egerton, Yeats, Wilde, Shaw, Synge, Joyce and, later, Bowen, Deevy, Salkeld, Johnston, Kate O'Brien, Flann O'Brien and Beckett. Writing of *An Giall*, Declan Kiberd claimed that its 'unashamed experimentalism and expressionist sequences proved that a Gaelic modernism had belatedly arrived' (*PPI*, 10). The recreation of *An Giall* as *The Hostage* would, of course, provoke lasting debate around authorship, with claims that Behan's reworking in English for Joan Littlewood's Theatre Workshop was largely authored by the English producer. This is an argument that can be rigorously challenged by tracing Behan's own aesthetics, as David Clare has done through his analysis that convincingly argues for *The Hostage* script as pure Behan.[1] Behan's literary output may be comparatively lean, but then, as Stephen Watt so aptly puts it, 'Happily, theatre and literary histories do not operate like accounting ledgers; more is not always more.'[2]

Even if it was obvious to the many intellectuals in Dublin of the 1950s that Behan was drawing on the familiar roots of European modernism (Carolyn Swift and Alan Simpson, to name just two), his subsequent fame notoriously eclipsed an appropriate critical appraisal of his writing. Certainly, biographical contexts inform his work. Behan was a republican who grew weary of political idealism; a writer who railed against the conservative social and sexual orthodoxies of post-independence Irish society; a gifted scholar who had little formal education but still acquired a rich knowledge of literature. However, of interest here is Behan's articulation of various socio-political realities through the modernist aesthetic. In this essay I explore Behan's formal strategies in *Borstal Boy* and his affinity with those of Samuel Beckett in his novel *Molloy*. I also discuss the significance of Dublin's Pike Theatre to Behan as a modernist writer.

Born in 1923, Behan practically grew up in the theatre due to the unrestricted access he enjoyed to the Queen's, which was managed by his uncle, the actor and dramatist P. J. Bourke. Behan's cousin, playwright Séamus de Búrca, described Behan as a 'precocious playgoer'.[3] His formative years were spent in a city that enjoyed the modernist plays being produced by the Dublin Drama League and the Gate Theatre.[4] Following his initial engagement with the late 1940s Parisian avant-garde literary scene, Behan fed his appetite for experimental work by attending the little theatre clubs of 1950s Dublin. In 1953, he attempted to have his work staged at the tiny 37 Theatre Club, which was then mounting productions of Elmer Rice (*The Adding Machine* in 1951) and Maurice Meldon (*Aisling, A Dream Analysis* in 1953).[5] It is likely that Behan attended the 37's 1953 production in translation of Jean Cocteau's play *The Eagle Has Two Heads*.[6] Following rejection of his work by the Abbey and the Gate, Behan's abandoned script of *The Quare Fellow* was rescued from the Gate offices by the actor, and niece of Micheál Mac Liammóir, Sally Travers, who alerted Carolyn Swift and Alan Simpson, directors of the Pike Theatre Club. The result was their introduction of Behan's work to the Irish stage on 19 November 1954 with the world premiere of *The Quare Fellow*.[7]

Behan immersed himself in Dublin's 1940s–'50s anti-authoritarian modernist milieu. His grandmother-in-law was the modernist poet Blanaid Salkeld, who, like Behan, came under the influence of T.S. Eliot[8] and who also adored the company and stories of the younger writer. She was, in fact, the 'only member of the family not to express surprise or even the slightest indignation' at her granddaughter Beatrice marrying Behan (*O'Sullivan*, 189). Behan befriended the modernist composer Frederick May, the artist Lucien Freud and in Paris, Samuel Beckett, James Baldwin and Albert Camus. He scribbled down the name and address of the avant-garde Paris publisher Sindbad Vail and sought him out.[9] Vail subsequently became the first to publish Behan's work internationally and the only one to publish 'After the Wake' in Behan's lifetime. Ireland's heightened conservatism and continued criminalisation of homosexuality ensured that Behan's treatment of the theme in his short story would see it consigned to relative obscurity until 1978.[10] While imprisoned in the Curragh Camp (1944–6), Behan enjoyed the mentorship of Máirtín Ó Cadhain, whose modernist novel *Cré na Cille* was published in 1949. In prison he was also tutored by Seán Ó Briain, who introduced him to, amongst other works, Merriman's *Cúirt an Mheáin Oíche*, and recalls Behan's love of the stories of Pádraic Ó Conaire.[11]

Stylistic features of Behan's writing reveal formal similarities with twentieth-century European literary modernism, such as fragmentation, narrative retreats and negation, inversion of narrative expectation, relocation of narrative to a psychological interior, role playing and performativity, and disruption of accepted chronological order in favour of recovering the past from the recesses of memory to make sense of the present. Behan's layering of genres frequently results in narrative digression, often into song and storytelling. This can give the impression of laxity, yet his departures have purpose. The self-awareness of his narrative style is linked by Colbert Kearney to the Irish tradition of the *seanchaí*, where the storyteller 'commands attention not merely by relating but also by re-enacting; he achieves depth not by commentary or analysis but by the dramatic power of his performance'.[12] To this could be added that Behan's re-enacting and *re*membering sees him build autonomy through his narration, at times creating contiguity between a disembodied past and the present, as when Behan moves his narrator Brendan into direct dialogue with the executed Irish revolutionary Tom Clarke in *Borstal Boy*. In Proustian fashion, the move rejects conventional temporality and attempts to make sense of a present that has proved disappointing for Behan in a post-1916, post-independence Ireland (a repeated theme in his work).[13]

Behan frequently reveals his engagement with the European modernists. His frustration with naturalistic readings of his work is palpable in his 1961 reaction to Sylvère Lotringer's suggestion that some found his depiction of IRA members in *The Hostage* 'a bit artificial'.[14] Behan invokes Bertolt Brecht and Jaroslav Hašek in defence of alternative readings: 'Well, it's artificial only to people who do not understand the theatre. Only to people who do not know music-hall, vaudeville [...] they have never seen the Berliner Ensemble by Bertolt Brecht. I don't imitate Brecht but . . . [sic] Have you ever read *The Good Soldier Schweik* by Jaroslav Hasek?'[15] When Behan categorically acknowledges Seán O'Casey's influence on his work, he intends the modernist rather than the realist O'Casey: 'the writing of *Borstal Boy*, in form, I think was finally decided by my reading Seán O'Casey's *Autobiographies*. [...] One of them, *I Knock at the Door*, where he brings in characters and sometimes they've got phoney names and sometimes they've got real names. He doesn't worry very much about time; he just tells you the story. And tells you what happened as he imagines it had happened.'[16] When it came to writing *Borstal Boy*, Behan chose an extract from Virginia Woolf's *Orlando* for its epigraph. The move is not only significant in its intertextuality with Woolf's novel about sexual identity, the inclusion also reveals Behan's interest in her literary style and her modernist aesthetic. Furthermore, as discussed below, Behan shares formal strategies with Jean Genet. He also displays an engagement with the work of the French writer and careful consideration of biographical similarities.[17]

Given Behan's engagement with experimental theatre, it is unsurprising that his first major modernist work, *The Quare Fellow*, should have been premiered at the Pike Theatre. Indeed, it was his success in fringe theatre that eventually brought acceptance for Behan by the mainstream. The Pike's director, Alan Simpson, demonstrated his hunger for avant-garde drama when he eagerly sought the rights to stage Beckett's 1953 *En Attendant Godot* in translation,[18] as well as Ionesco's *The Bald Prima Donna* and plays by Sartre.[19] When it came to the pioneering director Joan Littlewood, Behan's affinity with her working-class, socialist politics certainly eased the way for a professional collaboration. However, it was her commitment to modernist drama at the Theatre Workshop in east London that really drew him to her. When Behan endorses Littlewood's brand of political theatre, he simultaneously reveals his engagement with T.S. Eliot's philosophy of theatre by paraphrasing the modernist poet and dramatist with considerable accuracy. The occasion was

Behan's recollection of a 1958 rehearsal of *An Giall*, which was, of course, later directed by Littlewood in its reincarnation as *The Hostage*:

> While I admire the producer, Frank Dermody, tremendously, his idea of a play is not my idea of a play [...]. He's of the school of Abbey Theatre naturalism of which I'm not a pupil. Joan Littlewood, I found, suited my requirements exactly. She has the same views on the theatre that I have, which is that music hall is the thing to aim at for to amuse people and any time they get bored, divert them with a song or a dance. I've always thought T.S. Eliot wasn't far wrong when he said that the main problem of the dramatist today was to keep his audience amused; and that while they were laughing their heads off, you could be up to any bloody thing behind their backs; and it was what you were doing behind their bloody backs that made your play great. (*BBI*, 17)[20]

Given the sophistication of Behan's aesthetics, it comes as no surprise that he should express an affinity with Eliot's ideas on multi-layered drama.

If, as Behan states, 'music hall [was] the thing to aim at', he was drawing on his early exposure to music hall and Victorian melodrama, which was popular at his uncle's Queen's Theatre. However, in Behan's hands convention is employed to challenge hard-line nationalist rhetoric. He adopts stock ingredients of melodrama and music hall only to subvert them; he raises expectation of generic convention only to interrupt it with parody and farce, as seen in both *An Giall* and *The Hostage*. If Behan employs the stock hero/villain characters, the British soldier Leslie is the hero, and the villain the IRA officer; if nationalist sentiment is raised, it is refused and undercut by Meg Dillon's sardonic wit, and interruptions by characters of outrageously diverse identities who shatter the orthodoxies of normalcy. Behan's subversive deployment of melodrama and music hall participates in political theatre, not only practised by Littlewood, but also by playwrights from John Osborne to Shelagh Delaney.

Behan's modernist aesthetics invert and disrupt the boundaries of identity that were being so vigorously protected in 1950s Ireland. Dublin's little theatre clubs ran the gauntlet of the ultra-conservative 'lay clerics', as Seán Ó Faoláin called them, who acted as watchdogs for the authorities, monitoring theatre output for 'indecency'.[21] Charting the plays of Jack Yeats, Elizabeth Connor,

Donagh MacDonagh and Maurice Meldon, Ian R. Walsh documents Behan's interest in anti-mimetic drama, while noting that Behan's 'schooling took place in the experimental basement theatres, the ballad theatre of MacDonagh and the music-halls of Dublin'.[22] Mimetic drama, described by Desmond Maxwell as a 'self-enclosing realism [...] to the world which it is modelling',[23] was, notoriously, favoured by the Abbey's managing director Ernest Blythe during his long tenure from 1941 to 1967. Behan's experimental literary style departed from such realism and created a fluidity in identity. In the post-1932 de Valera years, innovation was met with resistance and global modernity was feared as conspiring to destabilise the fixed boundaries of Irish national identity.[24] In this climate of heightened conservatism, Behan's counter-cultural modernism unsettled such views.

Behan brought his increasingly ambitious aesthetics to his later prose work. When he chose to write a prison journal of his incarceration in England from 1939–41, it was retrospective and written with the benefit of mature reflection. Behan's choice of the hybrid genre of autobiography and novel for *Borstal Boy*, combined with the book's long gestation period from 1941 to 1958,[25] facilitated the writer's measured reconstruction of memory. Through the medium of the autobiographical novel, Behan was able to construct an alternative identity and a sense of inclusion in the liminal space of a prison. In doing so, he disrupts the nationalist binary of self and place, thereby subverting the notion of an essentialised Irish identity. His technique evokes that used by Beckett in his novel *Molloy*. Although Behan had published extracts from his prison journal in 1942, it was not until he moved to Paris in 1948 that he began to write the novel in earnest (*O'Connor*, 142, 150). Behan recalled his first four-month visit to Paris as taking place in 1947 and shared an anecdote about socialising with Beckett and his niece (*Confessions*, 147–54). Biographical accounts, however, record his stay in 1948. Either way, the timing is significant as work on his novel coincided with the early stage of his relationship with Beckett, at a time when Beckett was about to write *En Attendant Godot*. Behan was also in Paris in 1952 when Beckett was in rehearsal for the premiere of *Godot* at the Théâtre de Babylone, and certainly met Beckett at that time. As Anthony Roche argues, it is not hard to imagine that Behan had early access to the text.[26] Behan must surely also have been familiar with *Molloy*, which Beckett completed in 1947, although it was not published until March 1951 (in French). Behan had studied French while in prison, as documented in his 1943 letter to Séamus de

Búrca, when he requests the 'Maupassant in the French because I'm learning it now' (*Letters*, 24). Moreover, during the early 1950s, Behan associated with the influential group of writers and editors behind the Paris literary magazine *Merlin*, founded by Alexander Trocchi, that published early works by Beckett, Genet, Ionesco and Neruda. *Merlin*'s office was in Trocchi's apartment, which was also the site of the magazine's frequent readings and intellectual gatherings.[27] The office was in close proximity to Beckett's publisher, Les Éditions de Minuit, where copies of *Molloy* were prominently displayed in the picture window. Behan would have had to pass the display on his way up to the *Points* magazine office, which was housed in the same building. Behan also had time between the 1955 publication of *Molloy* in English and publication of *Borstal Boy* in 1958 to fully consider Beckett's aesthetics.

Although Behan's behaviour could, no doubt, be challenging, there is a genuine fondness expressed by Beckett for Behan. Both writers shared a sense of exile in Paris and both had suffered from rejection of their work in Ireland. The high regard in which Beckett held Behan's work is expressed in his 1955 letter to Alan Simpson, congratulating him on the Pike's success with *The Quare Fellow*, when he signs off by saying, 'Remember me to the new O'Casey.'[28] After visiting Behan in a London hospital in 1962, Beckett commented: 'I admired him for his marvellous warmth.'[29] This visit, so many years after they had first met, suggests a continued regard[30] and it is no surprise that following Behan's death in 1964 Beckett's tribute to Behan for the German magazine *Theater heute* should offer 'all homage and affection – and deep sorrow that no more'.[31]

Borstal Boy shares with *Molloy* the device of creating what Patrick Bixby identified in Beckett's novel as a deterritorialised space.[32] In *Molloy*, Beckett creates the character of the title as a nomad, thereby dislocating him from place. The action sees Beckett intervene in the space between self and place, which separates Molloy from his subjective present and communal past, thereby rupturing any sense of belonging and authenticity, central to the tenets of nationalism.[33] Molloy and his alter ego, the property owning Moran, are diametrically opposed and effectively cancel each other out through the metamorphosis of one into the other, as they endlessly circle in the episodic novel. Beckett's deterministic inclination in *Molloy* directly implicates nationalist ideology, employing, as it does, tropes of home and belonging to repeatedly show its lack of progress. Strategies used by Beckett to counter exclusionary nationalist discourse can also be read into *Borstal Boy*. Similar to the space which Beckett creates, the retrospective nature of Behan's autobiographical novel, along with its setting in the liminal space of a prison, allows Behan to create an autonomous space in which to intervene, imagine, and negotiate an alternative identity.

In the deterritorialised space which he creates, Behan interrogates exclusionary identity and posits alternatives. At times, coded language challenges a heteronormative hegemony by evoking homosexual desire. The vividness and detail of the narrative reconstruction of Brendan's first sighting of the character Charlie Millwall – a fictitious name designed to protect the anonymity of a friend who was killed in the Second World War (*O'Sullivan*, 312, n. 27) – follows the narrator's eye as he finds his point of attraction and, in turn, his gaze is returned:

> There were four bowls, all in use. A very old, or very down-and-out man, was replacing brown papers inside his shirt. A young man, in a bottle-green suit and a look of stupid conceit, was surveying his fingernails. There was a boy in a sailor's uniform, a little older than I, but lighter built. I took my place behind him, innocently admiring the back of his neck […] the sailor turned round. He had brown hair and long dark eyelashes. He rubbed his chin, and smiled. (*BB*, 9–10)

In the choreography between Brendan and Charlie that follows, there is a tenderness and intimacy as they fix each other's clothes; the scene is followed by one in which language expresses homoeroticism as they communicate through the walls of their cells, with 'lips [and] mouth to the spy-hole' (*BB*, 14, 18). Obvious parallels can be drawn here to Genet's 1950 film *Un Chant d'Amour*, where homosexual relationships between prisoners develop by communication through a minute hole in the wall. It is worth noting that, during moments of intense trauma, Genet's characters often retreat into an autonomous psychic interior, to which the action of the plot also transfers.[34] Behan frequently creates such interiority for Brendan. At times, the action involves a narrative retreat to the voice of historical heroes. On the occasion preceding his brutal beating in Walton Jail, Brendan withdraws to enter into dialogue with the executed republican revolutionary Thomas Clarke: 'Grip tight, and hold on, said Tom Clarke. [to which Brendan replies] I'd do my best'

(*BB*, 64). Writing as a mature man, Behan's reconstruction of the memory collapses time between past and present. If the retreat is triggered, Genet style, by a traumatic present, given that his own premature death was just years away, Behan's narrative is also infused with a sad irony when he draws the future into his present moment: 'maybe this bit of a belting they [his kidneys] got would be a contributory cause of my early death in the years to come, but sure what matter of that?' (*BB*, 68).

Behan creates a number of roles for Brendan as he navigates him between an interior and exterior space. In his comparison between the work of Behan and Genet, Stephen Watt notes that Genet will interrupt 'his narrative with thoughts of the outside world [to complete] the performing or becoming of the Other'.[35] In *Borstal Boy*, Behan uses a similar device for Brendan, as during his psychological retreat from his cell to think of his family: 'I only thought of them because I thought it was what I should do, in my situation; and it was only for a moment I went on thinking of them, and then I came back here to my cell in the cold' (*BB*, 112). Watt argues that performing is not only a 'process of re-entry to a lost or secret self [it is also] a method of world building'.[36] Brendan's frequent internal monologue throughout the novel expresses an inner voice, 'in my own mind', that cannot be articulated by his outer voice. This happens in the scene with the pious nationalist Lavery when Brendan's outward display of loyalty to the nationalist cause is inverted by his inner voice. To Lavery's comment that 'I can see a joke as well as the next sod' (*BB*, 186), Brendan responds internally: 'you could, be Jesus, if it was two feet from your nose written as high as the neon sign over Larne Harbour' (*BB*, 186–7). Coded language, psychological interiority and a recovery of the past become subversive in an attempt to create autonomy and explore forbidden identities.

When Behan was released from the Curragh Military Camp in 1946, he emerged from prison wary of political idealism. Behan's disillusionment is dramatised in *Borstal Boy* when the young Brendan grows impatient with political idealists. The onset can be seen in Brendan's early encounter with the republican fanatic Callan, who attempts to recruit him as a puppet for his political rhetoric, and which Brendan resists, before asserting his autonomy later in the narrative. The shift to greater defiance is figured in Brendan's encounter with Lavery, whose hard-line nationalist rhetoric is depicted as narrow and exclusionary. The heterogeneous identities of prisoners are often unified through song and language, such as when, at the close of *Borstal Boy*, Brendan's words are spoken 'with an almost Cockney accent' (367). The status of the IRA becomes increasingly diminished by the confusion of the prisoners, who argue if it is 'RIA [or] IRA', before raising the question: 'Whozamarafawgwohihis, if it's -ing 'ARP' man' or 'RIP man' (189). Defying Lavery's intentions, Brendan's instinct is to immediately divide up Lavery's gift to him of a 'large packet of Players, a box of matches, and six bars of chocolate' equally and indiscriminately amongst the seventeen prisoners (187). The action undermines Lavery's aim to create non-Irish nationals as a negative other as he simultaneously promotes essentialist views of nationality:

'But thon talk and jokes of theirs is animalism. A Presbyterian minister that comes in here is a Derry man, and although he digs with the other foot, he's still an Irishman and he says he thinks it a disgrace to put Irish lads in here with them. Catholic or Presbyterian, the Irish are reared the same, he said, and I agree with them, though it's only when you're listening to the English that you realize it. Now, you don't have too much to say to those fellows and never get into their dirty way of speaking. Remember that you're not a cat burglar or a – a – ponce, but a Republican soldier and carry yourself as such.' (*BB*. 187)

Lavery's outburst stumbles when associated with sex, represented by 'ponce', the prisoner's popular term for a pimp. Behan builds on the scene to demonstrate a nationalist piety that has no basis in Brendan's reality, which becomes evident as Lavery continues:

'a girl that lives here in London comes to see me every month'. 'Did you live with her outside?' said I. 'Of course I didn't,' said he, annoyed.
[...] His annoyance softened. 'Oh, of course, I took you up wrong. I've lived in London since I was fifteen. This girl went to the Gaelic League in Hammersmith and sometimes I used to leave her home.' (*BB*, 187)

As the references to the Gaelic League and the traditionally Irish area of Hammersmith signify, in contrast to Brendan, Lavery's circle is restricted to those with Irish connections. Distribution of Lavery's gifts by Brendan to the diverse borstal prisoners disrupts such attachments. Language is employed to further demonstrate unity as he does so: "'For the love of Jasus," said I, lapsing into the speech of my homeland [...] "Fur de luv ah Jaysuss." Someone was imitating my accent, and getting great gas out of it' (*BB*, 189). The interjection of the narrator maintains a control over the dialogue, while connecting a parody of 'homeland' with a sense of fun.

The tolerance displays a maturity by Brendan that has developed since his early days of detention when Callan attempted to employ him as a mouthpiece for his rhetoric: 'Uu – uuuuu – up the Rep – uuuuuuub – lic! [...] Get up and give a shout – a sh-oooooouuuuuuut!' (*BB*, 133). Brendan tries to defy Callan by giving a 'discreet shout [...] in a low tone' (*BB*, 133–4). The proposition that 'it's ventriloquism Callan should have gone for' (*BB*, 126), as Bernice Schrank argues, suggests that Callan is attempting to treat Brendan as a puppet and to deny him any autonomy. However, the image of puppet reduces the discourse of nationalism to a lifeless object,[37] over which Brendan asserts his autonomy in the scene with Lavery. The effect is to undermine an essentialised notion of nationality in favour of unity based on shared experience, while presenting a more pluralist and tolerant society.

In *Borstal Boy*, Behan's reconstruction of memory often facilitates a more liberal ideology. The narrator frequently lapses into the role of storyteller, lending authority to the account in the telling. To use Walter Benjamin's argument, he fashions 'the "raw material of experience" into something "solid [and] useful"' (*Brannigan*, 49). As such, power resides with the storyteller to refashion events to suit his purpose. Kearney observes that '[r]eading *Borstal Boy* is like being in the audience at a live performance'.[38] If written and oral storytelling was a popular form in early twentieth-century Ireland used to validate nationalist identities and ideologies (*Brannigan*, 60), in Behan's hands it becomes a device to challenge the limitations of such discourse.

Similar to the device employed by Beckett for his character Molloy, the use of memory, linked together by stories, creates a flexibility in identity, where fact and fiction are blurred, leaving room to recreate and reshape. In *Borstal Boy* the first-person narrator tells us 'What I told was ninety per cent lies, and that's being more than fair to myself, for I was an able liar, but my stories were often funny' (*BB*, 342). On the path to subjectivity, Beckett's Molloy also notes how important his stories and reflections have become to identity: 'What I need now is stories, it took me a long time to realise that.'[39] By contrast, as the coordinates of settled life for Molloy's opposite, Moran, unravel, and his identity becomes confused, he comments: 'Stories, stories. I have not been able to tell them. I shall not be able to tell this one.'[40] As fact and fiction fuse, and stories recreate an identity, Molloy tells us: 'Perhaps I'm inventing a little, perhaps embellishing', just as Brendan has been creative with the past.[41] For Behan 'it wasn't a matter of what [he'd] put in but what [he'd] leave out' for his narrator (*BB*, 268), while stories facilitate the desired reconstruction.

Behan complicates the denouement of *Borstal Boy* when he subverts the convention of the *Bildungsroman* by lending a negative connotation to Brendan's development and return home. On Brendan's approach to Dublin Port, stationary coordinates are used to measure progress, or lack thereof, as the case may be, and the passing of time. Fixed landmarks of Dublin Bay, the 'spires […] the Pigeon House […] the height of Howth Head' (*BB*, 371) register personal transformation against an unchanged landscape.[42] In the liminal setting of a prison Brendan was able to develop as an individual, much in the same way that Beckett's character Molloy develops once he is also 'detached'. In the process towards subjectivity, Beckett dislocates Molloy from place, as when the narrator tells us 'he seemed hardly to know, or not at all, for he went with uncertain step and often stopped to look about him, like someone trying to fix landmarks in his mind'.[43] Despite never having travelled more than fifteen miles from his hometown, Molloy cannot remember its name: 'X being the name of my town'[44].

As Brendan passes the landmarks of Dublin Bay, Behan invokes Samuel Ferguson's poem 'The Fair Hills of Ireland' for ironic effect. At the beginning of his borstal journey, in a moment of defiance of the British authorities, Brendan recites the T.D. Sullivan poem 'God Save Ireland', the scaffold-cry of the Manchester Martyrs, and from it includes the line: 'And our friends in Holy Ireland, ever dear …' (*BB*, 5). Behan also closes his novel with a reference to 'Holy Ireland' (*BB*, 371). This time, however, he uses Ferguson's poem, which, while celebrating Ireland's plentiful attributes, contains the refrain 'Uileacán dubh O!', a lament suggesting how the country is being stripped of them.[45] By using Ferguson's poem, Behan also invokes the 'keen *desiderium*' for Ireland expressed by John Mitchel upon sighting Bermuda from his prison ship in 1848, when Mitchel 'continually murmur[s]' Ferguson's poem to himself.[46] Through Ferguson's poem, Behan infuses the young Brendan's gaze over the familiar territory of Dublin with a sense of irony, which is accentuated by his final words uttered in *Borstal Boy*, 'It must': the young man's reply to the immigration officer's suggestion that 'It must be wonderful to be free' (*BB*, 372). Internally, Brendan is anything but free; on leaving prison, he has changed, yet he will not be able to translate his identity into reality in his home country.

By invoking Mitchel's *Jail Journal*, Behan also associates the image of home with Mitchel's creation of two 'Irelands'. Both Behan and Mitchel quote from Ferguson just before reaching 'home' – Behan on his return to Dublin, and Mitchel on arriving at his 'appointed *home*',[47] which he discovers to be a second 'Ireland', as it were, in Bermuda:

> At last we arrived at the anchorage in front of the government island, where the dock-yard is established. This island is at the extreme northwest of the whole group, and its name is nothing less than *Ireland*.[48]

Colin Graham argues that Mitchel creates two 'Irelands' by including, in parallel, the utopian image in *Jail Journal* of 'that green Hy Brasil of my dreams and memories',[49] and that in doing so he detaches Ireland from place, thereby turning 'signifier and signified loose from each other' only to be reunited once the individual is returned home to 'accommodate the duality of this "two sided psychological entity"'.[50] Graham sees Mitchel's action as a 'radicalism [that] becomes truly revolutionary'.[51] Perhaps significant to Behan's ambitions is Mitchel's 'desire to perpetuate "Ireland", to hold it in his mind as a place beyond the materiality of a world which is untrustworthy'.[52] At the close of *Borstal Boy*, Behan also creates 'two Irelands'. After Brendan picks out the visible landmarks of Dublin Bay he comments:

> I couldn't really see Kilbarrack or Baldoyle, but it was only that I knew they were there. So many belonging to me lay buried in Kilbarrack, the healthiest graveyard in Ireland, they said, because it was so near the sea, and I thought I could see the tricolour waving over Dan Head's grave, which I could not from ten miles over the Bay. And I could see Baldoyle, there, because it was the races. (*BB*, 371)

Behan makes explicit the physical impossibility of Brendan seeing the tricolour flying over the real-life IRA volunteer's grave while sailing into Dún Laoghaire, and his evidence for sighting Baldoyle 'because it was the races' (*BB*, 371) suggests a deliberate attempt to defy credibility, as a view of Baldoyle Racecourse is unlikely from his vantage point.[53] Like Mitchel, who through imagination draws on the 'resources of the past ("memories") and the future ("dreams")'[54] to create a utopian Hy Brasil, Behan creates a plurality of 'Irelands' in contention, where, internally, 'images and signs of Ireland circulate while attachment to the object itself wanes'.[55] Graham argues that by 'Detaching Ireland from its real place, [Mitchel] can replace himself there'.[56] He links the action to Jacques Derrida's term 'conjuration': in Derrida's words (and appropriate to Behan's purpose), 'a matter of neutralizing a hegemony or overturning some power'.[57] Behan challenges hegemony and creates a Beckettian 'deterritorialised space' by detaching the corporeal from the spiritual at the close of his novel. He casts the landmarks of Dublin Bay as a signifier to produce an alternative Ireland in Brendan's mind. Brendan's closing two words suggest that it is an alternative which may not materialise, as suggested by his wistful response of 'it must' to the remark that 'it must be wonderful to be free' (*BB*, 372).

In considering the aesthetics of *Borstal Boy* and *Molloy*, it is worth noting that, although he had started to write the play in 1946, Behan was also working on *The Quare Fellow* when he first met Beckett. The episodic nature of the play and denial of conventional plot structure evokes the endlessly episodic structure of *Molloy*. The endless sense of waiting as the condemned prisoners fret about their fate and experience the (non) arrival of the quare fellow has obvious parallels with Beckett's work.[58] The structure of *The Quare Fellow* invokes what might be described as Beckett's antinovel, which, contrary to conventional linear progression, subverts any notion of progress in its circular narrative. Much like the effect of Molloy's pattern of narrative advancement, then negation, as Walsh argues, stasis is created by the non-appearance of Behan's eponymous character.[59] Behan's use of prisoners A, B, C, D and E evokes Beckett's use of 'A and C' for Molloy's and Moran's counterparts.[60] Besides the expressionist characteristics, omitting a name creates space on which to write a new identity.[61]

Behan's attempt to find a mainstream theatre to produce his work would see him cast outside the Establishment. Early on, we see him dramatise his disillusionment with a censorious post-independence Ireland by invoking Ireland's first president Douglas Hyde (1938–45), whom he admired. Having written to Ernest Blythe in 1946 about one act of a play that would eventually become *The Quare Fellow*, Behan submitted his script to the Abbey Theatre managing director, who promptly rejected it. Behan later submitted a revised version, which he had translated into English. That too received a negative response. For the original title of his play, Behan had refashioned the title of Hyde's 1901 play *Casadh an tSúgáin*, calling his own *Casadh Súgáin Eile* (The Twisting of Another Rope), the word 'Another' suggesting the cyclical nature of an inherited judicial system, endorsed by the new Irish state. As Declan Kiberd argues, Behan sought to reclaim Ireland's heritage from a purely political nationalist imprint and to rewrite it in cultural terms:

> [Behan] came to endorse Douglas Hyde's doctrine that 'politics' do not equate with 'nationality'. Like Hyde he came to the realization that successive Irish political leaders had so exalted the fight against England into a self-sustaining tradition that they had imperceptibly abandoned those very things which made Ireland worth fighting for – a native language and literature, music and dance, an entire culture. (*PPI*, 9)

Given Behan's endorsement of Hyde's politics, he was being provocative in recasting Hyde's original title for his own play. Behan's title suggests his subversive desire to challenge a residual British imperialism and a hegemonic structure that largely controlled the national consciousness. John Brannigan argues that through the banishment of its protagonist Hanrahan, Hyde's play encapsulated themes of hanging and exile that were 'the twin forms of expulsion most familiar to nineteenth-century Irish nationalism'.[62] Hyde's play has been credited with being the first Irish-language drama to be presented on the Irish stage (*O'Connor*, 175), and Behan no doubt believed this, even if Robert Hogan later maintained that P.T. McGinley's play *Eilís agus an Bhean Deirce* was actually the first.[63] Behan, therefore, very consciously made reference to Hyde's play, believing it to be a landmark in Irish-language drama. He subverted its title before presenting it in English to the Abbey, which tended to favour plays in Irish. Rather than a straightforward homage to Hyde, Behan's play can be seen to challenge a regime that he sees as flawed.

Arguably, the characteristics of *The Quare Fellow* that caused Blythe to reject it were precisely those which attracted the attention of Alan Simpson and Carolyn Swift of Dublin's Pike Theatre, which they founded in 1953. Swift and Simpson sought to stage premieres of European plays in translation and, significantly, produced Beckett's *Waiting for Godot* in 1955. Given the Pike's hunger for European avant-garde, the directors no doubt recognised such form in *The Quare Fellow*. The Pike Theatre manifesto reads like anathema to the ideology of Irish cultural nationalism. Contrary to the Irish language revival agenda and deterrence of what was deemed foreign corrupting influence, the manifesto stated: 'Our policy is to present plays of all countries on all subjects, written from whatever viewpoint.'[64] The Pike's policy was in direct conflict with the Abbey's desire for Irish social realism. Blythe had stated: 'The Abbey doesn't do foreign plays.'[65] The Pike, by contrast, hoped 'to give theatregoers opportunities to see more of the struggle going on at present in world theatre to introduce new techniques and new subjects in play writing'.[66] This departure from the mainstream, however, would exact a heavy price in 1950s Ireland.

In the conservative mid-century period, Swift and Simpson were unconventional. Born in London, Swift was a Jewish woman in an era where moderate voices had been steadily sidelined, leaving space for a religious fanaticism and a chauvinistic nationalism, where anti-Semitic as well as anti-British sentiments were expressed.[67] Simpson was a Protestant captain in the Irish Army, the very same army which had guarded Behan while he was incarcerated in the Curragh Military Camp. The fact that Behan and Simpson would work together is testament to Behan's ability to overcome prejudice. Swift and Simpson shared an interest with Behan in the freedom of European avant-garde theatre. The challenge to fixed identity, portrayed in the Pike's 1954 intimate late-night satirical revues *The Follies of Herbert Lane* would attract international acclaim. Eventually, however, the theatre would fall victim to the government and church censorship that forced its closure following a production of Tennessee Williams' *The Rose Tattoo* in 1957. Behan's modernist approach and own brand of humour found a comfortable home in the Pike. Swift was the primary writer of the Pike's revues, and her style of Jewish-influenced humour undoubtedly appealed to Behan. Stephen Watt argues that Behan was influenced by Borscht Belt comedy, which was at its height amongst New York's Jewish community when Behan spent time in that city during the 1950s and '60s.[68] Elsewhere, Watt argues that self-parody, such as that seen in Behan's work and in Swift's revues, 'often involves significant playing or mirroring as well as the imaginative construction of worlds, the creation of a space of selfhood'.[69] Both *The Quare Fellow* and the revues display a fluidity of identity. Citing Lionel Pilkington, Walsh argues that the revues represented 'a cultural phenomenon that celebrated the arrival of a new, urban, liberal elite and a social space in which audience members could perform with brio this new identity'.[70] The performativity of society and its institutions in the Pike revues has parallels in Behan's use of European expressionism in *The Quare Fellow*. Presented as types and often without names, the characters play out a number of roles, such as when Prisoner C and Warder Crimmin step in and out of their official roles to unite in their loneliness as they talk 'for hours [...] through the [prison-door] spy hole, all in Irish' (*CP*, 95). If identity is performative it can be changed, but manipulation of the fixed identities enshrined in nationalist ideology would of course cause alarm amongst its advocates.

Behan's early gravitation towards experimental theatre would provoke and develop his interest in modernist writing. His move to Paris and exposure to Beckett's work, and the vibrant avant-garde literary scene, would hone that interest. As a writer, Behan constantly plays with the boundaries of identity – what is seen and unseen, allowed or forbidden. He frequently constructs an autonomous space for the creation of selfhood and subverts convention.[71] Behan creates an alternative, imagined space for his characters and pushes them through boundaries that are created by a restrictive, exclusionary, post-independence cultural nationalism. As Brannigan argues, Behan's Ireland was instead 'urban and modern; its modernity shaped and pulled "Irishness" into a diversity of cultural identities and affiliations which extended beyond the confrontational terms of Catholicism and Protestantism, Irish and English, Colonial and Nationalist' (*Brannigan*, 21). Behan's interrogation of Irish identity would see him marginalised by the establishment.

Naturalistic productions of Behan's work can entrap them in their historical moment and often ignore the complexity and formal ambition of his aesthetics.[72] Behan expressed his frustration with such interpretations. Fringe theatre enabled Behan's success as a playwright by attracting the international acclaim that his writing deserved. The Pike Theatre production of *The Quare Fellow* created the international awareness of his work that led the influential director Joan Littlewood to get involved. Her involvement, in turn, led to productions in London's West End, New York and elsewhere. Following initial rejection, success in the West End finally brought a broader acceptance by Dublin's mainstream theatres.[73] Ten years after Behan's 1946 approach to Ernest Blythe, *The Quare Fellow* was finally staged by the Abbey

Theatre. If success set Behan on a precarious course towards literary celebrity, the fame he achieved had the unfortunate effect of eclipsing his achievement as a European modernist writer.

5
EROS AND LIBERATION: THE HOMOEROTIC BODY IN *BORSTAL BOY*

MICHAEL G. CRONIN

In part three of *Borstal Boy*, which describes his time in the relatively benign regime at Hollesley Bay, Brendan Behan's narrator recounts an incident that takes place in the institution's library. Young Brendan finds a fellow borstal inmate reading Frank Harris' *Life of Oscar Wilde*. The narrator admits to us that in his childhood he had conflated the story of Wilde's imprisonment with the heroic tales of Irish rebels at the bar of British justice in which, as the child of a republican family, he was steeped. Even when he began to suspect that it had something to do with sex and asked his mother why Wilde was jailed, he remembers her replying vaguely 'his downfall – they brought him down the same as they did Parnell', a reply conceding that Wilde's was a sexual scandal, like Parnell's, while insisting on the interpretive framework of British injustice towards an Irish patriot. In the narrative's present, Brendan is told exactly why Wilde was imprisoned (though the dialogue in which this happens is alluded to rather than reproduced textually). He responds with studied insouciance – 'every tinker has his own way of dancing' – keen to stymie his worldly fellow inmate's satisfaction at shocking 'Paddy'.

Yet from reading the rest of the novel we might suspect that this revelation about Wilde is more intimately charged for young Brendan than his response suggests. This is particularly so given the emotional intensity and palpable eroticism of his friendship with Charlie, an imprisoned young English sailor. Clearly, in this apparently random incident Behan is purposefully deploying the figure of Wilde within the complex tempo of his young protagonist's political and sexual formation. As I will argue in this essay, the figure of Wilde stands at the nexus of two distinctive prison writing traditions – the Irish republican and the homoerotic – in which we can situate *Borstal Boy*. By mapping the compositional relationship between these two currents, we can also grasp the novel's imaginative vision of a radical sexual and political freedom; the potential of that vision for our own times remains untapped.

As the narrator tells us in the library episode, the first fact he knew about Wilde was that his mother was 'Speranza', whose poetry he learned in school. Through his mother, and her association with the Young Irelanders, as well as the younger Brendan's naïve assumption that Oscar must also have been a rebel, Wilde is associated in the novel with that tradition of prison writing – from Wolfe Tone's *The Autobiography* (1826) to Thomas Clarke's *Glimpses of an Irish Felon's Prison Life* (1913) – that was a key vehicle for the articulation of Irish anti-colonial and republican ideas from the 1790s onwards. *Borstal Boy* contains a dense web of intertextual references to these Irish republican prison writings, and to other significant modes of nationalist discourse such as ballads, poetry, speeches from the dock and Irish mythology.

As John Brannigan has delineated, Behan's novel takes its form from this current in Irish writing – it is, on the surface, another account of an imprisoned Irish republican – while also offering an ironic and subversively parodic commentary on that tradition (*Brannigan*, 126–50). Thus, when Brendan gives his own speech from the dock his earnest declaration of commitment to 'the Irish Worker's and Small Farmer's Republic' is undercut by a policeman comically mistaking the Hibernicism 'small farmer' as a commentary on the stature rather than the status of these farmers (*BB*, 4). Moreover, Brendan's commitment to the content of his statement sits alongside his sharp awareness that this is a performance rather than a spontaneous expression of ideals. His performance has been honed through immersion in notable examples of the genre, from Robert Emmet to the Manchester Martyrs (he explicitly links his use of 'God save Ireland' at the end of his speech to a ballad about them that he also quotes), to Roger Casement (disparagingly referred to by a prison officer a few paragraphs later). Brendan is also acutely conscious of his diverse audiences. The most significant audience is not in the courtroom but at home in Ireland, where the left and right wings of the movement will respond very differently to the speech. In addition, the adolescent Brendan excitedly reflects on how the reports of his speech will, he believes, burnish his heroic, sexy, manly image.

Nevertheless, as Colbert Kearney observes, 'he believes in his vision of himself' and that vision, along with the narrative act of sustaining it through singing and storytelling, is a source of comfort to Brendan amid the initial terror and isolation of prison life (*Kearney*, 92). The dialogism of Behan's text, and the interwoven perspectives of Brendan the protagonist, Brendan the narrator and Brendan Behan the author retrospectively moulding his youthful experiences into a narrative, has multiple political effects, in which, for instance, Brendan's speech from the dock is simultaneously a cynical performance, a source of comedy and a distillation of a revolutionary vision. The tissue of intertextual allusions to the various modes and styles of Irish republican discourse emphasises how young Brendan is sustained by, but also entangled in and struggling to make his own, this cultural and political inheritance. The formal complexity of the book's relationship to the inherited generic conventions encodes the dialectic of identification and disidentification in relation to inherited political models that drives the narrative of self-formation.

As its recurring references to Wilde suggest, *Borstal Boy* can also be situated in another prison writing tradition. This writing discursively connects a cluster of elements: same-sex passion between men; late nineteenth- and twentieth-century conceptions of homosexuality and masculinity; the spaces and characteristic social relations of incarceration. (We might note in passing that this narrative conjunction continues to have a flourishing, if culturally less prestigious, parodic afterlife as a staple *mise en scène* of gay porn.) Wilde's essay-letter *De Profundis* (originally written in 1897 but not published in complete form until 1962) is an originary text in this tradition. The essay offers an anguished and desolating anatomy of a relationship corroded from within by Alfred Douglas' personal and familial dysfunction.[1] But we must now also read that dysfunction historically as symptomatic of the instability, hypocrisy, paranoia and homophobia of late-Victorian bourgeois society in the age of high imperialism. For this social formation the newly minted figure of the 'homosexual' was just one of several spectres haunting the collective imagination and figuring the terrors of mass democracy or, worse, revolution;

similar figures of threat included the organised worker, the New Woman and the rebellious colonial subject. Incarceration, and the suffering which the imprisoned Wilde recounts was just the most visible and brutal manifestation of the reactionary drive to punish and extinguish such threats, and impose a phantasmal 'moral' order on to the objective instability and destructiveness of capitalism.

However, as readers of *Borstal Boy* will easily detect, incarceration in the novel does not, or at least does not only, bear this punitive and reactionary face. In a paradox we might justifiably call Wildean, in *Borstal Boy* the space of imprisonment is also a space of freedom. Politically the most intriguing and fruitful question is how the novel imagines such freedom. Unquestionably, the novel warrants a liberal interpretation in which such freedom is characterised in psychological and metaphysical terms. In this view, prison provides Brendan with the opportunity to achieve a more authentic self, which can also be translated into political terms as a more hybrid national identity, away from the burdensome, ensnaring and inauthentic demands of familial, political and national commitments. However, I believe it is also possible to glimpse, however partially and fleetingly, an alternative, radical vision of freedom in this novel. In other words, Behan's novel oscillates between a liberal humanism and what, in a different context, Lukács terms a 'revolutionary humanism'.[2]

Jean Genet's *Miracle of the Rose* (first published in French in 1946; in English translation in 1965) is a work from the homoerotic prison writing tradition that is chronologically and formally more comparable with Behan's work than is Wilde's *De Profundis*. Like *Borstal Boy*, *Miracle* is a fictionalised autobiography, structured as Genet's memoir of his imprisonment as an adult in Fontevrault prison and, woven through this, memories of his youth in the Mettray Reformatory.[3] Despite these generic similarities, Behan and Genet write in a very different style and register. Where *Borstal Boy* is a comic, realist, linear narrative, *Miracle* is a highly stylised, lyrical narrative, characterised by a shifting, unstable temporal fluidity. *Miracle* is also more explicitly homoerotic. Moreover, where *Borstal Boy* idealises erotic friendship between similarly aged adolescent boys and stigmatises as perverse any suggestion of sexual attraction between adults and boys, *Miracle* eroticises power. In Genet's fictional carceral world, erotic attraction between men is invariably pedaristic and propelled by hierarchies of age, status and physical strength. As Alan Sinfield observes, Genet shows 'that our sexual fantasies depend on the power structures in our societies'.[4] Genet also politicises the erotic, but does so through an existentialist hermeneutic in which abjection and masochism paradoxically generate a radical freedom, and in which, through the medium of erotic fantasy, the norms and morals of bourgeois society are turned on their head: the criminal is the hero; the sinner is the saint. In almost all respects this transgressive sexual vision is entirely uncongenial to the *Weltanschauung* of contemporary, post-Stonewall, lesbian and gay culture, with its political vocabulary of identities and civil rights and, as Kadji Amin puts it, its 'historically recent ideal of the coupled relationship as an authentic, consensual, contractual encounter of equals'.[5] (In a similar way, Genet's modernist aesthetic, with its pervasive recourse to imagery drawn from Catholic religious devotion, is in many ways uncongenial to a secular sensibility; here we might note an affective, though not stylistic, similarity with *Borstal Boy* where Brendan's exclusion from Catholic rites because of his republicanism is a source of political pride but emotional anguish.)

The homoeroticism of *Borstal Boy* is not characterised by the heightened emotional pitch and sadomasochistic fantasies we find in Genet. Nevertheless, there is a common structure of feeling, what Amin, writing about *Miracle*, describes as 'a distinct pre-Stonewall queer sodality characterised less by a shared sexual identity than by a queer fusion of pleasure and pain, togetherness and exile'.[6] Both works resist enveloping desire between men within a hermeneutic of identity, but we must be wary of reading that resistance as bad faith, as a manifestation of psychic and political 'denial' or, in Behan's case, as submission to the demands of respectability and literary censorship. As Amin argues, we must strive to avoid reading these earlier styles of writing same-sex passion as 'retrograde resistance to "progressive" politics or compensation for the impossibility of same-sex desire in the novel's present'.[7] In particular we must avoid reading them teleologically, as artefacts from an earlier stage in the evolution of a progressive narrative of sexual liberation that reached its apotheosis with the emergence of the modern lesbian and gay movement. Homoeroticism in Behan and Genet is striated by masculinist and misogynistic currents, but it is precisely that which is most disturbingly irreconcilable to our conception of sexual freedom in this writing that may most productively trouble our complacency about the regulatory frameworks that shape our lives. As Heather Love observes, in *Feeling Backward*, 'paying attention to what was difficult in the past may tell us how far we have come but that is not all it will tell us; it may also make visible the damage we live with in the present'.[8] Along with resisting the consolidation of homoerotic desire into identity, Behan's and Genet's eroticised idealisation of youthful delinquency – youth irreconcilable with the demands of productive and reproductive mature masculinity – offers a symbolic critique of the dominant temporality of capitalist modernity.

In an unpublished manuscript he prepared in the early stage of developing *Borstal Boy*, we can see Behan grappling directly with those reifying taxonomies of sexual identity which had first emerged in the late nineteenth century and which, in new variations, continue to underpin our own sex-gender system:

> I loved Borstal Boys and they loved me. But the absence of girls made it that much imperfect. Homosexuality (of our sort) is not a substitute for normal sex. It's a different thing, rather similar to that of which T.E. Lawrence writes in *The Seven Pillars*. The youth of healthy muscle and slim wrought form is not the same as the powdered pansy (who I hasten to add, as good as anybody else, has every right to be that and a bloody good artist or anything he wants to be). Our lads saw themselves as beautiful and had to do something about it … As I say however, without women it could not be a pattern of life, only a prolonging of adolescence – it was as beautiful as that.[9]

Here we have crystallised the dreary catalogue of stereotypes, illogical thinking and 'radical incoherence', as Eve Sedgwick terms it, that bedevilled Western sexual culture in the twentieth century and, to judge from the cultural fascination with gay sportsmen, continues to bedevil contemporary thought. There is the distinction between 'situational' homosexuality, to which any man may, in specific circumstances, temporarily resort and some more 'innate' homosexuality, which is confined to identifiable types of men; to use Sedgwick's formulation, this is the structuring contradiction in modern sexual thought between universalising and minoritising discourses. There is also a contrast between the authenticity and manliness of homosocial bonding, and the artificiality ('powdered') and effeminacy of the sexual invert. To invoke Sedgwick's terms again, this is the contradiction between a concept of homosexuality as gender separatism and as gender transitivity.[10] It is also notable that Behan's imaginary 'pansy' is more than likely working as an artist, evoking the association between 'innate' homosexuality, effeminacy, dandyism and aestheticism.

But Behan's writing also offers more nuanced and ironically knowing perspectives on the hegemonic categories of sexual definition. In 'After the Wake' the stereotypes are strategically and playfully deployed by the narrator. He begins his 'campaign' of seduction by encouraging his friend to 'think it manly, ordinary to manly men, the British Navy, "Porthole Duff", "Navy Cake", stories of the Hitler Youth in captivity … to remove the taint of "cissiness", effeminacy, how the German Army had encouraged it in Cadet Schools'. The other 'front' in the campaign was 'appealing to that hope of culture – Socrates, Shakespeare, Marlowe' (*Wake*, 48). In a grotesque denouement, the narrator is about to go to bed with his friend on the night of his wife's wake, with her corpse in the other room and the narrator imagining her face 'looking up from the open coffin'. In this Genetesque fusion of sex and mortality, the narrator is at once the vampiric predator of the homophobic imagination and the heroic object of sympathetic identification in the narrative.

Alan Sinfield argues that Wilde's three trials in 1895 produced a 'major shift in perceptions of the scope of same-sex passion. At that point the entire, vaguely disconcerting nexus of effeminacy, leisure, idleness, immorality, luxury, insouciance, decadence and aestheticism [...] was transformed into a brilliantly precise image [...] the principal twentieth-century stereotype entered our culture; not just the homosexual, as the lawyers and medics would have it, but the queer.'[11] In *Borstal Boy*, the Wildean or queer figure is identified only as 'the novelist's nephew' and Brendan is 'not surprised' to see him reading Harris' book on Wilde in the library. It is he who gleefully tells Brendan the truth of the Wilde trial, after which function he disappears from the narrative. Curiously, his distinguishing features have nothing to do with same-sex desire or his relationship with any of the other boys, but are entirely to do with his dandified appearance and pursuits. As Brendan magnanimously observes, 'he was altogether as decadent as our frugal means allowed. He was doing his best anyway, and not badly under the circumstances' (*BB*, 243).

By rigorously detaching homoeroticism from queerness, *Borstal Boy* reinforces the schema of 'situational' ('our sort') and 'innate' ('powdered pansy') homosexuality, and the regulation of masculinity ('gay' *and* 'straight') which it subtends. But since Behan's homoerotic writing dwells on bodies and affects, rather than on identities and discursive constructs, the novel simultaneously gestures towards a more humane alternative to that regulatory framework.

The homoeroticism is allusive and elliptical and yet, as John Brannigan notes, Brendan's relationship with Charlie 'occupies a muted but central role in the narrative' (*Brannigan*, 140). Their relationship has its beginnings in the physical intimacy of the wash room, with Brendan standing behind the young sailor 'innocently admiring the back of his neck' before describing his 'brown hair and long dark eyelashes'. When Charlie gives Brendan a gift of tobacco, matches and a newspaper he points out that Brendan's hands are wet and insists on rather elaborately placing the tobacco in his pockets and the newspaper inside his shirt, 'next my skin, putting his hand around me' (*BB*, 11). Later the emotional intensity of Brendan's relationship with Charlie is registered by Charlie's recurring anger and hurt when Brendan is cultivating his friendships with the other boys; given the elliptical quality of the text, Charlie's responses appear rather bafflingly opaque to the reader, and thus encourage speculation. Most painfully, this emotional intensity is registered towards the end of the novel in Brendan's mourning – falling into melancholic silence – on hearing the news of Charlie's death aboard a torpedoed ship (*BB*, 365–6)

From the beginning of Brendan and Charlie's relationship physical intimacy – touching, singing to each other, whispering through the spy-hole of their cells – is woven through acts of generosity, care and kindness. Moreover, as the novel unfolds, Brendan's relationship with Charlie is one intensified link in a web of such nurturing and sustaining relationships within the group of boys who form Brendan's closest friends. In this way, we could argue that the homoerotic is figured in the novel less as a site of identity than as a source of solidarity, and less as a distinctive current of sexual desire than as one component on an elastic continuum of bodily needs, affects and potentialities, what Ann Ferguson terms the 'sex-affective energy' that is a key component of all social relations.[12]

In *Eros and Civilisation* (1955), Herbert Marcuse argued against Freud's view that repression was an essential and necessary component of human culture. In contrast Marcuse outlines a vision of a 'non-repressive civilisation'; a human culture freed from the domination of the 'performance principle'. Central to Marcuse's vision is the distinction he draws between 'sexuality' and 'eros'. Sexuality, as Marcuse uses the term, describes a human instinct narrowly inhibited and confined to genital activity and reproduction – restricted to a specialised function, that of 'bringing one's own genitals into contact with those of someone of the opposite sex', as Marcuse puts it, citing Freud with a certain ironic relish – and confined to a socially and morally sanctified realm of marriage and the patriarchal family.[13] Historically this conceptualisation of sexuality has been inseparable from those rigid binaries underpinning bourgeois subjectivity; between the body as productive instrument and the creative soul or mind; between labour and leisure; between a masculine public sphere and a feminine private sphere; between political and moral actions; between individual relations and social relations. Sexuality, in Marcuse's usage, emerged in historically specific, material conditions and social relations; in other words, it is inseparable from the reification of human consciousness, affects and relationships under capitalism. By contrast, Marcuse's conception of eros describes a condition where the human body 'no longer used as a full-time instrument of labour would be resexualised … the body in its entirety would be an object of cathexis, a thing to be enjoyed – an instrument of pleasure'. For Marcuse, the transformation of sexuality into eros should not be thought of simply in terms of individual psyches throwing off the shackles of repressive morality, 'sexual liberation' as the 1960s counterculture understood it, but of a revolutionary re-ordering of social relations. This will require, he reiterates, 'not simply a release but a transformation of libido; from sexuality constrained under genital supremacy to eroticisation of the entire personality'. This transformation will be the result of 'a societal transformation that released the play of individual needs and faculties'.[14]

In *Borstal Boy* then we could argue that the erotic and affective intensification of his and Charlie's bodies is the indispensable first step in Brendan's growing solidarity with the other boys in the prison. One crucial feature of this growing solidarity is Brendan's gradual appreciation of the working-class culture he shares with boys from Liverpool, Glasgow and London. Here again, as with the question of same-sex passion in the novel, the temptation is to resort to a hermeneutic of identity, to project a distinction between a confected, politically problematic 'national' identity and a more authentic, properly political 'working-class' identity, and then to interpret the novel's *Bildung* narrative in terms of Brendan's movement from one to the other. However, we might profitably interpret his growing awareness of that shared working-class culture in different terms, as Brendan reformulating his cognitive map of empire. Rather than the relatively straightforward exploitation of colony by coloniser, he can now begin to grasp those imperial currents and flows of capital and labour in which his native Dublin and these other cities are interconnected in a much broader global system, and where the distinction between those who profit and those who are exploited must be conceptualised much more rigorously than any distinction between 'Irish' and 'English' would allow. (In this it might be said the novel is prescient of our own 'globalised' world, where formal colonialism has largely ended but the exploitative structures of the capitalist world system are stronger than ever.) In this view then, the trajectory of Brendan's emotional and political development can be understood less as a movement from a 'national' to a 'post-national' identity than the movement between the nativist and liberationist stages of anti-colonial consciousness charted by Franz Fanon; as with eros, liberation, as Fanon describes it, requires a transformation of social consciousness beyond national consciousness.[15]

Borstal Boy ends with Brendan's arrival at Dún Laoghaire port, arriving back to Ireland having served his time and been deported. Specifically, it ends with this exchange between Brendan and an immigration officer:

> I handed him the expulsion order.
> He read it, looked at it and handed it back to me. He had a long educated countryman's sad face, like a teacher, and took my hand.
> 'Cead mile failte sa bhaile romhat.'
> A hundred thousand welcomes home to you.
> I smiled and said, 'Go raibh maith agat.'
> Thanks.
> He looked very serious, and tenderly inquired, 'Caithfidh go bhfuil sé go hiontach bheith soar.'
> 'Caithfidh go bhfuil.'
> It must be wonderful to be free.
> 'It must,' said I, and walked down the gangway, past a detective and got on the train for Dublin.

Brendan appears to affirm the custom officer's complacent certainty that the conservative, repressive, bourgeois nationalist regime of the post-independence 'Free State' constitutes 'freedom', while actually asserting the direct opposite. Here we see something like the coded language (the open secret, the signal or gesture that can be read quite differently, but equally plausibly, by different audiences) that was part of the communicative repertoire of same-sex sub-cultures in the twentieth-century. One of the conditions of possibility for such sub-cultures was that they could be simultaneously recognisable and unrecognisable. For instance, while Wilde's dandified performance was read by some London contemporaries as disclosing his same-sex desires, others, including those close to him such as his biographer Frank Harris, were apparently genuinely shocked by the revelations at the trials.[16] But Behan's authorial decision to have this exchange take place in Irish, and to present it bilingually, as it were, with 'original' and 'translation' woven together on the page is also striking. In this way he reiterates how the grammatical structure of the Irish language makes possible this coded gesture of defiance. The novel ends with an expression of utopian aspiration – 'it must be wonderful to be free' – that is a sudden and unexpected eruption into a text that otherwise seems committed to a more reformist reconciliation with reality. This momentary utopian aspiration is made possible by the conjunction of a queer expressive strategy and an Irish linguistic register. This conjunction mirrors the book's twin generic legacies in the Irish republican and homoerotic prison writing traditions; it also mirrors that symbolic conjunction where Charlie's body, as a location of homoerotic desires and affects, sparks the fusion between the revolutionary possibilities of eros and liberation.

As Marcuse and Fanon each remind us so compellingly and as the history of the twentieth century so painfully insists, neither eros nor liberation will be easily achieved. *Borstal Boy* offers us a powerful emblem of this in the contrast between the beauty of Charlie's body in the washroom where Brendan first meets him – lustrous with the promise and potential of a transformed future – and the drowned body of the young sailor in the seas off Gibraltar, destroyed by the present reality of war. The novel's ending also reiterates that we can only grasp the idea of freedom in the conditional tense. Under our present conditions, we cannot know in advance what exactly eros or liberation will look like; we can only speculate, and hope, about how 'wonderful' they might be. 'Freedom,' as Marcuse writes, 'is an idea to which no sense perception can correspond.'[17] It is for this reason that Marcuse ascribes such strategic importance to the aesthetic, as a space of imagination and play, in the struggle to create a non-repressive civilisation. This also explains the thoughtful attention which Fanon gave to the complexities of creating a 'national culture' as a crucial element of decolonisation.[18]

The most astute criticism of *Borstal Boy* grapples with the relationship between the life experience and the literary work. To avoid reading this text as merely a transcription of Behan's own prison experience critics pay close attention to his careful construction of narrative structure; the creation of a persona, 'Brendan', that is intimately an aspect of, yet distinguishable from, 'Brendan Behan' the author; the linguistic playfulness, parody and intertextuality that are such characteristic features of the novel's prose style. In other words, we must be attentive to Behan's deliberate creation of a work of 'autofiction', as Bernice Shrank usefully describes it.[19] Nevertheless, even the most sophisticated critical interpretations still tend towards mapping an essentially biographical narrative that is psychological and providential; a developmental narrative moving from immaturity to maturity, and a salvation narrative, moving from the fallen state of political activism into the light of redemption that is liberal humanism.

The spatial-temporal structure of the narrative – moving from the oppressive hostility and alienation of Walton to the camaraderie and reforming encouragement of Feltham and Hollesley Bay – clearly encourages such readings. But what is most fascinating is how Behan's novel simultaneously resists its own narrative logic. Stylistically this is most apparent in the final section, where the tightly ordered pattern descends into a looser episodic sequence. Kearney offers a convincing historical and biographical explanation for Behan's loss of control when re-working this section; the IRA's bombing campaign in 1956 gave Behan a sense that this was an inauspicious time for such a work and made him reluctant to part with the manuscript; the London success of *The Quare Fellow* and *The Hostage* brought the distractions of celebrity.[20] Nevertheless we can also read this resistance to narrative as such as a compositional correlative of the novel's queer temporality, Behan's melancholic faithfulness to his younger self, his resistance to the developmental imperative of the 'production principle', and his insistence that homoeroticism and fiction can provide us with imaginative spaces where we might, however briefly, glimpse what freedom could look like.

6
BRENDAN BEHAN'S
IRISH-LANGUAGE POETRY
RIÓNA NÍ FHRIGHIL

B rendan Behan's poetic oeuvre consists of thirteen short lyrics, composed in Irish and mainly published in the Irish literary magazine *Comhar* between 1946 and 1952.[1] Behan was the youngest poet to have his work included in the esteemed anthology *Nuabhéarsaíocht 1939–1949* (1950), edited by Seán Ó Tuama, a clear indication that he was perceived as a poet of promise by his contemporaries. Although Máirtín Ó Cadhain rated him as one of the two finest poets in that anthology,[2] Ó Tuama identified Seán Ó Ríordáin, Máirtín Ó Direáin, Máire Mhac an tSaoi and Séamus Ó Néill as the leading lights of the emerging generation of poets.[3] The former three have come to be regarded as the great trinity of poets who championed the modern lyric mode in Irish. Behan, on the other hand, is now best known for his plays and novels in English. Nevertheless, his small but important contribution to modern poetry in Irish has been acknowledged in authoritative publications, including *The Field Day Anthology of Irish Writing* (1991) and *The Cambridge History of Irish Literature* (2006). *Poems and a Play in Irish*, a collection of Behan's thirteen Irish poems and the play *An Giall* was published by Gallery Press in 1981. English translations of the full texts of all thirteen poems have not been published to date. Colbert Kearney (1978) translated a number of stanzas and some complete poems into English as part of his seminal essay on Behan's Irish poetry. Likewise, Ulick O'Connor (1993) translated those poems or verses of poems which were relevant to his biography of Behan. In the interest of continuity and as they are more plentiful, the translations below are mostly Kearney's, although O'Connor's are arguably of equal literary merit.

Most commentary on Behan's poetry relies heavily on Kearney's influential analysis and seeks, above all else, to explain the poet's choice of language given that Irish was not his native tongue. Kearney has correctly pointed out that it was fortuitous that Behan's detainment in Mountjoy Prison and the Curragh Camp with a number of learned Irish speakers in the early 1940s coincided with a renewed impetus in the literary revival of Irish.[4] This exposure to the living language and to its literary tradition, as well as the opportunity to publish in the relatively new literary magazine *Comhar* (established in 1942), no doubt played a part in his decision to begin composing poetry in Irish. That the poem 'A Jackeen Laments the Blaskets' was dedicated to Seán Ó Briain, a schoolteacher and fellow republican prisoner from Ballyferriter, while the poem now referred to as 'Oscar Wilde' (*PPI*, 20) was originally titled 'To Seán Ó Súilleabháin' ('Do Sheán Ó Súilleabháin') when first published in *Comhar* in August 1949 attests to the influence that these native speakers of Irish had on Behan. Richard Rankin Russell contends that these friendships and Behan's interest in Kerry Irish influenced the portrayal of the characters 'the Quare Fellow' and 'Prisoner C' in *The Quare Fellow* (1956).[5] In a newspaper article published shortly after Behan's death, Ó Briain acknowledged Behan's genuine interest in the Irish language, his admirable understanding of canonical texts like Tomás Ó Criomhthain's *The Islandman* (*An tOileánach*, 1929) and his unsurpassed ability to recite large portions of Brian Merriman's eighteenth-century text *The Midnight Court* (*Cúirt an Mheán Oíche*).[6]

Behan's possible political motivation for choosing to write in Irish has been noted by both O'Connor and Kearney. Given, however, that only the first of Behan's poems is of an overtly political nature, it would appear that artistic motivation was of prime importance. The following discussion of Behan's poetry will examine how he reimagined or partially reimagined older poetic forms to explore contemporary themes and to develop a modern lyric mode. It will be argued that to designate Behan's Irish-language poetry as a transitory phase in his creative development anterior to his creativity in English is to overlook the bilingual nature of his literary imagination, which never expressed itself exclusively in one language or the other.

Behan's first and only overtly republican poem is an elegy to the IRA leader Seán McCaughey, who died on hunger-strike in Portlaoise Prison in 1946. 'The Return of McCaughey' ('Filleadh Mhic Eachaidh') is victorious in tone, the deceased being welcomed back to his native Ulster amidst the sound of guns and pipes:

> Cheapas ar dtús gur shochraid a bhí ar siúl acu
> Gur phíopa ag caoineadh a bhí ag osnaíl go géar
> Is na gunnaí – do cheapas gur bhuartha a nguth leis
> Ach is cosúil le buíon mhór chaithréimeach Uí Néill
> Ar a fhilleadh ón bPáil is an Gall faoi chrá fágtha –
> An Gael go gealmheidhreach is an chreach faoi lán seoil –
> Fáiltiú Mhic Eachaidh ar ais chuig an Tuaisceart
> – Mar sa deireadh is treise an bród ná an brón. (*PPI*, 13)

> I had expected to witness a funeral
> With pipes of condolence droning their keen,
> Had thought that the sound of guns would be mournful,
> But like the victorious host of O'Neill,
> Come from the Pale having crushed the invader,
> The Gaels are delighted to carry their trophy,
> To welcome McCaughey back home to Ulster,
> For pride is eventually stronger than woe. (*Kearney*, 49–50)

Kearney notes that the first four lines of Behan's poem are almost identical to the first four lines of the poem 'A Phádraig na nÁrann', composed by Liam Dall Ó hIfearnáin in 1760:[7]

> A Phádraig na n-árann, an gcluin tú na gártha –,
> An gcluin tú an pléaráca, an siosma is an gleó?
> Ar chualais mar tháinig
> Go Cúige Uladh an ghárda
> Thurot 'n-a shláinte le hiomarca scóip!

> Pádraig, my friend, do you hear the battle cries,
> Do you hear the revelry, the clamour and uproar?

Did you hear how to
the guarded Province of Ulster
Thurot came in full health and high spirits![8]

The intertextual reference is worth further consideration. Ó hIfearnáin's poem was purportedly composed to celebrate the capture of Carrickfergus in 1760 by French troops under Privateer François Thurot.[9] The poem contains Ó hIfearnáin's characteristic disdain for George III and the conviction, underpinned by Jacobean rhetoric, that Charles III (the Young Pretender) would, against all political and military odds, be restored as rightful heir to the throne of England, Scotland and Ireland.[10] 'A Phádraig na nÁrann' is therefore an enthusiastic call to arms. Behan's poem clearly references that Jacobean triumphant rhetoric and ideology, the return and restoration of the rightful leader, 'the lion', placing McCaughey in the same tradition as the Young Pretender. The irony that McCaughey's foe was no English monarch but a democratically elected Irish government is underscored by this intertextual reference. McCaughey's death by hunger strike is reimagined as a symbolic victory; mourners are compared to the followers of Hugh O'Neill (c. 1550–1616) when he returned victoriously from the Pale. The tone is one of moral superiority; the spiritual significance of the nationalist cause exceeds worldly concerns:

Inniu beidh an turas go Baile an Mhuilinn,
A mhuintir ina thimpeall, na mílte in ómós,
Is geall le turas taoisigh sheanaimsir ár saoirse
A shlí go réidh ríoga mall maorga tríd an slógh:
Na Fianna, ógthacaí dil Phoblacht na hÉireann,
Saighdiúirí na tíre idir fhir agus mhná
Cailíní beaga na gculaithe geala Gaelacha –
Buíon cheoil ag seinm agus móriompar brat –
Beidh na mílte go humhal ag leanúint a chónra,
Gealtaisce na hÉireann, croí dílis an leoin
Ag fáiltiú Mhic Eachaidh ar ais chuig an Tuaisceart
Mar sa deireadh is treise a bhás na a gcumhacht. (*PPI*, 13)

> His journey today will bring him to Milltown,
> Surrounded by thousands paying their respects,
> He'll pass like a prince in the old days of freedom
> Slowly and stately, through the host of his friends;
> The Fianna, young props of the Irish Republic,
> Men and women, all soldiers of our land,
> Young girls all dressed in their bright Irish costumes,
> Great banners being carried to the sound of the band.
> Thousands will humbly follow the coffin
> Of the darling of Ireland, the Lion-heart so bold,
> Welcoming McCaughey back to his homeland,
> For his death in the end is stronger than their force. (*O'Sullivan*, 129)

The repetition of the line 'For pride in the end is stronger than woe' ('Mar sa deireadh is treise an bród ná an brón') at the end of stanzas one and two affirms the ideology of self-sacrifice. The symbolic political importance of McCaughey's death is underscored in the ultimate line of the poem, which modifies the earlier refraining line 'For his death in the end is stronger than their force' ('Mar sa deireadh is treise a bhás ná a gcumhacht'). That Behan later had a fanatical Anglo-Irish patriot in the play *An Giall* sing lines from the poem is understood as a rejection of the effusive nature of the original poem and its uncritical appraisal of republican rhetoric (*Kearney*, 48). Given, however, that the character in question (Monsúr) does not recite the lines verbatim but chooses lines most appropriate to his own patriotic zeal, this could further be understood as a critical reflection on the appropriation of literary texts for political agendas, possibly even a self-censure by the poet himself.

The overt reference to Ó hIfearnáin's poem serves not only a political purpose but also a literary one. As a non-native Irish speaker, publishing for the first time in a language in which he had only recently immersed himself, Behan deftly creates his own literary genealogy, echoing the language, the imagery and the political rhetoric of an eighteenth-century predecessor to comment on a contemporary political event. Ó hIfearnáin's imagery clearly infused Behan's literary imagination and is echoed in his writings in English as well. 'The crash of drums and scream of pipes' is closely connected with descriptions of republican activities in *Borstal Boy* (1958) and with the character 'Monsewer' in *The Hostage* (1958). In the former, contemplating his incarceration in Dale Street Prison, Behan muses:

I could not even walk, but sat huddled on the bed in my blankets, with tears in my mind and in my heart, and wishing I could wake up and find out that I had only been dreaming this, and could wake up at home, and say, well, that's how it would be if you were pinched in England, and not attend any more parades, and drop out of the I.R.A. and attend more to my trade, and go out dancing or something, and get married; and if, watching an Easter Sunday parade and listening to the crash of drums and scream of pipes as the four battalions of the Dublin Brigade went into the slow march and gave 'eyes left', as they passed the G.P.O. with their banners lowered, and the crowds either side of O'Connell Street baring their heads, I felt my blood go to my scalp – I could always remind myself of the time I dreamt I was captured in Liverpool, and bring my blood back to my feet. (*BB*, 21)

Behan's conscious attempt to be part of the Irish-language literary tradition is again evident in the poem 'Repentance' ('Aithrí'), composed in 1947 during his detainment in Strangeways Prison, Manchester. The poem imitates an established genre of poetic repentances, such as 'The Repentance of Red-haired Donnacha' ('Aithrighe Dhonnacha Ruadh'), 'The Repentance of Blind Liam' ('Aithrighe Liam Daill'), 'The Repentance of Seán de hÓra' ('Aithrighe Sheáin de hÓra'), to name but a few. Behan's poem, however, proudly straddles two literary traditions. An explanatory note published with the original poem in *Comhar*, but not reprinted in the anthologised version, explains that the first verse is actually a translation of an English poem which Behan's great-grandmother recited. One is struck by Behan's own emphasis on the dual-language heritage to which he is heir, confirming that his great-grandmother 'was fluent in this language [Irish] and learned in English'. The fact that he wrote this poem while imprisoned in England, 'with the mail-bag needle as I had no other instrument with which to write', adds not only poignancy but a further layer of complexity to the politics of language and identity.[11]

The second and third stanzas of the poem draw on stock motifs of poetic repentances: the sinner lists his transgressions, including a self-indulgent life-style, repents and asks the Virgin Mary to intercede on his behalf on the Day of Judgement. There is, however, a sadistic tone in Behan's composition which undercuts any charge of mere ventriloquism. 'The time of terror' ('am seo an uafáis') alluded to in the first stanza is vividly imagined by the narrator in the two ensuing stanzas. The sinner of this poem lays bare his terrifying visions of being terrorised by memories of his decadent life on his deathbed. Like army sergeants calling orders, his memories of sins will hunt him down like hounds, pinning him to the ground while death on horseback will watch the pack maul him:

Is geall mo pheacaí le conairt chraosach,
Is í an chuimhne adharc a ngéimneach chugam,
An bás ar chapall, tar éis chúrsa mo shaoil-se,
Na blianta ina gclaímhte slán ar a chúl –
Is mise ar talamh, m'anáil ar taoscadh,
Caillte, cró-allas críoch sheilge ar mo ghrua,
Ag creathadh faoi dheargshúile con is a mbéicíl –
A Mhaighdean, ná diúltaigh áit shlán faoi do thrua. (*PPI*, 15)

Recollection hoots like a hunting-horn
Calling my sins like a ravenous pack;
To the end of my trail comes death on a horse,
Each year a jump behind his back;
As I wait for the kill, cornered and panting,
The bloodsweat breaking on my face,
As I tremble before their red-eyed howling,
Virgin, don't grudge me your merciful grace. (*Kearney*, 51)

Behan's elegy for Seán McCaughey was followed less than a year later by another elegy; this time for socialist and trade union leader Jim Larkin, who died in January 1947. Remarking on Behan's choice of language for this particular elegy, Kearney asserts: 'It is at first sight surprising that Behan should not think it more apt to honour Larkin in the language of the Dublin worker; a poem in Irish meant nothing to most of those with whom Behan had followed the coffin' (*Kearney*, 50). It would appear, however, that Behan's choice of language was determined less by the potential audience than by the subject of the poem itself; commemorating Larkin in the Irish language was entirely in keeping with Larkin's own commitment to the language movement as an essential part of radical Irish labour republicanism.[12] Larkin's renowned oratory skills are cleverly emphasised with the repeated use of the word 'clab' or 'mouth' in the first and second stanzas of the short elegy. Although translated below as 'the jaws of the city', a more literal translation would be 'the open mouth of the city' and 'the mouth of the city', respectively:

Ba mise é! Ba gach mac máthar againn é!
Sinn féin. Láidir. Mar ab áil linn a bheith,
    Mar ab eol dúinn a bheith.
Eisean ag bagairt troda is ag bronnadh fuascailte –
Is sinne ag leanúint a chónra trí chlabbhéal na cathrach
I mbéiceacha móra feirge.

Ag leanúint a chónra trí clab na cathrach aréir
An sinne a bhí sa chónra?
Níorbh ea: bhíomar sa tsráid ag mairseáil
Beo, buíoch don mharbh. (*PPI*, 14)

He was me – he was every mother's son of us,
Ourselves alone – strong as we wished to be,
    As we knew how to be.
He threatening fight and bringing freedom,
We following his coffin through the jaws of the city
    Amid great bellows of rage.
Following his coffin through the jaws of the city last night
Were we ourselves in the coffin?
No. We were marching in the street,
Alive – grateful to the dead one. (*Kearney*, 50)

As is the case in 'Return of McCaughey', the focus is less on the death of the individual than on the visionary's legacy; in both poems the deceased is portrayed as a leader who has inspired resistance to the status quo and who has emboldened the underdog. Ultimately, however, as Kearney has noted, this public poem lacks depth of emotion and conviction (*Kearney*, 49).

Behan's most famous lament and most anthologised poem is of course 'Jackeen ag Caoineadh na mBlascaod', variously translated as 'A Jackeen Laments the Blaskets',[13] 'A Jackeen Cries at the Loss of the Blaskets' (*Kearney*, 52), 'A Jackeen Says Goodbye to the Blaskets' (*O'Connor*, 133) and 'A Jackeen's Lament for the Blaskets'.[14] Behan, a self-confessed and proud urbanite for whom Irish was a second language, wrote this poem in 1948 while apparently grieving the gradual depopulation of the small south-western, Irish-speaking island. One of his biographers suggests that the poem could be interpreted as a farewell to Irish, an act of literary leave-taking as Behan would soon turn his attention to writing in English (*O'Connor*, 133). Kearney doubts this interpretation and posits that the deserted Blasket was a literary expression of Behan's own personal state of desolation: 'The poem, dedicated to Seán Ó Briain, is an effort to hold on to something of value at a time when his life seems to be slipping away from him' (*Kearney*, 53). Broadening the scope of this autobiographical reading, John Brannigan astutely observes that the dispersal of the Blasket Island community mourned in the poem is 'a refraction of his lament for the life of working-class communities in inner-city Dublin …' (*Brannigan*, 64), communities which were displaced to the newly built suburbs in the 1930s. The symbolic meaning of the Blasket Islands for Behan, however, should not be underestimated; they epitomised pre-colonial Gaelic culture and its vibrant oral tradition, an alterity which was becoming victim to modern times (*BB*, 70). In this poem, the imminent absence of human life and human noise on the island is juxtaposed with the noise of nature and of the elements:

> Beidh an fharraige mhór faoi luí gréine mar ghloine,
> Gan bád faoi sheol ná comhartha beo ó dhuine
> Ach an t-iolar órga deireanach thuas ar imeall
> An domhain, thar an mBlascaod uaigneach, luite …
>
> An ghrian ina luí is scáth na hoíche á scaipeadh
> Ar ardú ré is ag taitneamh i bhfuacht trí scamaill,
> A méara loma sínte síos ar thalamh
> Ar thithe scriosta, briste, truamhar folamh …
>
> Faoi thost ach cleití na n-éan ag cuimilt thar tonna
> Buíoch as a bheith fillte, ceann i mbrollach faoi shonas,
> Séideadh na gaoithe ag luascadh go bog go leathdhorais
> Is an teallach fuar fliuch, gan tine, gan teas, gan chosaint. (*PPI*, 17)

In the sun the ocean will lie like a glass,
No human sign, no boat to pass,
Only, at the world's end, the last
Golden eagle over the lonely Blasket.

Sunset, nightshadow spreading,
The climbing moon through cold cloud stretching
Her bare fingers down, descending
On empty homes, crumbling, wretched.

Silent, except for birds flying low
Grateful to return once more;
The soft wind swinging a half-door
Of a fireless cottage, cold, wet, exposed. (*Kearney*, 53)

Although the poem is ostensibly yet another example of the westward literary gaze from the modern metropole to the rugged, idyllic west, the reader's attention is drawn to this dynamic in the self-deprecating title which, in the original, reflects the linguistic and cultural divide: 'Jackeen' is left untranslated, the poet fully aware of the slightly pejorative connotation attached to the term by non-Dubliners, who consider the city dwellers the most Anglicised of the Irish population. The Blasket Islands of the poem are undoubtedly more imaginary than real; the harshness of the elements is completely absent from the poem; the ocean calm as glass, the wind softly swinging a half-door. Could the Jackeen of the title conceivably be lamenting the emblematic status conferred on the islands and its writers which, like the poem itself, glosses over the lived reality of the islanders and renders their alterity harmless? In a similar vein, Rankin Russell (2002) argues compellingly that *The Quare Fellow* is in fact an anti-colonial Irish drama, which critiques and laments the disappearance of the indigenous language in a neo-colonial Irish state.

As an Irish-language writer, enthralled by the Blasket islanders' auto-biographies – *The Island Man* (*An tOileánach*, 1929) and *Twenty Years a-Growing* (*Fiche Bliain ag Fás*, 1933) in particular – the prospect of 'a hearth without fire, without warmth, without defence' (my translation) was dismal indeed. Fire and warmth are synonymous with storytelling and this oral tradition was the cultural milieu out of which these texts were born. Their authors gave insider accounts of their lives without fully endorsing the romantic heroic narrative advocated by the Irish state.[15] What would this shift from oral culture mean for Irish-language literature? It is exactly this anxiety with regard to the future of the literary tradition which is the subject of the poem, 'The Rhymster's Wish' ('Guí an Rannaire'), published less than two years after Behan's lament for the Blaskets.

The self-effacing title draws a distinction between the narrator's own literary output, which he classifies as mere versifying, and the output of a true poet.[16] The narrator, apparently disillusioned by current literary output and trends in the Irish language, sets out his aspirations for Irish-language poetry:

Dá bhfeicfinn fear fásta as Gaeilge líofa
Ag cur síos go sibhialta ar nithe is ar dhaoine,
Ar mheon is ar thuairimí i ráite an lae seo
Soibealta sómhar soicheallach saolta,
Bheinn an-sásta a theagasc a éisteacht:
   File fiáin fearúil feadánach,
      Bard beo bíogach bríomhar bastallach,
      Pianta paiseanta pheannphágánach. (*PPI*, 24)

If some grown-up guy, with fluent Irish,
Wrote of people and things in a civilised style,
Of moods and opinions in the words of today,
Impudent, easy, expansive, *au fait* –
I'd happily hear what he had to say.
   A poet with punch, with power and plenty
   A burgeoning bard, blazing and brazen,
   Pained, impassioned, paganpenned. (*Kearney*, 57)

The narrator's contemporary concerns, expressed in alliterative language reminiscent of the work of Dáibhí Ó Bruadair (1625–98) and Brian Merriman (1750–1805), is a self-conscious attempt to marry the old and the new. It is also a reminder to readers of the wealth of literary forefathers available to them. The narrator's aspirations, his call for poetry that is contemporary in thought and speech but which also draws on the linguistic and intellectual resources of the native literary tradition, clearly echo Patrick Pearse's literary credo as outlined in his much-quoted article 'About Literature' (1906). Although cognisant of the fact that the literary revival was still in its infancy at that time, Pearse was clear about the literary goal:

> Of course, it were absurd at this stage of the movement to expect philosophical poetry, psychological novels and deep treatises on metaphysics. But we *do* think that a little more originality, a bit more boldness, a little more ambition on the part of Irish writers were both necessary and desirable. [...] Irish literature, if it is to grow, must get into contact on the one hand with its own past and on the other with the mind of contemporary Europe.[17]

The second stanza of 'The Rhymester's Wish' almost appears like an unequivocal affirmative answer to the question posed by Pearse, forty years previously:

> Do Kerry mountainsides and Iar-Connacht heights and Tirconnell glens nurture today a race in which there lingers no breath of the old daring spirit, no spark of the old consuming fire, no trace of the old high resolve?[18]

The rhymester's disdain for the conservative and self-serving elements of the language revival movement is unequivocal and similar in tone to Brian Ó Nualláin's acerbic novel *The Poor Mouth* (*An Béal Bocht*, 1941):

> Arú, mo chreach, cad é an fhírinne?
> Státseirbhísigh ó Chorca Dhuibhne
> Bobarúin eile ó chladaigh Thír Chonaill
> Is ó phortaigh na Gaillimhe mar bharr ar an donas!
> Gaeil Bhleá Cliath faoi órchnap Fáinní,
> *Pioneers* páistiúla pollta piteánta,
> Maighdeana malla maola marbhánta,
> Gach duine acu críochnúil cúramach cráifeach. (*PPI*, 24)

> But Jesus wept! What's to be seen?
> Civil servants come up from Dún Chaoin
> More gobdaws down from Donegal
> And from Galway bogs – the worst of all,
> The Dublin Gaels with their golden *fáinnes*,

Tea-totalling toddlers, turgid and torpid,
Maudlin maidens, morbid and mortal,
Each one of them careful, catholic, cautious. (*Kearney*, 57)

This derisive description of rural language enthusiasts is later repeated in *Borstal Boy*, as the narrator chauvinistically boasts of his urban working-class background:

I was no country Paddy from the middle of the Bog of Allen to be frightened to death by a lot of Liverpool seldom-fed bastards, nor was I one of your wrap-the-green-flag-round-me junior Civil Servants that came into the I.R.A. from the Gaelic League, and well ready to die for their country any day of the week, purity in their hearts, truth on their lips, for the glory of God and the honour of Ireland. (*BB*, 78)

Returning to the imagery of fire and heat in the final lines of the poem, the rhymester declares that he would defer to a true poet, if one were to emerge who would 'rekindle the embers' (ag séideadh gríosaí) of the literary tradition:

Dá dtiocfadh file ag séideadh gríosaí,
Rachainn abhaile, mo ghnó agam críochnaithe.
(*PPI*, 24)

If a poet came and inspired some spirit,[19]
I'd go home, my job finished. (*Kearney*, 57)

The gender ideology of the poem is worth noting. The true poet is imagined in masculine terms and exudes hypermasculine traits, being 'wild', 'manly', 'passionate' and 'bold'. In contrast, the respectable language enthusiasts with their bourgeois pretensions are 'effeminate', 'dull, lifeless, old virgins' who are too diligently pious for their own good. The great irony is, of course, that the poet who emerged shortly afterwards and who showed the linguistic accomplishment, intellectual verve and subversive creativity longed for in the poem was in fact Máire Mhac an tSaoi, poet, scholar and civil servant! Her employment of more traditional poetic forms and language has been described as a subterfuge, 'a cover for a more subversive enterprise', which challenged the established moral consensus of the time.[20]

Contrary to most authors who consider Behan's decision to write in Irish within a nationalist-historical framework, Barry McCrea focuses on the modernistic poetic impulse that may have inspired Behan.[21] McCrea's discussion is confined to an analysis of the poem 'A Jackeen Lamenting the Blaskets', and he speculates that Behan's homosexual longings and his choice of Irish as a literary medium were linked. The textual evidence appears scant if one examines Behan's poetry in Irish in isolation. A bilingual approach is undoubtedly revealing. When once asked why he originally wrote the play *The Hostage* (*An Giall*) in Irish, Behan avowed that 'Irish is more direct than English, more bitter. It's a muscular fine thing, the most expressive language in Europe' (Behan quoted in *O'Connor*, 204). The Irish language, grammatically a feminine noun, is exclusively imagined as female within the literary tradition. Behan's personification of it as male is openly transgressive and bears striking resemblance to the description of homoerotic love by the first-person narrator in Behan's short story 'After the Wake', first published in Paris in 1950 (*Wake*, 13). The narrator, a writer, is determined to initiate a physical relationship with a married man:

> The first step – to make him think it manly – ordinary to manly men [...] to remove the taint of 'cissiness', effeminacy, how the German Army had encouraged it in Cadet Schools, to harden the boy-officers, making their love a muscular clasp of friendship, independent of women ... (*Wake*, 48)

The first-person narrator employs an Irish love song to make coded references to his homoerotic longings for the male spouse:

> The night before she went into hospital we had a good few drinks – the three of us together. [...] I sang *My Mary of the Curling Hair* and when we came to the Gaelic chorus, 'siúl a ghrá' ('walk my love'), she broke down in sobbing and said how he knew as well as she that it was to her I was singing, but that he didn't mind. (*Wake*, 49–50)

The narrator exploits the ambiguities of the oral song tradition in Irish where men sang women's songs and vice versa, the narrative of songs being free enough to allow for reinterpretation from various perspectives.[22] This flexibility in the song tradition is exploited in the short story to undermine normative heterosexual assumptions. This is reminiscent of an incident in *Borstal Boy* when a fellow inmate, Charlie, whose physical attractiveness the young Behan had already noted, asks him to sing a song. Behan suggestively chooses a song about Bonnie Prince Charlie and provides the following lines in the book:

A bhuachaill aoibhinn, aluinn-ó,
Ba leathan do chroí, is ba dheas do phóg …
… beautiful, lightsome, awesome boy,
Wide was your heart, and mild was your eye,
My sorrow without you, for ever I'll cry,
… Is go dtéighidh tú, a mhuirnín, slán,
Walk my love, walk surely.

White as new lime, your thighs and hips,
Your clustering hair, and your sweet-bitten lips,
My last blaze of strength would die well in their kiss …

Is go dtéighidh tú, a mhuirnín, slán,
Walk my love, walk surely. (*BB*, 16–17)

In taking full advantage of the suppleness of the song tradition in Irish, Behan here was boldly striking at the very heart of the post-colonial state's puritan and Catholic ethos, as well as its sanitised version of the Irish language. In this he prefigured by many years the openly homoerotic aesthetic of poet Cathal Ó Searcaigh.[23]

There is little of this subversive reimagining of Irish literary sources in Behan's poetry, although there is clear empathy with one who led a hedonistic life in the poem 'Oscar Wilde'.[24] Most striking is the narrator's disturbing realisation that the ravishes of time tame even the most notorious non-conformist:

Aistrithe ón *Flore*
go fásach na naofachta,
ógphrionsa na bpeacach
ina shearbhán aosta,
seoid órga na drúise
ina dhiaidh aige fágtha

gan *Pernod* ina chabhair aige
ach uisce na cráifeachta;
ógrí na háilleachta
ina Narcissus briste
ach réalta na glan-Mhaighdine
ina ga ar an uisce.
(*PPI*, 20)

Exiled now from Flore
To sanctity's desert
The young prince of Sin
Broken and withered.
Lust left behind him
Gem without lustre
No Pernod for a stiffener
But cold holy water
Young king of Beauty
Narcissus broken.
But the pure star of Mary
As a gleam on the ocean. (*O'Connor*, 131)

The pathos of the poem is offset by a lighthearted *envoi*, which alludes to Wilde's deathbed conversion to Catholicism as well as his bisexuality:

Ceangal
Dá aoibhne bealach an pheacaigh
Is mairg bás gan bheannacht;
Mo ghraidhin thú, a Oscair,
Bhí sé agat gach bealach.
(*PPI*, 20)

Envoi
Sweet is the way of the sinner,
Sad, death without God's praise.
My life on you, Oscar boy,
Yourself had it both ways. (*O'Connor*, 131)

Although 'the not so subtle double entendre defuses the threat that might have been posed by a more overt declaration of Wilde's bisexuality',[25] nonetheless, the trace of admiration and affection for one who openly contravened the sexual mores of the time is daring and hints at the narrator's ambiguous attitude to sexuality.

Refuting Ulick O'Connor's assertion that Behan's Gaelic self and his gay self were discrete facets of his personality, McCrea draws on queer literary theory to explain Behan's choice as a conscious expressionistic literary device:

> For Pasolini and Behan, adopting a rural language of which they were not native speakers was a means to express a more generalized sense of not being at home in the world. For two queer poets, idealizing this language, and fetishizing its native speakers, echoes with the predicament of gay people, of being on the outside looking in, foreigners in the 'natural', organic world in which sexual desires are not singular, shameful internal states that set one apart from others but part of the unspoken order of things.[26]

Although one could question the extent to which Behan could be considered a 'queer' poet in the same way as Pasolini, who was openly gay and who wrote about homoerotic love in his poetry, there is no doubt that the poet plays with readers' expectations regarding sexual mores and desires in poems like 'Oscar Wilde' and 'Guí an Rannaire'. There is undoubtedly a sense of being on the 'outside looking in' in poems like 'Loneliness' and 'Grafton Street'. The first-person narrator in the latter poem is despondent about life in the capital city and sketches the tension between the emerging international popular culture and the conservative social and sexual mores stifling the high spirits of young lovers:

Chonac aréir na beo
Ar oileán na marbh,
Chuala caint in áit
Atá coiscricthe don bhalbh. (*PPI*, 21)

Saw last night the living
On death's island,
Heard talk in a place
Devoted to the silent. (*Kearney*, 55)

The advent of the so-called 'American way'[27] is welcomed in the second stanza of the poem: the narrator claims that he prefers the young female's fashionable blue coat with shoulder pads to homespun clothing. The strain between the new Hollywood-led definition of female beauty and the everyday reality of life in a country then devastated by tuberculosis[28] is inscribed in the language itself: the inclusion of English terms for beauty products ('shampoo', 'Max Factor') as well as the lighthearted laugh of the young woman, in contrast with the plight of a tubercular female:

> *Shampoo* ina folt órga
> *Max Factor* ar a leiceann,
> Ina guth tá gáire na hóige –
> Ní mar sin do Bhríd na heitinne. (*PPI*, 21)

This can be translated literally as:

> Shampoo in her blonde hair
> Max Factor on her cheek,
> In her voice, the laughter of youth –
> Not so for tubercular Bríd.

The allure of American culture is tempered by restrictive societal mores which apparently actively discourage young love:

> Cogar mar is cóir
> Faoin ngrá, i dtír na seirbhe,
> Sula dtéann siad isteach
> Chun damhsa san *Classic*. (*PPI*, 21)

> Whisper, as one must,
> Of love in this sour land
> Before they go in
> To dance in the Classic. (*Kearney*, 55)

One cannot but be struck by the contrast between the restrictive nature of social mores in the cosmopolitan centre, as depicted in 'Grafton Street', and the liberal attitude to adultery depicted in the seemingly more traditional poem 'To Bev' ('Do Bhev'), signed and dated Caherdaniel, Co. Kerry, 1949. In this, Behan resists the temptation to equate urban and fashionable with liberal and liberating. 'For Bev' is a lighthearted, superficial and indeed a surprisingly sanitised reworking of traditional *chanson de la malmariée* songs. The young woman of the song generally complains at being married to a much older man who is dull, as well as jealous or controlling. The songs usually contain bawdy details of his sexual ineptness and of her sexual desires. She often wishes him dead so that she can take up with her lover, with whom she is normally already involved.[29] The female narrator of Behan's poem, however, openly boasts about being married to an older man who can adequately satisfy her material needs, noting mischievously in the penultimate stanza that he will not live forever:

Níl aon ní in easnamh ná gátar ná easpa,
Ach gach rud is maith liom is rachmas dá réir,
Más aosta mo chéile, níl teorainn lena fhéile
Ar eagla go gcaillfeadh sé teideal ar mo bhéal.

Mo cheol thú, an tsaint is an gliceas chun cleamhnais,
Is mise ag glaoch ar chéadnótaí is ar ór,
Gan blas searbh riamh agam ar an gcaolchuid,
Ach gairm ar thogha gach bia agus óil.

Is é barr mo chuid áthais, nach bhfuil éinne a mhairfidh –
Dá mba dhearthair an diabhail féin é – níos faide ná an céad,
Agus idir dhá linn, cá mór daoibh an fhuinneog
Ar oscailt sa chistin is an doras ar théad? (*PPI*, 16)

I know nothing of scarcity, waiting or wanting;
I have all I desire and enjoy it in bliss.
If my husband is old, there's no end to his bounty
Lest he forfeit his conjugal right to my kiss.

My blessing on greed and intelligent marriage,
Bringing hundreds in banknotes and gold on request;
Utterly free from the sharp taste of shortage,
Of food and of drink I just order the best.

The height of my joy is that no one will live
(Not the devil's own brother) no more than five score,
And so, in the meantime, what harm if the kitchen-
Window is open and a string hold the door? (*Kearney*, 56)

Although Ó Briain attested to Behan's in-depth knowledge of Merriman's eighteenth-century text *The Midnight Court*,[30] the poem 'Do Bhev' exhibits none of the hard-hitting Rabelaisian parody of church and state that characterises the work of his literary forefather. Behan was no doubt impressed by the very bawdiness of *The Midnight Court*, a text which was at the centre of controversy when Frank O'Connor's English translation of it was banned by the state censor in 1946, while the original Irish-language text remained in print.[31] Years later in a letter to the *Irish Times*, Behan declared 'The Irish language is a bloody great land-mine, containing all sorts of explosive material from "The Midnight Court" to Padraig Pearse's essay on censors and craw-thumpers ... .'[32] Behan reportedly translated *The Midnight Court*; a small section is included in *Borstal Boy* but the complete manuscript was allegedly lost (*Kearney*, 58).

If critical of official orthodoxy, Behan apparently had little appetite for fashionable unorthodoxy either. 'L'Existentialisme' was his final poem published in *Comhar*, in March 1952. It is understood to be a doodle, an intentionally obtuse poem which mocks the existentialist discourse favoured in the literary coteries of post-war Paris (*Kearney*, 60). The subtitle 'An echo of St. Germaine-de-Prés' ('Macalla Saint Germaine-de-Prés') hints at the narrator's appraisal of existentialism as a vacuous discourse which reverberated in the literary cafés of St Germain. The poem bears out this assessment as the narrator observes a sentinel futilely, or maybe unwittingly, patrol a vacant building. The narrator poses philosophical questions to which no answers are provided and which will remain unresolved, rebounding in the echo chamber of metaphysical discourse:

A fhir faire atá ag siúl falla
foirgnimh fholaimh,
   cad é cúrsa na seilge?
Cúis reilige?
Turas go hIfreann?

Ní foláir é. Ach céard faoi d'intinn?
Cad a bhí ann romhainn?
Ní fios. Ní rabhas beo,
nílim fós.
Olc ár gcinniúint?
Róleisciúil
chun freagra a thabhairt.
Maitheas, níl a dhath,
ná ciall, ná pian, fiú amháin,
ná an fhírinne i m'abairt,
ná ina mhalairt. (*PPI*, 19)

Watchman, walking the wall –
of an empty hall.
What is the chase after?
a grave matter.
A journey to hell?
Of course, but your mind as well?
What was before our time?
Dunno. I wasn't alive,
amn't yet.
Evil our fate?
too lazy
to say.
Virtue, not a gleaning,
nor pain, nor even meaning,
nor truth in what I posit
nor in the opposite. (*Kearney*, 60)

Behan's scepticism was shared by a fellow Irish-language poet, Liam S. Gogan, who reportedly told Cumann na Scríbhneoirí (the Writers' Society) that he had coined an Irish term for existentialism – 'scoundrelism'.[33]

The edition of *Comhar* that contained 'L'Existentialisme' also carried an editorial entitled 'Examination of Conscience' ('Scrúdú Coinsiais') which critically assessed recent literary output in Irish. The anthology *Nuabhéarsaíocht* (1950) was cited as a beacon of hope, an example of emerging poetic talent, but there was a recognition that creative literature in the language was still

young and would benefit from rigorous literary review.[34] Although Brannigan
proposes that Behan may have ceased writing poetry in Irish because perhaps
'he realised then that the Gaelic literary culture of mid-century Ireland was too
close to his own satirical portrait of it in "Guí an Rannaire"' (*Brannigan*, 67),
this suggestion does not give due recognition to the subsequent publication of
the anthology, *Nuabhéarsaíocht*, and to the air of hope it engendered. Kearney,
on the other hand, surmises that it was his pessimism about the future of
the Irish language, along with a lack of confidence in his own ability as a
poet, which ultimately led Behan to cease writing poetry in Irish (*Kearney*,
61). Consciously or subconsciously, self-doubt about his own ability to write
creatively in Irish appears to have been a salient factor. Correspondence
between Behan and publisher Seán Ó hÉigeartaigh in 1953 clearly indicates
that Behan appreciated that he needed to improve his Irish in order to write
a proposed literary account of his involvement in IRA bombings in 1939
and his subsequent detention in Hollesley Bay. Ó hÉigeartaigh provided
financial support to allow Behan to live in the Gaeltacht while working on
the manuscript. Although Ó hÉigeartaigh received nothing in return for the
advance payments, totalling £107, the seeds for *Borstal Boy* had been sown.[35]
Former editor of *Comhar*, Riobard Mac Góráin, recalled Behan's tendency in
the last five years of his life to look for positive affirmation about his ability to
write and sing in Irish.[36] Whatever the reason, although he ceased to publish
poetry in Irish, Behan cannot be said to have abandoned poetry in Irish or to
have simply returned to writing in English. At critical points in *Borstal Boy*, for
example, Behan recalls lines from Irish poems that apparently best express his
state of heightened emotion or sensual pleasure. Carrying out manual labour
while in borstal in the midday heat, he unearths an apple and recounts:

> I took a few hurried bites from it and, with the juice sharp on my tongue,
> put it back in my pocket, and got on with work, with the morning well
> advanced and the springtime steaming off the trees and the grass.

> By God you weren't that blind, Raftery, that you didn't get the smell and
> feel of it:

> Anois, teacht an Earraigh, beidh an lá dul chun síneadh
> is tar éis na féile Bríde, ardochaidh mé mo sheol … (*BB*, 210)

For Behan, therefore, Irish not only offered an alternative mode of expression, but also an alternative literary tradition that he could exploit and mould to the needs of his own imagination and poetic expression. Far from paying pietistic homage to an ancestral tongue, Behan embraced Irish as a literary medium with the linguistic resources to articulate contemporary experience, whether rural or urban, Irish or Parisian. Critical of the conservative element of the language revival movement, he deliberately sought to embrace those elements of the literary tradition that undermined normative assumptions and refuted the sanitised versions of the language and its culture. Ultimately, the thirteen short lyrics point to a literary ambition that could not be sustained by the poet's own creative resources in Irish. Although Behan did not continue to compose poetry in Irish after the early 1950s, his command of spoken Irish, together with his considerable knowledge of its literary tradition and his personal acquaintance with native speakers of the language and their *Gaeltacht* communities, informs aspects of his literary work in English. To perceive Behan's Irish-language poems as a flirtation with the language, an apprenticeship anterior to his English-language success, is to grossly underestimate the complex workings of the mind that functions between and across languages. Brian Fitch's observation in relation to Samuel Beckett is equally pertinent in relation to Behan:

> In whichever of the two languages Beckett happens to be writing at a given moment, there is always the presence of the other language with its wholly different expressive potential hovering at his shoulder, always at arm's reach and within earshot.[37]

7

BRENDAN BEHAN'S *THE HOSTAGE:* TRANSLATION, ADAPTATION OR RECREATION OF *AN GIALL*?

CLÍONA NÍ RÍORDÁIN

Translation between a minoritised language and a majority one is often the topic of fraught debate. When the languages in question are Irish Gaelic (learned by an Irish nationalist political prisoner at the Curragh internment camp)[1] and the Queen's English, the question is complicated by issues of identity politics, colonialism, and the subaltern status of the Irish language and the Irish people. As John Brannigan has pointed out in his essay on the cultural hybridity of *The Hostage* (*Brannigan*, 100–25), the transfer from one language to the other in the case of *An Giall* has frequently been couched in terms of the betrayal of the notional (or national) purity of the form and language used in the original Irish text. This is the case in the critical responses of both Ulick O'Connor (*O'Connor*, 206–12) and Richard Wall.[2] In the movement between Irish and English it would seem the old Italian adage 'traduttore, traditore' gains a new and more deadly edge.

Brannigan himself explores the relationship between the Irish- and English-language texts in terms of hybridity, seeking to demonstrate that Behan's avant-gardism found a place within English theatre at the end of the 1950s. Central to Brannigan's thesis is a desire to escape the binaries of nationalism and imperialism by contextualising *The Hostage* within post-war cultural trends in England (*Brannigan*, 124–5). The present essay offers another alternative to these binaries, hinted at by Brannigan in his allusion to Marie-Louise Pratt's notion of 'transculturation' (*Brannigan*, 114) as a means of describing the absorption of colonised and post-colonial culture within the metropolitan fold.

Fidelity, purity, and dilution of the source text are tropes that have dominated thinking with regard to the relationship between a translator and the source text, since Roman times.[3] The emergence of translation studies as a discipline during the late 1960s has meant that the relationship between source text and target text has been reconsidered, leading to a less rigid and less judgemental approach.[4] Nowhere is this more relevant than in the field of theatrical translation.[5] Important also is the self-translational element in the movement between *An Giall* and *The Hostage*. While the practice has been attested to since medieval times, recent scholarship has examined emblematic self-translators such as Samuel Beckett, Julien/Julian Green, Nancy Huston, Vladimir Nabokov or Elie Wiesel. This phenomenon has been explored at length in essays and monographs,[6] starting with George Steiner's seminal text *After Babel*.[7] In what follows, I propose to outline the status of the translated theatrical text in contemporary translation studies, seeing how the movement from Dublin's An Damer to London's Theatre Royal can be reconsidered in the light of such findings. I will then turn my attention to the status of *An Giall/The Hostage* as a self-translated text, examining the definitions and conventions that govern such writing. In conclusion, I contend that it may be helpful to consider *The Hostage* as a co-authored text, suggesting that far from viewing *The Hostage* as an 'othered' version of *An Giall*, the relationship should be viewed in a more conciliatory vein as two texts that can exist simultaneously in a movement that can be seen through the prism of Paul Ricoeur's work in *La Mémoire, l'histoire, l'oubli*,[8] thus avoiding confrontation, betrayal, otherness and even hybridity.

TRANSLATING FOR THE THEATRE

Declan Kiberd's statement 'If that is true, then *The Hostage* rather than *An Giall* may be the definitive version of the play'[9] is indicative of the desire for absolute answers with regard to the status of *An Giall/The Hostage*. Yet, a translated text needs to take account of its target audience. As Susan Bassnett has underlined, 'Translators cannot possibly render the same networks because the frame of reference of the two sets of readers is bound to be different. All they can hope to do is to create an alternative web of inference.'[10] Bassnett's essay refers in this instance to a text that is to be received by a reader. The phenomenon is even more acute when the text is translated for the theatre, where reception is immediate and there is no time to re-read and re-appraise the text. As Kiki Gounardidou reminds us '[…] the translation of a dramatic text is a double act of cultural transformation: that of the literary text and that of the performance text at the same time'.[11] The addition of material that speaks to a British audience (class differences, references to the British politics of the period) is one of the contentious elements in the reception of *The Hostage*. The manner in which the material was developed is also important. Joan Littlewood's approach to theatre has been well documented.[12] Central to her technique was the use of workshopping. According to a variety of accounts (see *Brannigan*, 113 and Wolf Mankowitz qtd in *O'Connor*, 208), Littlewood and her troupe were responsible for the addition of 'British material' in what Ulick O'Connor has described as the gaps in the translated text (*O'Connor*, 206). In O'Connor's narrative of the events, Behan was pressured into adding extra characters who, in O'Connor's opinion, 'had no special relevance to the theme'. However, even O'Connor is prepared to acknowledge that this corresponded to Littlewood's habitual modus operandi (*O'Connor*, 207).

Central to our comprehension of this account is the status of the theatrical text. Unlike a translation for the page, the translation for the stage relies not just on the immediacy of impact but it is also dependent on the ability of the translator to produce translatable dialogue. A translated theatre text rarely remains identical to the text produced by the translator at his desk. It is the *épreuve de l'étranger* [test of the foreign] envisaged by Antoine Berman,[13] the litmus test for a translated text. Clifford Landers reminds us of this: 'Even style, which is by no means unimportant in dramatic translation, sometimes must yield to the reality that actors have to be able to deliver the lines in a convincing and natural manner.'[14] O'Connor dismisses Littlewood's motives, ascribing them to the basely trivial necessity of keeping the audience entertained. However, Brannigan astutely attributes this to the dichotomy between the melodramatic Irish tradition and the site of Littlewood's theatre, which was based in a building that had housed a music hall theatre (*Brannigan*, 102, 115).

The site-specific element here is important, as are the conditions in which *An Giall* emerged, produced on a shoestring in the Damer Hall.[15]

Perhaps the most problematic issue of all in considering the relationship between *An Giall* and *The Hostage* is the use of the word 'translation' itself to describe the process involved in transforming *An Giall* for the London stage. In most accounts, the process undertaken by Behan is referred to as translation. Etymologically, this is a pleasing concept, if one refers to the primary meaning of the term offered by the OED: 'Transference; removal or conveyance from one person, place, or condition to another'.[16] Nonetheless, while we may be charmed at the notion of Behan carrying the Irish language text across the sea, like booty to be deposited into the English language, in a reverse image of Seamus Heaney's famous metaphor of translation,[17] adaptation or rewriting seem to be far more appropriate terms. However, as Christine Raguet points out, these terms are very much interconnected:

> *Si des moyens différents peuvent recréer des effets identiques, l'adaptation ne s'oppose plus à la traduction, mais en est l'une des manifestations, l'un des modes les plus adéquats, les plus efficaces.*[18]

> If different means can recreate identical effects, then adaptation is no longer to be viewed in opposition to translation but should be seen as one of its most suitable and effective manifestations. (*translation mine*)

What emerges in translation theory with regard to the definitions of the various terms is a continuum, where translation in its primary sense involves a high degree of fidelity to the source text, and other modes of translation, such as adaptation, transmogrification, version and rewriting, are placed further along the continuum. However, as Raguet suggests, they can be viewed as other manifestations of the same original phenomenon. As one moves further along the spectrum, cultural additions and creative freedom become increasingly important. Should *The Hostage* then be viewed as a rewriting of *An Giall*? This would seem to be the case if one considers André Lefevere's definition of the term:

> Translation is the most obviously recognizable type of rewriting and [...] is potentially the most influential because it is able to project the image of

an author and/or a (series of) work(s) in another culture, lifting that author and/or those works beyond the boundaries of their culture or origin …[19]

Yet, this convenient classification ignores the self-translational dimension of the *An Giall/ The Hostage* relationship.

AN GIALL/*THE HOSTAGE* AND SELF-TRANSLATION

Rainier Grutman defines self-translation as 'the act of translating one's own writings or the result of such an undertaking'.[20] The translator who undertakes the translation of his/her own work should therefore be the ideal translator, as questions of sense, intentionality and fidelity can be evacuated via the relationship between the self and the source text. Yet, while the writer is not writing an entirely new text, he/she is free of the constraints that might ordinarily be applied to an anonymous translator. In a recent article that outlines the choices made by various self-translators, Valeria Sperti suggests that the self-translating author should produce a work that incorporates the following features:

> *Chaque autotraducteur doit quand même tenir compte des objectifs de toute transposition: maintenir les informations complètes du texte premier; atteindre une qualité esthétique comparable et veiller à ce que le texte ait une même fluidité et un même naturel dans l'autre langue. Par sa réaffirmation de l'œuvre et par le processus auquel elle soumet la première version, l'autotraduction se manifeste ainsi comme une continuation du texte premier.*[21]

Every self-translator should nonetheless take account of the objectives of any act of transposition. They should ensure that all the information available in the original text is contained in the new one, attain an aesthetic quality that is similar to the original text and they should be attentive to the fluid and natural quality of the text produced in the other language. As a result, because of the reaffirmation of the original work's importance, combined with the process undertaken in transforming the first text, a self-translation can be viewed as a continuation of the first text. (*translation mine*)

Any assessment of the translation of *An Giall* recognises the salient narrative features of the original text and the fluidity and natural dimension of the English used in *The Hostage*. Critical attention has been focused on the aesthetic element, where differences persist between what Colbert Kearney has referred to as a 'naturalistic tragedy' versus a 'musical extravaganza' (*Kearney*, 131). Others, like Clive Barnes, are intent on the experimental nature of the final performance:

> When it was first produced 14 years ago by Joan Littlewood's Theater Workshop in London – the production later went to Broadway – it was almost as much a play by Littlewood as a play by Behan. The staging took the script and made a paper dart of it, and let it fly in the face of the Establishment. The written script was only the basis of a rollicking theatrical experiment.[22]

However, Barnes also draws our attention to what can be seen as the co-ownership of the English-language text (he is obviously unaware of the existence of *An Giall*). This dimension of the self-translated text has often been ignored. It is indisputably a common feature of the genre. The status of the resulting text produced in collaboration may possibly be seen as a collaborative translation. Recent work undertaken in Paris by Anthony Cordingly and Céline Frigau-Manning[23] attempts to establish a taxonomy of collaborative translation. Their research draws attention to the possibility of simultaneous co-authorship in the Renaissance period and underlines the emergence of the concept of 'singular genius' during the nineteenth century, reinforcing the *auctoritas* of the author for much of the twentieth century,[24] as Michel Foucault highlighted in his essay 'What is an author?'[25]

It is the criticism practised by French genetic critics that has allowed the position of the collaborative compositional process to be reconsidered. As Cordingly and Manning underline: 'The methods of textual genetics have been applied to translation, leading to the emergence of "genetic translation studies" … which generally accounts for collaboration when it becomes manifest (material) in the genesis of a translation.'[26]

In the absence of a genetic analysis of the manuscript of *The Hostage* and/or a recording/journal account of the workshopping of the play, it is possible to suggest, tentatively, that co-authorship could be attributed to the

Behan–Littlewood dyad for the English-language text. This hypothesis can be supported by comparative analysis of both texts. Some additions to the text can be read as mere 'explicitation', in an attempt to make the text more comprehensible for the target audience. This is the case with regard to the complement of information given for the hanging of the Belfast man in the opening scene (*CP*, 128). The original text makes reference to the young man hanging as high as the Busáras in Dublin ('Crochfar chomh hard leis an mBusáras é' (*PPI*, 29)). This local and quite banal Dublin reference[27] is transformed in *The Hostage* to a more internationally recognised summit: 'Tomorrow at eight, he'll hang as high as Killymanjaro' (*CP*, 131). While cultural adaptation of references between one text and the other is a common practice in translation, the substitution of the highest mountain in Africa for a locally controversial building could seem to be a metaphor for the translation strategy at play between the two texts.

Other additions to *The Hostage* are more difficult to attribute to translation strategies. From the same opening scene we can see the way in which the stage directions themselves have been expanded at length. The Irish text is sober and descriptive in introducing Monsúr and it has been mentioned earlier that the tune he plays on the pipes is 'Ó Dónaill Abú':

> *Isteach le MONSÚR. Tá filleadh beag a chaitheamh aige agus a chuid píob faoina ascaill aige. Séideann sé nota fada deireanach ar an bpíb.* (PPI, 30)
>
> *In comes MONSÚR. He is wearing a kilt and he is carrying his pipes under his arm. He blows one last note on the pipe.* [my translation]

Contrast this with the English version:

> *A blast on the bagpipes and MONSEWER enters along the passage looking like Baden Powell in an Irish kilt and flowing cloak. The noise from the bagpipes is terrible. Everyone but MEG springs smartly to attention as MONSEWER passes and salutes. MONSEWER lives in a world of his own, peopled by heroes and enemies. He spends his time making plans for battles fought long ago against enemies long since dead.* (CP, 133)

The expansion of the stage directions provides a narrative for the character that is not available in the Irish-language text. In terms of helpful stage directions, only the addition of 'the flowing cloak' can be regarded as practical. The bagpipe music – a recognisable marching tune connected to Ireland's revolutionary past, with its key refrain 'onward for Éireann, O'Donnell Abú' ('abú' meaning 'for ever'[28]) – has become 'a blast', or 'noise'. There is no identified tune. The music has become cacophony. Graphically, the title 'MONSÚR', a phonetic transcription of 'Monsieur', has become MONSEWER. While on a phonic basis no difference is perceived, the English transcription indicates a semantic pathway to the reader that goes some way to explain the obscenities and the bawdy dimension, features that distinguish *An Giall* from *The Hostage*. A genetic analysis of the English manuscript might provide pointers as to the reason for this narrativisation, which, from the outset, indicates to the actors (and not to the spectators) the fey, demented characterisation of Monsúr in English.

It is likely, nonetheless, that the hypothesis of co-authorship would not be satisfactory for all readers, not least for those who continue to regard *An Giall* as the 'true source text'. If we accept that the English text was conceived of *ex novo* as opposed to *ex nihilo*,[29] perhaps we can envisage another solution that takes into account the linguistic asymmetry of the Irish and English languages,[30] an historical fact that dates back to the nineteenth century.

CONCLUSION

The unbalanced relationship between the two languages is rooted in the colonial past that links Ireland and Britain; it is to be seen in the resentment experienced as a result of the loss of the Irish language, and the presence of what John Montague referred to as 'the grafted tongue' continues to preoccupy.[31] French philosopher Paul Ricoeur has done much to explore questions of historical resentment and the persistence of unhappy memories.[32] The tension in the reception of *An Giall* and *The Hostage* can be understood as a reminder or a remainder of this painful colonial past. The present state of the Irish language itself can be seen as a legacy of this supreme moment of subalternship. Ricoeur suggests that the third term in the triptych of his title 'oubli' [forgetting] may enable people to escape from the painful experience of history. This gift can be seen as a means of avoiding what Ricoeur in earlier work has referred to as 'le pathétique'[33] [the pathetic], in a movement that he characterises as 'la synthèse pratique' [the practical synthesis] where he promotes a duality allowing us to imagine an existence where both remembering and forgetting can be envisaged simultaneously. In such a scenario, it is possible to consider both *An Giall* and *The Hostage* as consecutive, yet equally valid, manifestations of the same creative impulse, thus resolving the tension and foregoing all thoughts of purity, infidelity and hybridity.

8

BRENDAN BEHAN AND ELIE WIESEL: *AN GIALL* AND *L'AUBE*

MÍCHEÁL MAC CRAITH

In April 1953 Brendan Behan wrote to the Irish-language publishing house Sáirséal agus Dill offering to write an account of his experiences during the Irish bombing campaign in Britain in 1939 and his subsequent imprisonment and detention in the Hollesley Bay Borstal. Behan hoped that the publishers would be able to offer him a scholarship to spend a few months in the Gaeltacht to produce the book, making the not unreasonable point that living in an Irish-speaking atmosphere would help to hone his literary and linguistic skills. The completed work would come to about 120,000 words.[1] Seán Ó hÉigeartaigh, one of the co-founders and directors of Sáirséal agus Dill, was impressed, as was his wife Bríghid. Already acquainted with Behan's work in Irish as a contributor of poetry and essays to the literary journal *Comhar*, Ó hÉigeartaigh replied in a very encouraging manner, sent Behan an initial sum of money and suggested the Aran Islands as the best location in which to write. By mid-May Behan wrote in an upbeat fashion from Inis Mór, the largest of the Aran Islands, that he hoped to have 20,000 words written within a fortnight. Unfortunately, that was as good as it got. Despite Ó hÉigeartaigh's support, both moral and financial, his confidence in Behan's ability to produce an Irish-language version of *Borstal Boy* proved sadly misplaced. By the end of March 1954 not a page of the projected work had appeared and even the optimistic Ó hÉigeartaigh finally gave up on the abortive scheme.

Despite his failure to deliver, it is interesting that Behan actually considered Irish as the medium for his first major work. He had already supplied a series of six articles on the 1939 IRA bombing campaign in Britain for *Comhar*, between October 1952 and April 1953, and these may well have been the source of Ó hÉigeartaigh's optimism. The editor of the journal, Roibéard Mac Góráin, was also involved, in 1953, in the founding of Gael Linn, which soon proved to be a new dynamic language revival organisation. When Gael Linn established a theatre for fostering Irish-language drama in 1956, Mac Góráin realised that it would be a major coup for the new theatre if Behan, fresh from the international success of *The Quare Fellow*, were to write a play in Irish. Behan readily agreed to Mac Góráin's suggestion and commenced work on a play in March 1957. The author himself claimed to have written the play in twelve days while the producer, Frank Dermody, complained that the final revisions came 'scrawled on the backs of cornflake bags' (*O'Connor*, 192). On 16 June 1958, Behan's play, *An Giall* (The Hostage) opened in the Damer Hall. It was an instant success, with crowds packing the theatre each night. Such was the demand that *An Giall* was staged for a second week, thus becoming the first ever play in the Damer to run for more than a week.[2]

At the same time Joan Littlewood's Theatre Workshop at Stratford was in financial difficulties and needed a big hit to bail it out. She approached Behan for a translation of *An Giall* and he was more than happy to oblige. Behan went to Sweden in August 1958 both to work on the translation and to complete the proofs of *Borstal Boy*. He found the task of translation a challenge but managed to complete his English version by mid-September. His text, however, was ramshackle and full of gaps. According to Colbert Kearney, what Behan produced was more 'the basis of a workshop play rather than a script in the traditional sense' (*Kearney*, 131). Given Littlewood's avant-garde approach to theatre, this was not necessarily a major obstacle. As far as she was concerned the dramatist was only one member of a team and the script did not have to be treated as if it were sacrosanct.[3] Whereas playwrights who stood up to Littlewood were usually over-ruled, Behan offered no resistance and actually contributed to the metamorphosis of his original script.

The Hostage opened on 14 October and like its predecessor proved an immediate success. The critics were highly complimentary. As Kenneth Tynan commented in *The Observer*: 'It seems to be Ireland's function every twenty years to provide a playwright who will kick English drama from the past into the present' (quoted in *O'Connor*, 199). Some of those who had seen the original Irish play, however, were not as enthusiastic as the English critics, claiming that the integrity of the original naturalistic tragedy had been transmuted into a musical extravaganza. While acknowledging Littlewood's role in ensuring that *The Hostage* became an international success, Ulick O'Connor was scathing in his judgement:

> Nevertheless, *The Hostage* as it was performed in the West End and Paris version is a blown-up hotch-potch compared with the original version which is a small masterpiece and the best thing Behan wrote for the theatre. The first production relied for its effect on a quality which is missing from the West End one. This is the contrast between the innocence of the two central characters and the atmosphere of violence and lust in which they become involved. (*O'Connor*, 200)

O'Connor was supported in this assessment by the Abbey actor and producer Eddie Golden, who had been present at the premiere of *An Giall*: 'Though the action of the play took place in a brothel, there was an extraordinary air of innocence about it. At the end I felt as if there had been a falling of flower petals through the air. I could almost smell them. It was uncanny' (quoted in *O'Connor*, 194).

Flushed with widespread acclaim, Behan himself opted for the superiority of the translation over his original play and endorsed Littlewood's contribution:

> I saw the rehearsals of … *An Giall* and while I admire the producer, Frank Dermody, tremendously, his idea of a play is not my idea of a play. I don't say that his is inferior to mine or mine is inferior to his – it just so happens that I don't agree with him. He's of the school of Abbey Theatre naturalism of which I'm not a pupil. Joan Littlewood, I found, suited my requirements exactly. She has the same views on the theatre as I have, which is that the music hall is the thing to aim at for to amuse people and any time they get bored, divert them with a song or a dance. I've always thought T. S. Eliot wasn't far wrong when he said that the main problem of the dramatist today was to keep his audience amused; and while they were laughing their heads off, you could be up to any bloody thing behind their backs; and it was what you were doing behind their bloody backs that made your play great.[4]

Behan's brother Brian, however, recalled him passing a less than complimentary comment on Littlewood. One night during a performance of *The
Hostage* before a packed theatre in Stratford, Brendan turned around suddenly
to his brother and said, 'Fuck Joan Littlewood.' As Brian reminisced:

> I was surprised and looked at him closely. He looked suddenly as if he
> knew that he had been 'taken for a ride', that he had been adopted as a
> broth of a boy, that they had played a three card trick on him. I think he
> suddenly had a moment of insight which was gone as soon as the next joke
> or drink came around. (quoted in *O'Connor*, 207–8)

While a play on the 'Irish Question' would not have interested London theatre circles in the late 1950s, Irish critics and audiences resented what they
saw as a stage-Irish play by a notorious stage-Irishman.[5] If Behan was gifted both as a serious writer and a performer-cum-entertainer, it seemed that
Behan the performer had taken over from Behan the writer when he collabo-
rated with Littlewood.

Recent criticism has not been so polarised in comparing *An Giall* with
The Hostage. John Brannigan has argued in favour of Behan attempting not
so much a translation as a transformation of *An Giall*, when he worked on
The Hostage (*Brannigan*, 105). Rather than bring *An Giall* to an English
audience, Behan wished to convert his play into a form sensitive to the
theatrical vocabulary of an English audience.[6] While conceding that *The
Hostage* can be taken as a relentless parody of *An Giall*, Brannigan suggests
that the former is best seen as 'a play inscribed within the codes and contexts
of English theatre and culture, which resituates the subversive potential of *An
Giall* within the language, forms and cultural politics of mid-century England'
(*Brannigan*, 123). Whereas in *An Giall* Behan subverted the structures of late
nineteenth-century Irish political melodrama to attack the myths of post-
independence nationalism, in *The Hostage* he subverted the cultural politics
of music hall entertainment to attack the myths of both Irish nationalism
and English nationalism or imperialism.[7] Rather than simply seeing Behan
acquiescing to Littlewood's demands, Brannigan's approach has the advantage
of rehabilitating him as an author in control of his work.

In this essay I would like to take a fresh look at *An Giall* and to distance myself from the comparison between the original and its 'translation'. To facilitate

this new approach I propose to compare Behan's Irish-language play with Elie Wiesel's short novel *L'Aube* (*Dawn*) published in 1961. An observant Jew, Wiesel was born in the Transylvanian town of Sighet in Romania on the last day of September 1928. Due to German pressure, Northern Transylvania was ceded to Hungary in 1940. In 1944 the Jews of Sighet were deported to Auschwitz where Wiesel's mother and youngest sister were sent immediately to the gas chambers. In early 1945, the German authorities started transferring prisoners to Buchenwald ahead of the advancing Russian forces. Shlomo Wiesel, Elie's father, died in Buchenwald on 29 January. When Buchenwald was liberated by American troops on 10 April, Elie was taken to Paris. Here he discovered that his two older sisters, Hilda and Beatrice, had also survived the camps. Believing that he had been spared for a reason, Elie decided to become a witness to the evil of the camps, but first took a ten-year vow of silence about the Holocaust in order to prepare himself for this mission. He learned French and studied philosophy and literature at the Sorbonne. Following the establishment of the state of Israel in 1948, he got a position as Paris correspondent for *Yediot Aharonot*, a newspaper published in Tel Aviv, and he visited Israel for the first time the following year. In 1954, he was assigned to interview Pierre *Mendès-France* the Jewish prime minister of France. The premier did not give interviews, however, but Wiesel tried again through the intervention of the well-known Catholic writer François Mauriac, who had been awarded the Nobel Prize for literature in 1952. Wiesel recounted his meeting with Mauriac as follows:

> A few days later he received me into his home [...]. To put me at my ease, he began speaking of his feeling towards Israel: a chosen people in more ways than one, a people of witnesses, a people of martyrs. From then he went onto discuss the greatness and the divinity of the Jew Jesus. An impassioned, fascinating monologue on a single theme: the son of man and son of God, who unable to save Israel, ended up saving mankind [...].

All this proved too much for Wiesel, who then interrupted Mauriac's monologue:

> 'Sir,' I said, 'you speak of Christ. Christians love to speak of him. The passion of Christ, the agony of Christ, the death of Christ. In your religion,

that is all you speak of. Well, I want you to know that ten years ago, not very far from here, I knew Jewish children every one of whom suffered a thousand times more, six million times more, than Christ on the cross. And we don't speak about them. Can you understand that, sir? We don't speak about them.'[8]

Thinking that he had blown the interview, Wiesel, in complete disarray, made for the door.

At the same moment I heard the door opening behind me. With an infinitely humble gesture the old writer was touching my arm, asking me to come back. We returned to the drawing room and resumed our seats, one opposite the other. And suddenly the man that I had offended began to cry. Motionless, his hands knotted over his crossed legs, a fixed smile on his lips, wordlessly, never taking his eyes off me, he wept and wept. The tears were streaming down his face, and he did nothing to stop them, to wipe them away [...].[9]

When Mauriac recovered he asked Wiesel details about his experiences in the camps. When Wiesel refused, Mauriac persisted. Why hadn't he written it all down? The survivor explained that he had taken a vow of silence but also signalled that he would never forget this encounter. When the interview was over, Mauriac escorted Wiesel to the door of the elevator, embraced him and assumed a grave, almost solemn, mien: '"I think you are wrong. You are wrong not to speak ... listen to the old man that I am: one must speak out – one must *also* speak out." One year later I sent him the manuscript of *Night*, written under the sign of memory and silence.'[10]

In 1958 Wiesel finally published an 800-page work in Buenos Aires, based on his experience of the Holocaust. Written in Yiddish it was entitled, *Un di Velt Hot Geshvign* (And the World Kept Silent). It began as follows:

In the beginning there was faith, a naïve faith; and there was trust, a foolish trust; and there was an illusion, a terrible illusion. We had faith in God, trust in man, and we were living an illusion. We made believe that a holy spark glowed in each one of us; that the image was mirrored in our eyes, and that it rested in our soul. Alas, this was the source, if not the cause of misfortunes that befell us.[11]

Also in 1958 Wiesel published a pared-down version (160 pages) of the original Yiddish in French entitled *La Nuit* (Editions de Minuit). Mauriac not only provided the foreword, but actually hawked the manuscript around until he found a publisher willing to accept it. The English translation, *Night*, was published in 1960.[12] In the introduction, Mauriac recalled his initial meeting with Wiesel:

> That morning the young Israeli who came to interview me for a Tel Aviv paper immediately won my sympathy, and our conversation very quickly took a personal turn. It led me to recall memories of the Occupation. It is not always the events that we have been directly involved in that affect us the most. I confided to my young visitor that nothing I had seen during those sombre years had left so deep a mark upon me as those trainloads of Jewish children standing at Austerlitz station. Yet I did not even see them myself. My wife described them to me, her voice still filled with terror [...] at that time we knew nothing of Nazi methods of extermination [...].
>
> This, then, was what I had to tell the young journalist. And when I said, with a sigh, 'How often I have thought about those children!' he replied, 'I was one of them.' He had seen his mother, a beloved little sister, and all his family except his father disappear into an oven fed with children. As for his father, the child was forced to be a spectator day after day to his martyrdom, his agony, and his death. And such a death! The circumstances are related in this book, and I will leave the discovery of them and of the miracles by which the child himself escaped to its readers, who should be as numerous as those of *The Diary of Anne Frank*. [...] And I, who believe that God is love, what answer could I give my young questioner [...]? What did I say to him? Did I speak of that other Israeli, his brother, who may have resembled him – the Crucified, whose cross has conquered the world? [...] But I could only embrace him, weeping.[13]

Though considered to be one of the bedrocks of Holocaust literature, *Night* is not easy to place in a particular genre.

> The work defies all categories. It has been described as personal memoir, autobiographical narrative, fictionalised autobiography, nonfiction novel and human document. Essentially it is a *témoignage*, a first-hand account of

the concentration camp experience, succinctly related by the fifteen-year-old narrator, Eliezer.[14]

Wiesel then wrote five novels, in quick succession, with *Night* as their starting point: *Dawn* (1960), *The Accident* (1961), *The Town beyond the Wall* (1962), *The Gates of the Forest* (1964), *A Beggar in Jerusalem* (1968). The link between the first three works is better expressed in their French titles, *La Nuit*, *L'Aube*, *Le Jour*. As the author himself expressed it:

> *Night*, my first narrative, was an autobiographical story, a kind of testimony of one witness speaking of his own life, his own death. All kinds of options were available: suicide, madness, killing, political action, hate, friendship. I note all of these options: faith, rejection of faith, blasphemy, atheism, denial, rejection of man, despair, and in each book I explore one aspect. In *Dawn* I explore the political action; in *The Accident*, suicide; in *The Town beyond the Wall*, madness; in *The Gates of the Forest*, faith and friendship; in *A Beggar in Jerusalem*, history, the return. All the stories are one story except that I build them in concentric circles. The centre is the same and is in *Night*. What happened during that *Night* I'm afraid will not be revealed.[15]

L'Aube/Dawn is a slim novel of ninety-six pages, dedicated to Mauriac. As this novel serves as a very interesting counterfoil to Behan's *An Giall*, it is necessary to give a summary of the plot. Elisha, an eighteen-year-old survivor of Buchenwald, has been recruited in Paris for 'the Movement' to fight in the Israeli war of independence, which in the initial stages was primarily directed against the British Mandate in Palestine. He is enthralled by his leader's stirring words:

> The English government has sent a hundred thousand soldiers to maintain so-called order. We of the Movement are no more than a hundred strong, But we strike fear into their hearts. Do you understand what I am saying? We cause the English – yes, the English – to tremble!

> This was the first story I had ever heard in which the Jews were not the ones to be afraid. I had believed that the mission of the Jews was to represent the trembling of history rather than the wind which made it tremble.[16]

For two hours each day Gad, the leader, indoctrinated the young freedom fighters with the movement's ideology: 'the goal was simply to get the English out; the method, intimidation, terror and sudden death [...]. On the day when the English understand that their occupation will cost them blood they won't want to stay.'[17] Despite the stirring words, the survivor of Buchenwald does not easily take to the role of becoming a killer:

> The first time I took part in a terrorist operation I had to make a superhuman effort not to be sick at my stomach. I found myself utterly hateful. Seeing myself with the eyes of the past, I imagined that I was in the dark grey uniform of an SS officer. [...] It was then that nausea overcame me. I saw the legs running like frightened rabbits and I found myself utterly hateful. I remembered the SS guards in the Polish ghettoes. Day after day, night after night, they slaughtered the Jews in just the same way ... They too ran like rabbits sotted with wine and sorrow, and death mowed them down. No, it was not easy to play the part of God, especially when it meant putting on the field-grey uniform of the SS.[18]

As Elisha wrestles with his conscience, the movement raids a British Army barracks for arms, in a ploy reminiscent of the spectacular IRA raid on Gough Barracks in Armagh on 12 June 1954. Unlike the Armagh raid, a sentry becomes suspicious and shoots after the departing truck, puncturing a tyre. Two Israelis hold off the advancing paras while the tyre is changed. Although the truck manages to escape, one of the Israelis is killed while the other, David ben Moshe, is captured and sentenced to death by hanging by a military tribunal. By means of posters and underground-radio broadcasts, the movement issues a solemn warning: 'do not hang David ben Moshe; his death will cost you dear. From now on, for the hanging of every Jewish fighter an English mother will mourn her son.'[19]

In retaliation, the movement kidnaps an English officer, Captain John Dawson, and holds him as hostage. The whole country is plunged into a state of tension:

> The English army proclaimed a forty-eight hour curfew, every house was searched, and hundreds of suspects were arrested. [...] The whole of

Palestine was one great prison, and within it there was another, smaller prison where the hostage was successfully hidden.[20]

When the high commissioner of Palestine announces that the entire population will be held responsible if John Dawson is killed, the Zionist leaders counsel prudence, for fear of a pogrom. The head of the movement, however, rejects their counsel: 'If David ben Moshe is hanged, John Dawson must die. If the movement were to give in the English would score a triumph ...Violence is the only language the English can understand. Man for man, death for death.'[21] As the stand-off continues, it becomes a major international story. Dawson's mother intercedes with the Colonial Office requesting a pardon for the Jewish boy. The secretary of state for colonial affairs tells her that her son will not die but the high commissioner is not so optimistic. He recommends clemency on the basis that it would turn worldwide public opinion in Britain's favour. His recommendation is turned down. England would become the laughing stock of the world should she cave in. Still confident that the Jewish underground will not carry out their threat, the English authorities announce that David ben Moshe will be hanged at dawn the following day. At this point the underground galvanises itself to put its retaliation into effect. Elisha is chosen to execute John Dawson: 'All I knew was that he was an Englishman and my enemy. The two terms were synonymous.'[22]

At this stage the similarities between *An Giall* and *Dawn* should be quite obvious. Mícheál Caoimhín Ó Néill, an eighteen-year-old IRA volunteer, has been sentenced to death for shooting two policemen and the Northern Irish government is not prepared to submit a plea for clemency to the crown. In retaliation the IRA kidnap eighteen-year-old Private Leslie Alan Williams from the military barracks in Armagh and take him to a brothel in Dublin, which they are using as a safe house.

Despite these similarities, however, the development and dénouement in both works are quite different. In *Dawn*, Elisha is very disturbed in the hours before the execution. He is already carrying a heavy burden of post-traumatic stress as a survivor of the Holocaust. This is compounded by his military activities in the Jewish underground, as the erstwhile victim-become-killer feels that he is wearing the grey uniform of the SS. And now he is to become a killer in a one-to-one situation for the first time. The stuffy room feels to him as if it is filled with people from his past, including his parents and the little boy he used to be:

'We are here to be present at the execution. We want to see you carry it out. We want to turn you into a murderer [...]. You are the sum total of all we have been,' said the youngster who looked like my former self. 'In a way we are the ones to execute John Dawson. Because you can't do it without us. Now, do you see?'

I was beginning to understand. An act so absolute as that of killing involves not only the killer but, as well, those who have formed him. In murdering a man I was making them murderers.[23]

Ilana, one of the female members of the underground, tries to comfort him, but to no avail:

There are not a thousand ways of being a killer; either a man is one or he isn't. [...] He who has killed one man alone is a killer for life.[24]

The night passes slowly. At four o'clock Gad gives Elisha a revolver but he is afraid to even touch the weapon that would make the all-important difference between what he is and what he risks becoming. Eventually he decides to go downstairs, unaccompanied, and talk to his intended victim. He feels an irrepressible urge to see, talk to and get to know John Dawson:

It was cowardly, I said, to kill a complete stranger. It was like war, where you don't shoot at men but into the night, and the wounded night emits cries of pain which are almost human. You shoot into the darkness, and you never know whether any of the enemy was killed, or which one. To execute a stranger would be the same thing. If I were to see him only as he died I should feel as if I had shot a dead man.[25]

When Elisha confronts his enemy he is disconcerted both by John Dawson's composure and by the fact that he actually likes him. In different circumstances they might even have become friends: 'We were the first – or the last – men of creation; certainly we were alone. And God? Perhaps he was incarnate in the liking with which John Dawson inspired me. The lack of hate between executioner and victim, perhaps this is God.'[26] Dawson asks Elisha his name and age, tells him twice that he is sorry for him and then, in a strange inversion of the roles of victim and executioner, invites him to sit down. He tells Elisha that he has a son the same age as him, a quite normal young lad who has none of Elisha's anxiety and unhappiness. The executioner gives his victim a pencil and paper to write a note to his son, which he promises to deliver. As the decisive moment approaches, Elisha becomes even more confused, and vainly tries to overcome his confusion by thinking of the death of David ben Moshe instead of that of John Dawson: 'I wanted to hate him. Hate would have made everything more simple [...]. Why did you kill John Dawson: I killed him because I hated him.'[27] Elisha fires the fatal bullet at the stroke of dawn, just as John Dawson pronounces his name, Elisha, a biblical name that means God saves. 'The shot had left me deaf and dumb. That's it, I said to myself. It's done. I've killed. I've killed Elisha.'[28]

At the beginning of *Dawn*, Elisha looks out a window and sees a face, his own. He remembers how a beggar once taught him to distinguish night from day: 'Always look at a window [...]. If you see a face, any face, then you can be sure that night has succeeded day. For, believe me, night has a face.'[29] In the concluding paragraph of *Dawn*, Elisha again goes to the window:

> The night lifted, leaving behind it a greyish light the colour of stagnant water. Soon there was only a tattered fragment of darkness, hanging in mid-air. Fear caught my throat. The tattered fragment of darkness had a face. Looking at it, I understood the reason for my fear. The face was my own.[30]

As Robert McAfee Brown, one of Wiesel's most perceptive and sympathetic critics, notes: 'The title *Dawn* is ironic. It is still night. The road to emancipation through becoming an executioner has been a cul-de-sac, for murder is only another form of suicide [...]. Darkness is still eclipsing night.'[31]

Despite the basic similarities of the plots of *Dawn* and *An Giall*, fundamental differences remain. First and foremost, Wiesel's work is a novel, whereas Behan's is a play.[32] Even if most of the novel is written in the form of soliloquies, with only brief interludes for conversations when conversations do occur, the sentences are interspersed with Elisha's silent reflections. The sparseness and tautness of Wiesel's writing is totally alien to Behan's rollicking style. And while *An Giall* lacks the metaphysical and ethical angst that pervades *Dawn*, Behan prefers to use the innocent relationship between Treasa and the captured English soldier in Act II to deal with the same issues. The actor Eddie Golden's reaction to this act on the opening night bears repeating: 'Though the action of the play took place in a brothel, there was an extraordinary air of innocence about it. At the end I felt if as there had been a falling of flower petals through the air. I could almost smell them. It was uncanny.'[33] The relationship between Treasa and Leslie is Behan's way of undermining the assumption that Englishman and enemy were synonymous terms, a notion that was taken for granted by Elisha on the very first page of *Dawn*.

Treasa is very innocent, not realising that she is working in a safe-house, let alone a brothel. She and Leslie are both eighteen-year-old orphans whose common experience of orphanages facilitates their conversation. Leslie is quite like the young English teenagers Behan would have encountered in Borstal. He is even sympathetic to the young volunteer who is due to be hanged in Belfast. Treasa and Leslie know little and care less about partition and the Irish question. If *Borstal Boy* can be read as a deconstruction of the idea that the terms Englishman and enemy are synonymous, this process is actually taken a step further in *An Giall*. It also should be acknowledged that Behan's encounters with enlightened adults like C.A. Joyce during his time in borstal also aided this process of deconstruction. And while one may fault Act I, with its witty banter and puns, for making little contribution to the development of the plot apart from setting the scene of the play, the portrayal of Monsúr, Pádraig and the un-named volunteers can be taken to describe the pitfalls involved in any revolutionary movement when common humanity is sacrificed at the altar of fanatical idealism. Monsúr is mad, Pádraig turned into a cynic after the disillusionment of post-Civil War Ireland, and the contemporary volunteers are puritanical. Monsúr is so deranged that he does not even realise that the safe house is a brothel, thinking instead that the clients are volunteers on the run, and the molls members of Cumann na mBan. Treasa is equally unaware of the regular function of the safe house, yet despite her innocence she is astute enough to question Monsúr's lauding the death of a young man prepared to die for Ireland.

It could be argued that Act I is actually a wrestling match between Behan the performer and Behan the writer who just about manages to win out. But if all the characters apart from Treasa are crippled in their humanity, with Pádraig's physical handicap (*ar leathchois*/one-legged) acting as a symbol for his emotional frustration, humanity takes centre stage literally and metaphorically in Act II when Treasa and Leslie fall in love. While Elisha is unable to respond to Ilana's attempts to comfort him in Wiesel's novel, in *An Giall* the budding relationship between Treasa and Leslie is central. Ilana and Elisha are both committed to the struggle for Israeli independence but Treasa is both unaware of and unconcerned about the Irish question, while Leslie is an unwitting victim of a struggle not of his own making. While we know from the very beginning of *Dawn* that John Dawson is going to be executed, it is only at the very end of Act II that we know that the same fate is in store for Leslie. Treasa and Leslie are rockin' n' rollin' to Tommy Steele crooning 'Singing the Blues' on the radio when the music is followed by a news bulletin. The government of Northern Ireland will not appeal for clemency for Mícheál Caoimhín Ó Néill and as a result he will be hanged the following morning as arranged:

Mar gheall ar an saighdiúir a gabhadh dhá mhíle taobh amuigh d'Ard Mhacha san oíche aréir, Private Leslie Alan Williams, eisíodh ráiteas inniu á rá gur gníomh díoltais in éiric an phríosúnaigh i mBéal Feirste a bhí ann. Dúradh sa ráiteas sin dá gcrochfaí an príosúnach, Mícheál Caoimhín Ó Néill, go gcuirfeadh Arm Phoblachta Éireann an saighdiúir, Private Alan Williams, chun báis mar dhíoltas.[34]

Wall's English translation reads:

Regarding the soldier who was captured two miles outside Belfast last night, Private Alan Williams … and a statement was issued today saying that he was a hostage for the prisoner in Belfast, and if the prisoner Michael Kevin O'Neill is hanged, the Irish Republican Army will execute Private Alan Williams as a reprisal.[35]

Treasa cries out in shock, throwing her arms around Leslie. The curtain falls with Pádraig's futile attempt to turn off the radio in time.

In the short final act, Pádraig tries in vain to reassure Leslie that it is all a game of bluff and that nothing untoward will happen to him. Similarly to John Dawson in *Dawn*, Leslie composes himself and informs Pádraig that an English soldier can die as bravely as anybody else. But where John Dawson's captivity becomes an international story, Leslie is under no illusion about the possible impact of his own situation. He feels it will not overly disturb the peace of the establishment. He also finds it ironic that he and his fellow squaddies in the barracks in Armagh had some sympathy for the fate of the IRA volunteer, who was hanged at such a young age. Pádraig's reassuring words notwithstanding, he becomes quite gruff with Treasa when she suggests going out for fish and chips (an excuse to inform the Gardaí). Equally ominous is the fact that the house is well guarded by the IRA, something that has not evaded Leslie's attention. The Special Branch, however, succeed in making a surprise raid, but not before Leslie, unknown to Treasa, is bound, gagged and hidden in a large cupboard. Despite the ensuing confusion, with guards and detectives scouring the house, Monsúr succeeds in giving his word to Treasa that no harm will come to Leslie. Eventually the brouhaha dies down and the police depart, but by the time the cupboard is opened, Leslie has suffocated and cannot be resuscitated. The play ends with Treasa cradling Leslie's head in her arms. The fact that Leslie's death is unintentional makes it all the more futile, a feature that clearly differentiates *An Giall* from *Dawn*.

In a tendentious article in the *Irish Times* in autumn 2014, Fintan O'Toole made the following comments:

> In some ways *Borstal Boy* is Behan's *The Hostage* in reverse. In that play a young English soldier is held hostage by the IRA and a mutual affection develops in spite of everything. In *Borstal Boy* the same things happens [sic], but it is to Behan himself. There is, though, one huge difference. In *The Hostage* the IRA kills their prisoner anyway. In *Borstal Boy* they simply kill his fanaticism with kindness.[36]

In pursuit of his argument, O'Toole has conveniently omitted to mention Leslie's 'resurrection' at the end of *The Hostage*. Furthermore, he either completely ignores or is unaware of *An Giall*, where Leslie actually dies by accident and is not killed by the IRA at all. Far from offering contrasting points of view, the futility of fanaticism and political violence is underscored in *The Hostage* every bit as much as it is in *Borstal Boy*. This is equally true of *An Giall*. Our comparison between Behan's play in Irish and Elie Wiesel's *Dawn* shows both works, for all their differences, to be at one in subverting the premise that Englishman and enemy are synonymous.

9

'NOT EXACTLY PATTERNED IN THE SAME MOULD': BEHAN'S JOYCE

JOHN McCOURT

In 1962, Brendan Behan delivered a lecture to the James Joyce Society at the Gotham Book Mart in New York City. This was recorded by Folkways Records and later sold as a long-playing record with the simple title, 'Brendan Behan on Joyce'. The beautifully designed record cover contains a pencil portrait of Joyce by American sculptor Jo Davidson (1883–1952), whom Joyce had known in Paris. Decades earlier, Davidson had done a terracotta sculpture of Joyce (casts can today be seen at the Metropolitan Museum in New York and in the Harry Ransom Center at the University of Texas) and had given Joyce's friend Arthur Power his first start in the French capital, finding him a position as an art critic for the Paris edition of the *New York Herald*. This brought Power into contact with many leading artists of the day, including Modigliani. The considerable presence of Davidson in the 1962 Joyce Society production offers a direct connection between Joyce's Paris of the 1920s and '30s and that, a couple of decades later, of Brendan Behan.

In *Inventing Ireland*, Declan Kiberd has described the importance of Paris as a refuge for Irish writers from Oscar Wilde onwards. Kiberd sees 1892 as a key year: 'It was in London in that year that Oscar Wilde was not allowed to stage his play *Salomé*. Consequently, he had *Salomé* published in Paris with 'the assertion that Paris was now the true home of personal freedom'.[1] Paris would be the home of personal freedom for Behan too in the years following his release from prison. It would also be the site of literary emancipation, the place where he would find the psychological space to begin moving beyond the years of study in prison into a more exclusively creative moment, particularly with the writing of *Borstal Boy*. Over almost two decades from 1948 until his death in 1964, Behan enjoyed several sojourns of varying length in the French capital where he made a host of friendships and acquaintances, many of them literary (significant among them, Samuel Beckett, Albert Camus, James Baldwin). Many other acquaintances were merely passing through or were American GIs willing to feed his alcohol needs in return for good stories, many of which would be about Joyce.

A second sketch by Davidson is printed beside the accompanying text of the talk, which, unfortunately, is riddled with errors, not committed by Behan but by his (presumably American) transcriber who clearly struggled with Behan's Dublin (and perhaps drunken) English and who also does not appear to have known much about Joyce. Despite this, Behan's text, in both spoken and written form, provides a vivid portrait of both its subject, Joyce, and of Behan himself. The entire production illustrates a core characteristic of Behan's output (and not just of his 'talk books'): that intricate counterpoint of the spoken voice and the written word in which the power of the original spoken word is only partially rendered in the written version, which struggles to convey the human energy, perception and depth of what was intended to be delivered orally.

The experience of reading Behan's Joyce lecture is akin to reading his *Brendan Behan's Island: An Irish sketch-book*, which was published in the same year. It could well function as a chapter within that same volume. While there is much truth in Louis MacNeice's comment that Behan 'writes like a talker with plenty of hyperbole and emphasis, with humanity, gusto and formidable wit' (quoted in *O'Connor*, 251), he seems to forget that *Brendan Behan's Island* actually *was* a talk book, in Enrico Terrinoni's words, 'the first of his three talk books or confessional publications which were mostly talked into a tape-recorder with the assistance of an editor'.[2]

Behan's interest in Joyce, whom he describes in his talk as 'the man that was able to use the right words in the right place',[3] was longstanding. As early as 6 June 1946, while still imprisoned in the Curragh, Behan made mention of Joyce in a letter to Ernest Blythe, then director of the Abbey Theatre. The purpose of the correspondence was to try to convince Blythe to read drafts of what was eventually to become *The Quare Fellow*. Behan's first 'Dear Sir' letter concludes with him telling Blythe that 'there is nothing political in it [his draft]'. A second letter, sent less than a month later, reads: 'I should like to enter the competition which the Oireachtas has for a novel. Could you give me permission to go in for the competition?' This earnest and seemingly straightforward approach is undermined by Behan's almost comical follow-up in which he tells Blythe: 'I have no novel written, but for a hundred pounds, I could translate *Finnegans Wake* into Irish. Here is the third Act of *The Landlady*' (*Letters*, 32). Not surprisingly, nothing came of either of these proposals. Behan's knowledge of Irish was still at an early stage and so was his familiarity with *Finnegans Wake*. Behan makes it clear in his New York Joyce lecture that although he dabbled in the *Wake* he certainly was not in any position to make a translation: 'About *Finnegans Wake* I can refer you to either Padraic Colum or Thornton Wilder, because for me, as I say, it is a frequently opened and as frequently closed book and just about baffles me.' Later, Behan directly connected his disappointment at his treatment by the Abbey with Joyce's earlier rejection there: 'Like Joyce, I put it aside and went on with my other writing' (*Confessions*, 242).

The New York lecture was the public culmination of what was a decades-long interest in Joyce, whose life and works provided Behan with an important template for his own semi-autobiographical writings. From Joyce's *A Portrait of the Artist as a Young Man*, Behan would have learned how to turn the facts of a life into fiction, that the writing of the self is never a neutral transcription of events that took place, but is a stylised, selective, distorted rendering, a conscious and often ironic re-fashioning designed to be read in a different moment and mood to those in which the narrated happenings were lived. In Behan's own writings there is a probing exchange between a forceful dynamic of raw self-exposure and a necessarily revisionist counter-thrust of self-concealment, disguise and disavowal. Behan's works are always, like Joyce's, autobiographical, but treacherously so, teasing the reader with detail, using but at the same time twisting the facts of original lived life, consciously playing up the unreliability of the finished fictional version, purposefully drawing the reader into a constant double-take that shakes accident and incoherence into pointed thematic heft. It is no accident that Behan himself entitled one of his later books *Confessions of an Irish Rebel* or that Colbert

Kearney's influential article on his writer uncle bears the distinctly Joycean title of 'Borstal Boy: A portrait of the artist as a young prisoner'.[4] Somewhat tragically, in his later writings Behan struggled for control over his material and was no longer able to differentiate between the fictive and the real, sometimes dipping into his own plays and fiction while attempting to give voice to his own biographical journey. Or, to say it with Terrinoni: '[I]n Behan, fiction and truth, like stories and reality, go hand in hand',[5] and in his latter years he struggled to distinguish between the two.

The affinities between Behan and Joyce are many, as Moore-Gilbert (among others) has illustrated, even if his initial claim that Behan became an '(ex)-Nationalist' seems a little simplistic:

> There are certainly enough specific echoes of *A Portrait of the Artist* to justify seeing Behan's text as 'A Portrait of the Artist as a Young (ex-) Nationalist'. Specific echoes include the Christmas sermon in Walton (compare Chapter 3 of *A Portrait*) and Behan's revelatory experiences on the seashore at Hollesley Bay (compare Chapter 4 of *A Portrait*). *Borstal Boy*, too, describes the formation of an artist's mind, in the process of which Behan reports the lesson that Stephen draws: in order to succeed, he must escape the nets of nationality and religion. In exile, moreover, Behan often survives through the silence […] and cunning […] which Stephen advocates.[6]

Moore-Gilbert also draws attention to what he calls 'Behan's affinities with Joyce's cosmopolitan conception of a decentred, postnational, but still relational conception of identity' which, he says, 'can be traced in the linguistic hybridity which does so much to reflect the protagonist's shifting negotiations with various collectives'.[7] In following Joyce, Behan would walk a path previously trod by earlier intellectual or literary Irish republicans, such as P.S. O'Hegarty, Eimar O'Duffy, Brinsley MacNamara and Eoin Ryan, all of whom had grown disenchanted with the republican cause and with the Ireland that it had produced. They turned to Joyce as a way of negotiating their way through their disappointment and sense of constriction in the new Ireland. Ryan spoke with deep appreciation in 1934 about Joyce's liberating influence in terms that might help explain his usefulness to Behan. Ryan described how it was through Joyce that he had acquired freedom in his use of language at a time when there was precious little literary freedom in the country. The presence and the impact of Joyce liberated him 'to evoke all, or most of the sides of Irish life we had known, and as the sides were different, we changed the style to suit the side; and, in that, brazenly and openly and with deep gratitude, took several leaves from the book of Mr James Joyce'.[8] In Ryan's view, Joyce uniquely captured the complexity of Ireland, both at home and abroad, and paved the way for others to create liberating spaces for themselves despite the squinting-windows mentality of an increasingly conservative country.

Joyce's unique capacity to capture the complexities of 'dear, dirty Dublin' also served and impressed Behan, who professed 'for those who favour Ireland, for myself it was ever Dublin' (*Confessions*, 201). He would turn to Joyce (and, even more so, to Seán O'Casey) as a model of how to impose a city setting, city voices and a city aesthetic on his writings at a time when there was an undoubted supremacy of the rural in Irish writing. He alludes to this in the lecture, where he interestingly pairs off the two writers as two giants that could not be contained in a brief description:

> My attitude to Joyce as a writer is similar to my attitude to Seán O'Casey. My wife said, when she was asked here what did she think of Seán O'Casey, she said 'What do you think of Niagara Falls?' When you're asked what you think of Joyce only thing you can say is 'How's the world using yourself,' because Joyce was a … he was a world … .

The sense of writing in the wake of two such colossal figures did not ease Behan's isolation as an almost lone figure writing about the city in the middle decades of the twentieth century. As he put it to Sindbad Vail in a June 1951 letter:

> Cultural activity in present-day Dublin is largely agricultural. They write mostly about their hungry bogs and the great scarcity of crumpet. I am a city rat. Joyce is dead and O'Casey is in Devon. The people writing here now have as much interest for me as an epic poet in Finnish or a Lapland novelist. (*Letters*, 45)

Thus, while he laboured alone in the physical absence of Joyce and O'Casey, Behan was comforted and enabled by the very real presence of their writings as he attempted, almost single-handedly within his generation, to give voice to the Dublin working class and to Dublin republicanism, two elements of the city that had not been a part of Joyce's central focus. Behan would also learn much from the multimodality of *Ulysses*, which draws on the conventions and techniques of cinema, music, popular culture, theatre, music-hall and vaudeville, pushing the limits of what had up to then been rendered in prose fiction. In his talk, Behan stressed that *Ulysses* was read in the Behan household 'as a sort of a gag-book which is as it should be and as a sort of very funny account of things of conversations that they had'. He then resorts to song, announcing that 'I can do something that nobody has ever done on this stage before', which is, somewhat underwhelmingly, to sing 'Love Is Teasing'. Apart from being a way of killing five minutes, by singing Behan was drawing attention to the love of music that he shared with the older writer and to the music that is such a vital component of their literary works. For both, song was a shorthand version of history. In all of Behan's writing, the use of song was a natural and almost unconscious act. Communicating through music was a vital technique, the extension of a family tradition (as it was too for Joyce). In *Confessions of an Irish Rebel*, Behan explains:

> In addition to other extraordinary abilities I'm a pretty good singer – or at least I was until my larynx gave in to too much of the gargle and too many cigarettes. And I had an extensive repertoire of songs, many of which I had learnt from my Uncle, Paedar [sic], and from my mother who has never stopped singing, not even the depression could stop her [...]. No matter what anybody mentioned, she'd sing a song about it. (*Confessions*, 219–20)

Behan would have appreciated how Joyce's experimental and cacophonous prose challenged and destabilised the more sedate and harmonious tones of much late-Victorian literature and the rhyming pleasantries of some early Revivalism. Joyce also introduced a very distinct set of urban Dublin voices and accents into Ireland's prose literature, just as O'Casey would later do on the stage. Behan would learn and borrow from both. The almost unplayable *Richard's Cork Leg*, for example, is surely a kind of fusion of the dark humour of 'Hades' and that other almost unreadable and certainly unplayable play-like episode 'Circe' with its, at times, seemingly shapeless hodge-podge, its amalgam of puns, snippets of music-hall, its comedy, songs, parody. It is hard not to see

Behan's prostitutes, Rose of Lima and Maria Concepta, who dominate the first act of *Richard's Cork Leg*, as the literary descendants or as the counterparts of Joyce's Bella Cohen. Where 'Circe' challenges boundaries, pushes the limits of what was considered morally and even narratively acceptable (in terms of both content and form), and makes huge demands on the reader, *Richard's Cork Leg* also seems to delight in similarly challenging and disorienting the viewer.

In his New York lecture, Behan made a point of connecting his play not with *Ulysses* but with Joyce's *Exiles* (something he was also doing in conversation and in print elsewhere):

> Somebody asked me why I called this play *Richard's Cork Leg*. Well, the reason I called it *Richard's Cork Leg* is that in Shakespeare and Company Miss Beech [sic] has a story of James Joyce sending a play called *Exiles* to the Theatre de Louvre on the Boulevard Cliché .... The aforesaid Theatre de Louvre sent a letter to Joyce about *Exiles* and he said 'Mr. Joyce, France has just come through a terrible war and we're all very sad despite the fact that we got a victory, it was a terrible price and there are cripples walking along the Boulevard Cliché but some of them are able to get into a theatre, they're that ambulant and they surely want something a bit more cheerful than Exiles.' So he said bitterly to Sylvia Beech [sic], 'I suppose I should've given Richard a cork leg.' So in my play I decided to give somebody called Richard, who is totally irrelevant to the plot, if any there be, a cork leg.[9]

Behan had probably been reading Beach's book about Shakespeare and Company which recounts what happened, but he may also have heard the story directly from her when they met at the Joyce Tower on Bloomsday 1960. An Irishman's Diary in the *Irish Times* reported: 'Brendan Behan was also present and "climbed the Tower like a mountain goat" before leaving a message for Miss Beach which read: "Throwaway is a Good Thing for the Gold Cup. Signed. Nosey Flynn".'[10] In any case, Miss Beach's written version reads as follows:

> Lugné-Poe spoke very apologetically about his failure to produce Joyce's play. ... 'You see,' he said, 'I have to earn my living. That's my problem. I must consider the demands of present-day theatregoers, and all they ask

today is something that makes them laugh.' I could see his point. Joyce's play was not at all funny, but neither, for that matter, was Ibsen. That's one thing about Bill Shakespeare, he let his clowns put a lot of gags in his plays. Obviously, I could urge Lugné-Poe to take the risk with *Exiles*. ...When I reported the interview with Lugné-Poe to Joyce, his only comment was, 'I should have made it funny. Richard should have had a peg leg!'[11]

Behan clearly believed in the power of humour and somewhat incongruously cited T.S. Eliot to back up his belief:

Joan Littlewood, I found, suited my requirements exactly. She has the same views on the theatre that I have, which is that the music hall is the thing to aim at for to amuse people and any time they get bored, divert them with a song or a dance. I've always thought T.S. Eliot wasn't far wrong when he said that the main problem of the dramatist today was to keep his audience amused; and that while they were laughing their heads off, you could be up to any bloody thing behind their backs; and it was what you were doing behind their bloody backs that made your play great. (*BBI*, 17)

Of more long-term value to Behan was the manner in which Joyce's writings were genuine chronicles of Dublin and of Irish life. Partly for this reason, he enjoyed delving into their detail. An example of this is to be found in his unfinished novel *The Catacombs*. In one of the many digressions in that rambling, entertaining work, the narrator describes the 'large cattle-owning colonies of Irish people descended from settlers who emigrated in the 1840s and '50s from the grazing country of the Irish Midlands' to 'many countries of South America' (*Wake*, 59). He points out that they

are now an immensely wealthy group, and their eldest sons are sent home to Mullingar and Athlone and Kildare to be educated. One of them is mentioned in James Joyce's *Portrait of the Artist as a Young Man*: 'The higher line fellows began to come down along the matting in the middle of the refectory – Paddy Rath and Jimmy Magee, and the Spaniard who was allowed to smoke cigars and the little Portuguese who wore the woolly cap'. (*Wake*, 60)

Behan's quote is characteristically less than precise. Joyce's text reads: 'He heard the fellows of the higher line stand up at the top of the refectory and heard their steps as they came down the matting: Paddy Rath and Jimmy Magee and the Spaniard and the Portuguese and the fifth was big Corrigan who was going to be flogged by Mr Gleeson.'[12] But this does not change the substance. Behan continues: 'These South American Irish were intensely proud of their ancestry, and have a snobbish horror of Irish-Americans from the United States' (*Wake*, 60). Behan had in mind the Irish diaspora in Latin and South America, figures such as Guillermo (William) Brown, the Mayo-born founder of the Argentinian Navy, and Don Bernardo O'Higgins, who led the forces in Chile's fight for independence from Spain and became first leader of Chile. It is singular that Behan would provide evidence for his claim by referring not to a book of history but to Joyce's novel, which pays but passing heed to this often forgotten, but significant, Irish diaspora.

Behan also took an interest in teasing out some of the historical models for characters in Joyce's *Ulysses*, writing a letter to the *Evening Herald* in Dublin in response to an article by Anthony MacDonnell entitled 'Two Dublin Tragedies', published in November 1957. The tragedy that caught Behan's attention was that involving Constable Henry Flower and thirty-year-old Bridget Gannon, who was found drowned in the River Dodder on 23 August 1900. Constables Henry Flower, John Hanily and Constable Toal of the Dublin Metropolitan Police were sent to investigate. The coroner deemed that the death had been caused by drowning and the body was buried in Glasnevin Cemetery. However, on 11 September, Constable Henry Flower was charged with murder. He had proposed marriage to Bridget Gannon but because he was Protestant and she Catholic, she refused. Gannon's friend, Margaret Clowry, had also been dating a constable called Dockery and they had gone on a double date to Davy's pub on Baggot Street. The two couples walked home separately and Clowry said that she left Bridget and Flower to walk on alone and that was the last she saw of her friend. The case took another twist three days after Flower was charged, when Constable John Hanily was found dead in the police station, having cut his own throat. There was insufficient evidence to convict Flower who, after his acquittal, resigned from the force and left the country. In the 1930s in a deathbed confession, Margaret Clowry admitted killing Gannon in a robbery and claimed she did so because she had recently lost her job and was desperate for cash.[13]

Behan responded to the *Herald* article connecting this tragic real-life story with *Ulysses*, writing:

With regard to to-night's piece about Constable Henry Flower and the drowning of poor Bridget Gannon, Henry Flower was one of the aliases James Joyce gave to Leopold Bloom in the latter's love letters in *Ulysses*. Joyce also uses the initials of the witness, Bridget Gannon's friend, Margaret Clowry:

What object did Bloom add to this collection of objects?

A 4th typewritten letter received by Henry Flower (let H. F. be L. B.) from Martha Clifford (find M. C.).

This is in page 683 of the Bodley Head edition and the parentheses are Joyce's. (*Letters*, 138)

From this letter we can safely assume that Behan possessed a Bodley Head *Ulysses* and that he read it closely enough to annotate this Dublin news reference. This vignette of Behan as a *Ulysses* annotator aligns him with a number of contemporary Irish intellectuals of his generation who were defensive about the Irishness of Joyce and about the role they felt they could play in teasing out local references in Joyce's works. But Behan was more straightforward in his appreciation of Joyce and more tolerant of the Joycean scholars than most of his Irish literary contemporaries. (Brian O'Nolan dismissed them as the 'shower of gawms who erupt from the prairie universities to do a "thesis" on James Joyce'.)[14] Another of Behan's letters is telling with regard to how he sees Joyce as *the* figure to which to aspire. This time it is to Iain Hamilton, who commissioned *Borstal Boy* for Hutchinson. Behan is replying to Hamilton, who had quoted William Koshland's very positive report in which Koshland declared that he was 'overwhelmed by the writing itself, and the general excitement of the prose, its moving quality. ... Literature with a capital "L". Behan thanks him in a comment that is deeply revelatory of his own insecurity: 'We have no proper view of our own work – we think we're James Joyce one minute and plain gobshites the next' (*Letters*, 147).

Whatever his esteem for Joyce, however, the task of labouring in his shadow took its toll. In *Confessions of an Irish Rebel* Behan recounts how he was asked, in the Paris bars, to talk about Joyce and Ireland. His response was understandably ambivalent. Real respect for Joyce too often morphed into yarn-spinning in return for free drinks. This process is also the subject of his

Irish-language poem 'Buíochas le Joyce' which was first published in the Irish-language journal *Comhar* in August 1949. This early poem, and indeed all his subsequent Irish-language writings, owes much to the fact that he spent much of his imprisonment in the mid-1940s learning Irish (Behan was incarcerated following his attempt to murder a police detective after the annual Easter 1916 commemoration at Glasnevin Cemetery in 1942, but served only four of his fourteen-year sentence, thanks to a general amnesty for political prisoners in 1946). During his time in Mountjoy, in Arbour Hill and finally in the Curragh he had the time to engage seriously with the Irish language, taking lessons with the Kerry schoolteacher Seán Ó Briain and later with novelist and short-story writer Máirtín Ó Cadhain (who, it should be remembered, is the Irish-language equivalent of Joyce both in terms of his linguistic exuberance and his groundbreaking literary techniques). In such hands, Behan gained the skills needed to begin to write in Irish and the Joyce poem is one of the earliest published examples:

'Buíochas le Joyce'

Annseo i Rue Saint André des Arts
i dtábhairne Arabach, ólta,
míním do Fhranncach fiosrach thú
Ex-G.I.'s Rúiseach ólta.
Molaim gach comhartha dár chuiris ar phár
Is mise san Fhrainc ag ól Pernod dá bharr,
Maidir le conteur is bródúil sinn díot
Is buíoch den Calvados ólaimid tríot.

Dá mba mise tusa
Is tusa mé féin
Ag teacht ó Les Halles
Is ag iompar an méid seo cognac
Ag seinnt ar lánbholg
Scríofá-sa bhéarsa nó dhó do mo mholadh![15]

The poem suggests Behan's ambivalence at being left in Joyce's wake in a Paris where he finds himself repeatedly talking about his predecessor as a means of being plied with free drink. The poem, with its French, Russian and American presences is caught between evoking the openness of cosmopolitan Paris and the closure of an expat community of passers-through. The fact that it is written in Irish, which Declan Kiberd controversially calls Behan's 'truest medium, the language in which the bilingual Behan expressed that part of himself which was incorruptible',[16] is also his way of attempting to declare some measure of independence from Joyce who, it was presumed at the time, had distanced himself from Irish and, more loudly, from the Irish-language movement. Ulick O'Connor's English translation, which is probably the most cited of the English-language versions, reads as follows:

'Gratitude to Joyce'

Here in the Rue St André des Arts,
Plastered in an Arab Tavern,
I explain you to an eager Frenchman,
Ex-G.I.s and a drunken Russian.
Of all you wrote I explain each part,
Drinking Pernod in France because of your art.
As a writer we're proud of you –
And thanks for the

Calvados we gain through you.
If I were you
And you were me
Coming from Les Halles
Roaring, with a load of cognac,
Belly full, on the tipple,
A verse or two in my
Honour you'd scribble. (*O'Connor*, 136)

Read in this translation, which lacks the buoyancy of the original, it is hard not to agree with John Brannigan's downbeat assessment:

In ['Gratitude to Joyce'], Behan reveals his anxiety about his parasitical relationship to Joyce, living (or in this case drinking) off the stories that he can tell to foreign audiences eager to hear about the great Irish author. Behan is describing the sterile function which he performs, reduced to glorifying the works of the dead in return for the anaesthetic rewards of drunkenness. (*Brannigan*, 133)

It is not clear, however, why O'Connor provides his own translation of the poem and ignores the version by Valentin Iremonger, which was published with Behan's imprimatur in *Brendan Behan's Island*. Here the poem appears in English with the less formal title 'Thanks to James Joyce' and under the throwaway title that suggests a round of drinks: 'A couple of quick ones' (the other 'quick one' being 'Oscar Wilde', dedicated to Seán Ó Súilleabháin/Seán O'Sullivan). Together they might be taken as an example of what Brannigan describes as Behan's subsuming of 'canonical figures of modern Irish literature within a diffuse, popular folk tradition'. (*Brannigan*, 36)

'Thanks to James Joyce'

Here in the rue St. Andre des Arts
In an Arab tavern, pissed,
For a studious Frenchman I construe to,
Ex. G.I.'s and a Russian, pissed.
All of those things you penned I praise
While, in France, I swill Pernod in return:
Proud of you as a writer we are
And grateful for the Calvados we owe to you.
If you were me
And I were you
Leaving Les Halles
Holding all this cognac,
On a full belly bawling,
You'd write a verse or two in my praise. (*BBI*, 179)

Although it is not clear why Iremonger inverts the 'If I were you and you were me', this version of the poem captures better the conversational, throwaway, wilfully irreverent tone of Behan's poem. Lines like 'Ex G.I.'s and a Russian, pissed' and 'On a full belly bawling' are closer to Behanspeak than 'Ex-G.I.s and a drunken Russian' and 'Belly full, on the tipple'. Thomas O'Grady has commented cogently on the qualities of this translation:

> Slightly better than O'Connor's 'Roaring', Iremonger's 'bawling' likewise derives from *seinnt* – 'Warbling, chattering' – but given Behan's direct oversight of Iremonger's translation, it surely conveys the spirit, if not quite the letter, of the original word choice; … Iremonger manages to alliterate 'belly' and 'bawling' in the spirit of the verbal philandering noted by Heaney. By translating *lánbholg* as 'full belly' he also allows Behan's mentioning of Les Halles to resonate with *Le Ventre de Paris*, the title of Émile Zola's well-known novel set in that *quartier*, conventionally translated as *The Belly of Paris*.[17]

O'Grady is ever so slightly stretching it with 'warbling, chattering'. The most common meaning of *seinnt* would refer to playing a musical instrument with *seinnteoir* meaning a music player or performer. Warbling and chattering are acceptable secondary meanings. Behan's frustration remains evident in both versions and is presumably caused by difficulties with focusing on his own writing, with forging his own way in the cosmopolitan French capital instead of hanging out with expatriates and repeatedly reanimating Joyce's ghost in return for drink. And yet, as O'Grady notes, there is irony and humour in his treatment of Joyce. He argues convincingly that a better title for the poem would be the almost biblical 'Thanks be to Joyce'[18] which would convey the appropriate 'whiff of blasphemy' but also a large dose of irony towards Joyce himself. Again, irony is present in the poem's closing words:

> Very simply, that final phrase – 'ólaimíd tríot' – translates readily as 'we drink [ólaimíd] on your account [tríot]. Clearly, Behan is playfully acknowledging that Joyce not only provides the occasion for a drinking session but, in a sense, is also paying the tab.[19]

O'Grady's positive reading of the poems paves the way for Behan's later lecture, which is the work of a writer who has enjoyed international success and is now more at ease in celebrating an important predecessor. Yet Behan continues to vacillate, not so much in his appreciation of Joyce but in his understanding of his own worth. Ultimately, he remains unsure of himself in Joyce's company. Even when he compares himself directly with the master in terms of the Joycean (or, better, Dedalian) weapons of 'silence, exile and cunning', Behan's response in his New York lecture is self-deprecating: 'as is known I'm not a very silent man, I don't think I'm a very cunning one, and I'll be going home for Christmas. So I'm not exactly patterned in the same mould.'

Behan does not have a particularly well-prepared 'lecture' to give; rather, he offers a rambling, anecdotal and at times repetitive talk, sometimes bordering on stand-up comedy. Bemused at being defined as a 'Caucasian according to American statistics' and describing himself as being 'a European by promotion', Behan starts off with a diversion about the colour of his own skin, which is not, he says, his usual 'cholesterol red'. But then, he jokes, he has 'never seen a really white person, only a dead one'. He then gets to the problem of talking about Joyce and especially about *Finnegans Wake*. Although he claims to have dipped in and out of it, and although he has sought aid in finding a way through it, Joyce's final novel remains a tough nut to crack: 'I have met very few people who could explain it to me in ordinary terms because it's written in its own language, and they say that the wind bloweth where it listeth.' Here he is quoting from the King James Bible, from one of the great foundational texts of English itself, using John 3:8 to establish a basic rule of *Finnegans Wake*, that is, that it makes its own rules and the reader can only assent to be carried along by the flow. The full biblical quote reads: 'The winde bloweth where it listeth, and thou hearest the sound thereof, but canst not tell whence it commeth, and whither it goeth: So is every one that is borne of the Spirit.' This leads him to talk about Joyce's style through Frank Swinnerton 'for whom', as he says, 'I've great affection' (*Confessions*, 101). As John Brannigan has pointed out, many of Behan's opinions on Joyce (and indeed on Yeats) are second-hand and lifted quite directly from Frank Swinnerton's 1935 *The Georgian Literary Scene*. Swinnerton regarded Joyce

> as one of those writers who notice and remember for ever headlines and solecisms in newspapers, the clichés of barmaids, slips made by common, genteel and ridiculous persons, smells, lingerie, betrayals of vulgarity, scandals about well-known persons, and the faux pas of ingénues'. (*Brannigan*, 37)

Whatever reservations Swinnerton may have had, these were elements that Behan would have warmly appreciated. One of Behan's approaches to Joyce is through his personal knowledge of the Joyce haunts described in *Ulysses* (he was brought up very close to the Monto area of Dublin where the 'Circe' episode is set). Behan points out that he is well-acquainted with Barney Kiernan's pub and 'the marvellous scene' that Joyce describes there ('Cyclops'). Behan calls the pub the 'Court of Appeals where the Citizen has the row with Leopold Bloom': 'As a matter of fact, I drank a pint in it with the first money I ever received as wages or a fee.' Behan falls into line here with many Dublin Joyceans who believed their intimate knowledge of the city gave them a special importance in Joyce studies. At the same time he seems to castigate the same Dubliners for singularly failing to take a lead in Joyce scholarship. Richard Ellmann's monumental biography had recently been published and clearly occupied centre stage and Behan was unusual among his Irish literary peers in treating it with relative generosity:

> About Kellman's or Ellman's is it ... – Ellman's life of Joyce, I thought it a very conscientious piece of work. There are 618,000 inhabitants of the city of Dublin that – no, you have to leave out the children – there are ½ million citizens of that city who think that they could have written it better, but opening times and closing times pressing on them so hard they never got around to it.

Very often in his talk, Behan focuses on an element in Joyce that is of particular relevance to his own experience and his own thematic priorities. This we see, for example, in the anecdote about the sermons in *A Portrait of the Artist as a Young Man* and, in particular, Father Arnall's words about the 'four last things':

> 'During these few days I intend to put before you some thoughts concerning the four last things. They are, as you know from your catechism, death, judgement, hell, and heaven. We shall try to understand them fully during these few days so that we may derive from the understanding of them a lasting benefit to our souls.'[20]

In Behan's telling, in which he is clearly relying on memory rather than text, this becomes:

> But the other thing that I remember shortly before I left home was the four last things, that's not what I remember before I left home but it just happened to come into my mind – that's the way I prepare my lectures.

The four last things: Death Judgement, hell and heaven wherein the blessed saint Ancelin tells us the damned in Hell are so helplessly bound they
cannot pluck from the eye the worm that gnaws. Christ or Barabbus!
(Christ but by Jesus don't keep us all night!)

Behan then 'annotates' this with a story of meeting someone who as a young
man had been to Gardiner Street church where 'he met the priest who was an
old man, who was giving the sermon that Joyce described (Belvedere I think
it was) and the priest said that the sermon was exactly as he had delivered
it. The man said to me, Hadn't Joyce a great memory? And I said to him,
Hadn't the priest a cheek?' Even allowing for a dodgy transcription, Behan's
lack of preparation and accuracy – which, to be fair, he himself flags – is all
too apparent here. He also muddies the distinctions between life and fiction,
between biography and fiction, by reading the sermons in *A Portrait* as reliable
versions of what Joyce would have heard in school. Of course what Joyce was
obliged to listen to in school may well have been his point of creative departure
but there is little doubt that Joyce embroidered and strengthened the sermons,
drawing on a variety of source texts. Behan quotes a third-hand source, whom
he claims spoke to the original priest of the sermons. We might wonder about
the reliability of such a source but Behan's most essential point is to take a
swipe at the Irish Catholic Church for instilling fear into defenceless youth.
There is more than a hint of his own hurt towards the church and his sense
that the Irish were often not well served politically by their Catholic priests.[21]

In the 'Epilogue Appointed to be Read in Churches' to *Brendan Behan's
Island*, Behan leads with a broadside against the church by aligning himself
with Joyce:

James Joyce was forever referring to Hadrian the Fourth, the only English
Pope, a man called Nicholas Breakspear. It was he who gave Henry II a Bull
authorizing him to go and impose some discipline on the Catholic Church
in Ireland. The Church in Ireland has always tended to be somewhat
independent of Rome. The granting of the Bull was ironic, as it was the
Irish that converted the English and Scots to Christianity. The Bishops
decided to give fealty to their liege, Henry II, and all down the centuries
they have tended to side with the English authority. (*BBI*, 185)

Behan then goes on to talk about the horrors of the Irish Famine – comparing it to the Holocaust – before condeming both the British government and the Irish church for their inadequate responses:

> The great disaster to happen to any one nation, in Europe, until the murder of six million Jews in the last war, was the Irish Famine of 1847. Eight million people lived in Ireland at the time, but when the famine ended there were only four million left. … The Bishop of Kildare and Leighlin, who was known as J.K.L., said that he was proud that the people of his diocese were so God-fearing that they would sooner die of starvation than refuse to pay the rent. Well, die they did, and they weren't helped much by Government or Church. Queen Victoria was very distressed at the famine among her loyal subjects and she sent £5 to the Famine Relief Fund; then in case she might be thought to be showing open sympathy with a crowd of rebels, she sent £5 to the Battersea Dogs' Home. (*BBI*, 186)

The concluding comment about Queen Victoria, although widely believed, was inaccurate. She sent £2,000 to the Famine fund and whatever donation she made to the dogs' home was not in any way connected. This of course does not undermine the basic intent of Behan's words: that the British response to the Famine was shamefully inadequate. This was a claim that Behan believed throughout his life and this version is little more than a recycling of the words uttered by Pat in *The Hostage*, who is partly based on Behan's father:

> PAT. I'll tell you what you've done. Some time ago there was a famine in this country and people were dying all over the place. Well, your Queen Victoria, or whatever her bloody name was, sent five pounds to the famine fund and at the same time she sent five pounds to the Battersea Dog's [sic] Home so no one could accuse her of having rebel sympathies. (*CP*, 215)

Behan continues by denouncing the role of the Catholic Church in helping suppress the Fenians and Irish Land League agitators and in bringing down Parnell. (Here he is also deep in Joyce territory with regard to the church; one only needs to think or the depiction of 'Christ and Caesar / hand in glove' in 'The Holy Office', of the Christmas dinner scene in *A Portrait*, or of the 'Scylla and Charybdis' episode of *Ulysses*, which so brilliantly illustrates the connivance of the two powers.) As a result, Behan opines, there 'always has been a certain amount of anti-clericalism in Ireland. … It's the Church's own fault for always being against the people's political inclinations towards independence' (*BBI*, 189). At the same time, unlike Joyce, Behan writes far more as one who, despite everything, still appears to feel he belongs within the broad embrace of the church. In *Brendan Behan's Island*, he writes warmly of the current clergy at work in Ireland and considered himself a Catholic, albeit a 'bad Catholic', right up to the end of his life.[22] Bryan MacMahon also recalled Behan's response to Eamon Andrews' questioning as to whether he was a Catholic during their BBC interview: 'Certainly I'm a Catholic – a bad Catholic.'[23]

He also uses his lecture to underline a substantial class difference between himself and Joyce and the Joyce family. He does so by talking about Eileen Joyce, the Joyce sister who had returned from Trieste to live in Ireland and a woman who was, in Behan's slighting words, 'a very elegant, a very arrogant woman' (the irony of the Joyce family's collective fall into poverty is clearly not lost on Behan). He points out that he had come to know her in Dublin because he used to deliver milk to her:

> But I gave Mrs. Joyce or Mrs Schaurek a sup of the whiskey and I said 'Well Eileen, good luck to you.' No she said, 'Eileen?' and I said 'Well isn't that your name?' I said. 'I can't pronounce your second name because it's as easy to pronounce as my own which is called variously Ba-han, Bayin, Bean, Ben however I was rather pleased to notice that the Joyces had not lost sight of the fact that they were a step above and that their father was at Cork University after it was a Hedgeschool and he was something in a distillery up in Chapelizod.

Behan overplays his own family's poverty. His grandmother, after all, was a successful landlady, although clearly without the pretensions of the Joyces. He does, in any case, acknowledge that Eileen 'turned out to be a most entertaining citizeness' and he clearly enjoyed listening to her praise Joyce and her father:

> she didn't want anyone to forget that his father before him was a great man and that his grandfather had a house out in (she was full of Cork snobbery) yes a relation of the great liberator which I wouldn't have thought was a

recommendation for anyone because he sold out the 40 shilling freeholders for the right of the middle-class Irish to become judges and to sentence the Athenians.

This reference to Catholic Emancipation would have been lost on most of Behan's American audience. In 1829, the bill granting full emancipation for Catholics was passed in parliament but the income necessary to qualify as a voter was raised from 40 shillings to £10. With this, most of those supporters who had helped O'Connell to win the measure in the first place found themselves disqualified from voting. Behan, like many an Irishman, had a long memory, but also a deep awareness of how personal and communal memory is shaped by class issues.

The fact that Behan agreed to lecture publicly on Joyce is a sign of his ongoing interest in and sense of alignment with his predecessor. In his manner of writing about Ireland from afar but with the power and penetrative insight of one who never left, Joyce represented a model for Behan, an important predecessor whom he seemed to admire in a far more straightforward way than his contemporaries, such as Flann O'Brien and Patrick Kavanagh, would ever do. Perhaps this was because, for all his troubles and for all the sense of wasted opportunity, Behan truly did enjoy international success in his own lifetime. And perhaps because, like Joyce, he managed to put the previously unwritten on the page and on the stage of Irish writing. In a 1957 letter, discussing *Borstal Boy*, he wrote: 'Some people may say that my book shouldn't be read, then I say that adolescence should not be lived' (*Letters*, 114). It may be casual but here Behan echoes Joyce's words in the face of opposition to *Ulysses*: 'If *Ulysses* isn't fit to read, life isn't fit to live.'[24] Both writers, ultimately, were united in their desire to express in fiction everything that life threw their way, and both would pay a heavy price for doing so, especially at home in Ireland.

10
SECRET SCRIPTURES:
BRENDAN BEHAN IN THE
CRUISKEEN LAWN
PAUL FAGAN

Brian O'Nolan's 1939 debut novel *At Swim-Two-Birds* (published under his 'Flann O'Brien' pseudonym) sold a mere 244 copies in its initial run, before 'being consumed, along with Longman's London warehouse, [...] into obscurity and legend by a Luftwaffe bombing raid'.[1] Its reputation among Dublin writers as the 'lost masterpiece' by notorious *Irish Times* columnist 'Myles na Gopaleen' (O'Nolan's most prominent pen name) was assured, but it was not until the novel was republished by Timothy O'Keeffe in 1960 that its broader significance to Irish modernist experiment-ation was fully acknowledged. In assigning a reviewer for the reissued cult text, the *Irish Times* chose O'Nolan's fellow traveller Brendan Behan. The 30 July 1960 review acknowledges the novel's storied history and reputation with its evocative title 'Secret Scripture', and opens with an appropriately digressive Mylesian anecdote set in the White Horse at Burgh Quay (a regular haunt of journalists and writers owing to its proximity to the *Irish Press* headquarters). Behan relates an encounter with 'Three businessmen' whom he characterises as 'The complete Dublin literary pub Chamber of Horrors': an unholy trinity comprising a 'spare time' 'Catholic intellectual' who talks about 'old Aquinas'; 'a liberal Protestant – viz., one who votes for Fianna Fail' and reads the *Irish*

Times; and 'a cultured Jew, and sympathetic to writers'.[2] When the first of the troupe approaches, Behan squirms under a catechism of cliché:

'What are you having?' asked he.
'Hard times' [...].
'Ah, come on, have something – have a half one. Have – a ball of malt.' [...]
'No thanks.'
'Ah, take something.'
'Would you do something for me?'
He sighed, nodded with a resigned and indulgent smile, and put his hand in his pocket. 'All right. What is it?'
'—— off!'
His friends, from the bar, murmured, 'Filthy tongue', 'He's famous for it.'
But the Aquinas man tried to laugh, and said:
'Myles is in very bad form this morning.'

Considering the shared commonplaces that shape their public and critical reputations, the Aquinas man might be forgiven for confusing Behan with Myles. Each is renowned for his caustic wit, his drinking and his mastery of the anecdote. Myles is cast typically as 'the licensed jester of the Dublin intelligentsia',[3] with Hugh Kenner asking, representatively, 'Was it the drink was his ruin or was it the column? For ruin is the word. So much promise has seldom accomplished so little.'[4] This language echoes intimately the standard rehearsal of Behan's literary trajectory: 'Behan the carouser and jester became addicted to his hellraiser image and self-deprecating wit, describing himself as "a drunk with a writing problem"; we can only surmise what other literary accomplishments he might have been capable of.'[5] Declan Kiberd reinforces this account with his estimation of 'Myles na Gopaleen' as 'the fatal clown, the licensed jester' in a 'doomed and drink-sodden triumvirate' with Behan and Patrick Kavanagh.[6]

In recent years, critics have begun to re-evaluate these writers and their work away from the overworked narratives of drink and wasted talent to gauge their more complex and pivotal roles in twentieth-century Irish writing as formal innovators and cultural critics. Initial interventions have parsed the aesthetic politics of Behan and O'Nolan's bilingual writing alongside their mutually in-fluential deconstructions of mid-century cultural nationalism.[7] Yet, given the extent to which their reputations are interlinked, this ongoing re-evaluation necessitates a larger-scale relational approach to Behan and O'Nolan's shifting positions and shaping interactions with and within the spaces, networks and institutions of the Dublin literary field.[8] Such a project would also reflect their central importance to new modernist studies as late modernists who decamp to the marginalised forms of column writing, new media and anecdotal performance in ways that test routine binaries of mass and coterie readerships, parochial political engagement and modernist formal experimentation. In this essay, I mean to lay the groundwork for this future work by bringing to light Behan's many previously undocumented appearances in O'Nolan's *Cruiskeen Lawn* column throughout the 1950s and early '60s.[9]

Behan's tale of mistaken identity provides an appropriate launching point for this investigation. While the anecdote is stylistically and thematically germane to the subject of his review, what might be lost on present-day readers is the extent to which it engages in a series of self-reflexive nods to Behan's own appearances in *Cruiskeen Lawn* throughout the previous decade. The gag is both a direct recycling of an anecdote Myles himself had related to his readership in 1957 and a sly allusion to the columnist's regular wilful confusions of himself with Behan.[10] In addressing Behan's increasingly central appearances as a 'character' in *Cruiskeen Lawn* throughout the 1950s (a critical gap in both Behan and O'Nolan studies), I suggest that Myles' characteristically idiosyncratic gloss on the Behan phenomenon offers a peculiarly intimate view of these writers and their cultural milieu alongside more standard accounts.

The columns considered here document a dual trajectory, which traces the overlapping public and personal dimensions of the writers' relationship. In the first movement, I observe a gradual shift from Myles' initial jockeying for superiority over the upstart Behan to his later mixed feelings of pride and envy at his apprentice's success on the international scene. These pieces shed new light on the integral role of Behan's art and reception in O'Nolan's skewed take on the aspirations and resentments of a Dublin literary generation, which shared 'the common experience of neglect – financial and critical'.[11] In the second movement, I note a trajectory from Myles' exploitations of Behan's notoriety to foment a series of quasi-comic political and cultural insurrections amid the 1959 presidential elections, to his valuations, in the column's waning years, of Behan as his sole companion in the Lemass-era Ireland from which he feels increasingly alienated. Seemingly minor in their individual battles, these discrete sketches – by turns humorous and derisive, self-ironic and cautiously revealing – capture a certain camaraderie between these kindred spirits amid the restrictive, at times destructive, codes of literary competitiveness and male companionship that shape and delimit their professional and personal relationship.

MASTER AND APPRENTICE

The 3 April 1954 issue of the *Irish Times* was a simultaneously inauspicious and auspicious occasion for Behan, as it included both his arrest notice for drunken and disorderly conduct[12] and his first appearance in *Cruiskeen Lawn*. Given that O'Nolan and Behan had certainly known each other professionally and personally from at least the mid-1940s,[13] it is noteworthy that Behan had theretofore not featured in the column's biting takes on the Dublin literary scene. In the early months of 1954, Behan had appeared regularly in the paper because of his role in the high-profile Kavanagh–*Leader* case, which had established him as 'a media darling of sorts', with his photograph featuring prominently in the *Irish Times* front-page trial coverage on 11 February.[14] It is possible that Behan's growing public profile threatened O'Nolan, and he first appears in a column in which Myles seems anxious to re-establish his own anti-authoritarian credentials and literary standing after years of drifting out of the spotlight. The 1 April column by the paper's radio critic G.A. Olden, had ended with a call for 'a revival of that wildly funny play, Myles na Copaleen's [sic] "Faustus Kelly"'.[15] Myles picks up on this rare praise in the 3 April *Cruiskeen Lawn* to re-evaluate his unsuccessful foray into dramatic writing as 'a masterpiece, saturated with a Voltaire quality, and penetrating human stupidity with a sort of ghoulish gusto'.[16] Olden's title 'More Irish Comedies Wanted on R.E.' may well have brought Behan to O'Nolan's mind, as the writer's gradual metamorphosis from 'pub character' into 'public personality', accelerated by his recent press coverage, had definitively started with his broadcasts on Radio Éireann starting from 1951 (*O'Sullivan*, 162). Myles shares the supposed 'rumour that Cyril Cusack is going around pestering everybody, including Brendan Behan, for plays', which he exploits to further his own cause ('Cyril could do worse than produce "Faustus" and play his own old part in it'). However, the reference to Cusack soliciting a play from Behan was likely ironic, or at least a sly in-joke, as Behan had sent

The Twisting of Another Rope to the actor after that play had been rejected by the Gate, only for Cusack to reject it in turn (*O'Sullivan*, 178). Whether a suspicious acknowledgement of Behan's growing cultural capital, a salute to a fellow neglected artist, or a dig at a rival's inability to have his plays staged (before the debut of *The Quare Fellow* at the Pike Theatre that November would decisively reverse that failure), the brief cameo begins the process by which Behan would become one of the column's featured characters by the end of the decade.

Shortly thereafter, in mid-April, Behan became Myles' direct competitor when he was commissioned to write a regular column for the *The Irish Press*. When he next appears in *Cruiskeen Lawn*, in 'A Square Root' on 6 October, Behan has been welcomed into the column's intellectual coterie with his inclusion among the few 'friends' Myles invites 'out to [his] place in Santry for afternoon tea'.[17] Myles' soirée comprises writers, performers and renowned Dublin wits ('there was Captain Joe Pike, Lennox Robinson, Brinsley, Harvey Duclos, The Pope O'Mahoney, Jimmy O'Dea, Brendan Behan, Nul Cowd'), and is an exclusively male affair ('The maids had been given the afternoon off and it was myself who attended to the guests personally'). If, as Sarah Cole argues, male friendship has been imagined historically 'as a vital, masculine counterpart to domestic life',[18] here Myles ironises this association by relocating from the more realistic venue of such encounters – McDaid's pub – to a domestic space and its attendant concerns: 'Our object was simple, and so was the fare I proffered – black coffee, biscuits, a spoonful of tinned peas.' There is an ambivalently queer subtext to the scene, which both upturns masculinist myths (and realities) of the carousing Dublin writer and fosters comic incongruity from static assumptions about gendered space. While they enjoyed varying degrees of achievement, there is also a subtle gesture to the literary group's neglected status in the Spartan serving of 'a spoonful of tinned peas', which functions also to underscore their unaffected lack of pretention in contrast to the 'corduroys' (Myles' term for the self-styled Dublin intelligentsia) that the column excoriated regularly. These subtexts are expressed obliquely when, rather than relay to his readership the content of their 'by-play with the coloured ball of high-class conversation', Myles reveals that his ulterior motive in recounting the assembly is to lodge his complaint with W. & R. Jacob regarding the biscuit tin he proffered his guests: 'two sides of the lid (and of the tin) were, by a microscopic fraction, longer than the other two sides';

a 'silly damn situation' that, Myles estimates, 'causes the loss *per annum* of 100,000,000 domestic man- and woman-hours' in 'disastrous attempt[s] to replace the lid'. This figurative play with wasted creative labour (as we shall see shortly, the column regularly conflates creativity with digestion) and a sense of not fitting (or fitting obliquely) 'in the box' would have been particularly pointed for Behan at this stage in his career. Despite his growing cultural cachet, 'there was a cohort of young Dublin literati who resented [...] the uneducated jailbird' for encroaching on what they conceived to be their territory (*O'Sullivan*, 173–4). While the scene is framed ironically, a sense of camaraderie comes through in Myles' avowal that 'We enjoyed ourselves and enlightened each other thoroughly'. His public association with Behan here, and identification of him as his 'friend', can be read as a demonstration of solidarity not only with a fellow Dublin drinker and wit, but also with a fellow misfit.

The 'scale of [Behan's] international success had been one of Dublin's major sensations in 1956'[19]; accordingly, Myles upgrades Behan's status from hanger-on to the main subject of the 23 July 1956 column, titled 'Behanism'.[20] To explore this reversal of fortune, Myles returns to his favourite narrative situation (which Behan would appropriate for his *At Swim-Two-Birds* review): the disturbance of his peace by a pub bore. In this case, a plumber probes Myles on whether he 'know[s] that man Been?' Myles disavows any knowledge of his friend, but the drinker asks suspiciously whether he has 'any objections to himself having his own notions about art'. Myles replies 'NO' ('I was sure he would hit me if I said YES'). The plumber persists that 'Mr Been was a tradesman, and his faaather was a tradesman [...] and what about it?' 'Nothing about it,' Myles responds, attempting to relieve 'the mounting tension somewhat by saying we were all tradesmen in our own way'. But the plumber, becoming increasingly heated, proceeds to characterise Behan's trajectory from his own perspective:

Mr Been [...] wrut a play. [...] It was turnded down be that crowd in the Mechanics Theatre, th'Abbey, and had to be put on at the heel of the hunt in some sort of a somewhere. Now it's in the middle of Lunnon. And they tell me it's going across to America. What's wrong with that?
Nothing at all.

[...] There's another crowd in this country that gets out a wee book now and again and has a whole crowd over the head of it drinking small sherries in the High Berinian. Your man just clatters a play off the typewriter and takes the whole world into his lap. What's wrong with THAT?

Not a thing . . .

The plumber contrasts the inauthenticity of Dublin's public intellectuals with the authenticity of Behan's counter-image as a working-class 'tradesman as poet' (as opposed to Myles' suggested formulation of 'poet as tradesman'). This construction draws heavily on the formula, which had been a recurring crutch in media reports on his meteoric rise, of Behan as a labourer artist.[21] The cliché enables Myles to set his sights on dual targets: on the corduroys' bad faith self-presentations as the authoritative voice of an Irish people from which they are economically and culturally detached; but also on the bland banalities of The Plain People of Ireland who 'flattered the prejudices of the "keltured idiocated"' with their 'antiquated taste for the plain, simple and homespun'.[22] The implication appears to be that Myles both shares the appreciation of Behan's achievement and is suspicious of the regional and class lenses through which that achievement is being packaged for and received by local and international audiences. The plumber's declaration that 'Mr Been is a class of a pote' strengthens this sense in so far as it boxes Behan into the role of 'people's poet'. O'Nolan had satirised this cultural category previously in *At Swim-Two-Birds*, through the populist doggerel of the proletarian 'Jem Casey, Poet of the Pick', whose 'Workman's Friend' the Plain People prefer to the Old Irish poems and narratives.[23] As Maebh Long underlines, in that novel 'The type of knowledge respected and possessed by the class that creates the Plain People of Ireland is mocked [...], and their relation to Ireland and self-identity repeatedly problematised.'[24] Yet, the emerging cult of 'Behanism' furnishes Myles also with new material for his related theme of the questionable function of art in the censorious, isolationist and chauvinist culture of post-independence Dublin. Behan's unique combination of working-class *bona fides*, local celebrity and international acclaim offers the column a new vantage on the tension between 'the currency [...] of what remains irreducibly local in [...] culture (idiom, accent, humour, barroom politics)',[25] the localist discourses by which class differences are trivialised, and the dubiously authenticating gaze of the international audience, with its unnuanced assumptions (from Myles' perspective) about Irish culture and character.

And yet, these thematic and cultural concerns are framed by O'Nolan's personal response to the Behan phenomenon, especially given that his own early hints of international fame had come to nothing.[26] Myles introduces the pub anecdote with a punning invocation of the Behan phenomenon, acceding that 'It is not unexpected that people should ask this simple question – *is he a human Behan at all*'. In establishing his own authority to confirm Behan's humanity ('I believe he is. I seen him'), Myles eschews the bond of friendship evoked in 'A Square Root' in favour of an ironic claim to paternity as the father of Behan's style:

> I know him for years. Matter of fact, you could say that I reared him, paid his university fees (he never qualified for anything in that quarter but forthwith resumed his studies in the competing academy, the university of life), though he always acknowledged his obligation to me, and in his queer way harbours a little respect for me still. I intend no pun when I use that word 'still'.

The equanimity of friendship is abnegated in favour of relationships that imply a power imbalance and the recurrence of debt: father and son, literary master and apprentice, sponsor and drinker. Yet, despite Myles' broader attempt to re-establish his primacy over Behan, this last gesture towards their shared reputations as drunken jesters acknowledges, obliquely, their interrelated fates. Beyond its knowing comic deflection from the more immediately obvious homophony of 'queer', the declined pun on 'still' as an apparatus for distilling alcoholic drinks deepens the impression that Myles' claim to have paid his protégé's fees in the university of life is a euphemism for supplying him with drink, and that the respect Behan harbours for Myles is as a source of liquid rather than literary inspiration.

On 18 May 1957, Myles returns to this theme in a column titled 'A Liquid Acid'. Discussing the value of the artist over the recording device as a transformer of raw material and filterer of relevance rather than a bland documenter of facts, Myles again employs the cliché of Behan as labourer-artist to complicate his coordinates:

What was said, merely repeated, has not the same effect on the new listener. The artistic digestive organ takes in some materials, ejects others. That is what the artist is for – unless it be for a higher purpose, as when Mr Brendan Behan recently threatened to paper my bedroom.[27]

Literalising (and thereby banalising) this figurative image of the 'artistic digestive organ', the column goes on to record a tedious encounter with another pub bore who complains of indigestion due to the predominance of acid in the Irish diet: 'Toast in the morning for breakfast with maringlade on it. Full of acid'; for dinner every day a 'Big plate of rheugarg [...]. Full of acid'. The bore's condition is then cast as a national affliction, as he laments that Ireland is 'destroyed with acid'. As digestion is introduced as Myles' operating metaphor for the artistic process, this image of a nation suffering from acid indigestion bespeaks a creatively blocked community. Supported by the column's title, the unspoken implication of the dialogue in this pub setting is that it is neither 'maringlade' nor 'rheugarg' that is the cause of the country's acid problem, and that Myles and Behan's shared reputations are metonymic of a national condition.

The 4 September 1957 entry, 'Brendan Being', opens with Myles declaring his intention to depart from the column's regular function as a digestive organ in order to report the 'straight news' that 'for the first time in the history of this earth ... Mr Behan has written a play *in Irish*'.[28] Myles exploits the announcement to further leverage his insider status: 'I have seen the script – full of excoriations, deletions, changes, after-thoughts.' Taking up the mantle of critic, Myles comments that the play seems 'full of possibilities' but finds fault with the impossibility of having the grandmother 'die in the drawing-room in Act I and then join an assembly toasting a newly-married couple in Act III [...] unless [Behan is] organising some Sam Beckett job'; a charge which reportedly evokes 'Various linguistic explosions' from his companion. Given the dynamic developing between Myles and Behan in the column, and Behan's known admiration for Beckett,[29] this sideswipe is telling in its attempt to ally the Ireland-based writers in opposition to continental avant-garde theatre. However, Myles appears to acknowledge a change in their relative status when he, unusually, allows Behan to undermine his critical authority:

He looked at me in a stare composed of friendship and pity.
—Look at the title again, he said.

I did so. It is 'An Giall', which, in English, means *The Hostage*.
—Get my point?
—I don't, I said truthfully.

Deflecting from this diminishing stare 'of friendship and pity', Myles changes the subject to safer ground, teasing the authority of the international gaze that Behan's celebrity brings to his work and to Ireland more broadly:

I [asked] him whether he had the Abbey in mind [...]
—Hollywood.
—In Irish?
—Yes faith. Half of the crowd over there are native speakers from Ireland.
I didn't pursue the argument.

The impasse between the two men – their diverging satirical and quasi-modernist aesthetics, their differing professional trajectories, their local and international audiences – leads Myles from 'factual' reporting to the realm of the anecdote (as ever in the column, the distinction is dubious). Here, Myles relates the same tale of mistaken identity that Behan would recycle three years later for his review of *At Swim-Two-Birds*. The general shape of the anecdote is the same: Behan is accosted in a tavern one Sunday morning by 'a nest of overdressed gents' who attempt to buy him a glass of malt and, when curtly rebuked, declare: 'I'm afraid Myles is in a bad temper this morning!' Both Myles and Behan relate the encounter as a humorous acknowledgement that, for better or for worse, they find themselves becoming one another's double. However, Myles frames this conceit with the puckish dig that the story's central confusion of the two writers 'is probably much against myself'. (He does diffuse, but not reverse, the slight by admitting in a parenthetical aside that 'Never having heard a story in favour of myself I don't suppose this one is unique'.) While Behan's review briskly skims over the motivations that brought him into the pub ('I was feeling somewhat in need of a restorative one morning')[30], Myles lingers on the writer's mid-morning craving in a sketch of the compulsive drinker: 'On a certain Sunday morning Mr Behan was not feeling too well at all. In ghastly slow motion, the clock crawled around to half one. He had the price of a bottle of stout and entered a tavern.' This ambivalence is indexical of the column's dynamic, as Myles and Behan's shared reputations as heavy drinkers are claimed as a mark of solidarity in one column and used as brickbats in another.

Myles' responses to the increasing disparity in their situations continued to vary between the humorous, the ironical and the passive aggressive. As Behan's international celebrity grows,[31] Myles jokingly declares himself 'the most important and influential man in the town next to Brendan Behan'.[32] At times, however, he reverts to language that positions Behan as his apprentice: when asked in one column how he had got on the previous Friday, Myles responds '*I cannot recall. Perhaps I was correcting Behan's new play.*'[33] He continues to poke fun at the myth of Behan's character, as when he glosses the figure of the 'Eulenspiegel' as 'a jester, a bit of a rogue, a sort of Brendan Behan of the Middle Ages'.[34] Yet, elsewhere he alludes more openly to their relative situations, as when he reports that for the upcoming Easter he 'will be in the torment of [his] definitive exegesis of J. Joyce, and Brendan Behan will be in Moscow impatiently instructing Ulanova how to do the "Quare Fellow" ballet without breaking her sconce'.[35] These diverse vantages on Behan are informed by 'the nuanced interplay among literary celebrity, bohemian Dublin, the politics of cultural criticism, postwar isolationism, and economic need in midcentury Ireland',[36] a background which comes to the fore in the 14 November 1957 *Cruiskeen Lawn* column, 'Tell of Vision'. Myles exploits news that 'the Feena Fayl Crowd are going to authorise the start of a TV station' to paint a devastating sketch of the paucity of the Irish domestic cultural scene in which he was trapped and from which Behan's celebrity had ostensibly freed him:

> Who on earth in this depopulated paradise is going to run this station? All our bad actors are either in the Abbey or the various small stable-theatres, we have hardly any competent instrumentalists or singers, [...] and I am very busy myself. If the new doctrine of therapeutic foreignism propagated by Mr Lemass means that the job will be done by inviting in a horde of aliens, I suppose it is all right and that Ireland will in time grow up to be a proud little republic like Luxembourg.[37]

The coordinates of local cultural production and the international gaze lead Myles to his now go-to point of reference, and he asks, with a trace of envy, whether the initiative is merely 'another plan for keeping Mr Brendan Behan in the public eye?'[38]

MYLES/BEHAN FOR THE PARK, 1959!

As the 1950s draw to a close, Myles' evocations of Behan begin to take on a political, even insurrectional dimension. For instance, his scheme to employ Behan 'to sabotage certain letters' of Dublin signs to make them say 'something very remote from that intended' is presented as bearing 'formidable political, moral and even military possibilities'.[39] These possibilities were borne out in the mock 'Behan and/or Myles for President' campaign of 1958–9.

When Dr Noël Browne TD was reported as saying that 'It is time we put our President to live in a detached house in Blackrock', Myles took to his column to declare that Blackrock 'is no place for the President' and to inquire, cheekily, 'What is wrong with Santry?'[40] While Myles' palatial residence in Santry is a recurring gag in *Cruiskeen Lawn*, O'Nolan himself had lived at 4 Avoca Terrace and 81 Merrion Avenue, Blackrock. This inside joke, and its attendant suggestion that Myles himself (rather than O'Nolan) might assume the office, leads the columnist to ponder who else might run in the 1959 presidential elections. He lists off some prominent politicians (Fianna Fáil TD Seán MacEntee, independent republican Patrick McCartan), before coming to his plum candidates: 'it is practically a certainty that Brendan Behan is going up. Myself? Mmmmyes … but Dr Browne must come with me as a counsellor.'

Behan's next appearance comes with a standard dig at his non-literary labouring talents, as Myles claims that the author had previously worked as a department store Santa Claus in Todd Burns on Dublin's Mary Street ('I know that your man would take on anything, but that seemed a rather extreme exercise of his diverse talent').[41] Yet Myles' throwaway jab might have seemed prescient to those who witnessed Behan switch on the Parnell Street Christmas illuminations in December 1958.[42] As reported in 'An Irishman's Diary', Behan, dressed 'like a young Conservative, with a tie to match', used the occasion to emphasise his local *bona fides* at the expense of his international fame, remarking: 'the only serious thing I have to say is that the opinion of the people of North Dublin about myself – a neighbour's child – is more important than the opinion of anyone on the whole globe'.[43] This self-positioning appears to have struck Myles as carrying the air of a political speech. In his 4 December column 'Above in the Park' (on the same page as the 'Irishman's Diary' report on Behan's speech at the illumination ceremony), he plays with Behan's tags of working-class people's poet and international celebrity without explicitly referencing the honour bestowed on the author by the Parnell Street Decorations Committee. Myles sets his sights rather upon the announcement of 'The William J.B. Macaulay Foundation in honour of the President of Ireland, Seán T. Ó Ceallaigh' to provide fellowships to 'young creative artists',[44] writing:

> I can think of one young writer who has almost simultaneously produced a most vigorously acclaimed best-seller and a play that has been loudly applauded in Dublin, London and New York. His name is Brendan Behan. How much of this petty patronage did *he* get or look for, for that matter?

At this juncture, Myles pivots to his 'real subject': the pressing question of 'Who is next for the Park?' He pooh-poohs the apparent contenders for president (McCartan, Fianna Fáil's Frank Aiken, and the two eventual nominees, Fine Gael's Seán Mac Eoin and An Taoiseach Éamon de Valera) with a dismissive caricature of their inevitable public gatherings: 'Think of the gay garden parties, the dinners, the card school, and the flunkey going in and out with trays full of usquebaugh, with the Gaelic cods turning up in kilts.' This sketch of aloof political decadence and superficial cultural nationalism both calls on the plumber's condemnation of the 'crowd [...] drinking small sherries in the High Berinian' in the 1956 'Behanism' column and is implicitly contrasted with the frugal, salt-of-the-earth domestic gathering Myles shares with Behan and their friends in the 1954 'A Square Root' column. All of which leads to Myles' petition that

> the office should be held not by any ego-obsessed politician, but by a person of international distinction who is withal an excellent man in his humour, *and that person is Brendan Behan*. I am perfectly serious, and his chance would be excellent if he went forward. [...] He has the ultimate qualification: he has been in jail![45]

And yet, perhaps because of his characteristic aversion to being aligned too closely with any one cause or side of a given argument, in the 27 January 1959 column Myles distances and differentiates himself from Behan's politics. At the outset, Myles sets his sights on de Valera's proclamation that the solution to the 'problem of partition' is to revive the Irish language '*as a band to keep us together*' – a policy Myles derides as 'nauseating drivel' emanating from 'a cloud-cuckoo-land inhabited by pookas and banshees living in sin'.[46] To bolster his opposition, Myles recalls an episode from his youth, when his grandfather supposedly dismissed the Irish as 'a crowd of guttersnipes'. He assures the reader that he 'hotly denied' this slur and 'quoted the opening part of Robert Emmet's speech from the dock', for which rhetoric he was labelled a 'bowsie' by his senior. Myles breaks off his reminiscence in exasperation: 'I am terribly angry. I am being confused with Brendan Behan.' Thus, Myles at once defines his platform in opposition to de Valera's cultural nationalism and distinguishes himself from an ally with whom he had found it advantageous to confuse himself in the past. At the same time, the ironic allusion to the opening of Emmet's speech on the eve of his execution hints that what is at stake in the mock campaign is Myles' sense of his own diminishing standing and reputation. In the relevant passage, Emmet speaks passionately of how his loss of life will weigh less heavily on him than his maligned reputation, which 'should be rescued from the load of false accusation and calumny which has been heaped upon it'.[47] Emmet's speech would be evoked again in a later column as a cipher of Myles' perceived slights and defamations at Behan's hand.

In a more playful mode, throughout late February and early March 1959 the column gave its space over to the fictional reporter 'Miss Shuecra O'Sleveen', whose four-part serialised report 'The Real Man' details her trip to Myles' Santry residence. The eccentric columnist gives O'Sleveen her scoop with his announcement that he is 'going to have a bash at the Presidency'.[48] Here, Myles appears to reverse his endorsement and reassert his dominance over his former apprentice: 'By domm but I would make a right President. I will appoint Behan my secretary and footman.' Pressed on whether he would take up residence in Áras an Uachtaráin, Myles retorts that he and Behan would serve instead from a disused distillery in Chapelizod. It transpires that Myles' political project is rather malevolent (and somewhat silly), as he has invented an 'anti-vote miracle drug' that abolishes elections by inducing total apathy in the electorate.[49] Myles' vision, in effect, is of a benign dictatorship, assisted by Behan, over the drugged and apathetic Irish people. Implicitly, the scheme is a grotesque enactment (and warped logical conclusion) of de Valera's cultural nationalist 'scheme of reviving the Irish nation'[50] by linking it with its mythical-historical past:

Did you ever hear of Niall of the Nine Ostriches holding elections?

—Well … no.

—Or Brian Boru?

—No but they lived in different ages.

—[…] they were sterling Irishmen. They are ancestors of Behan and myself.[51]

By the end of the week, *Cruiskeen Lawn* was back to its regularly scheduled programming, and Myles and 'Sir Brendan Behan, O.B.E.' were back on cordial terms, drinking malt in Ballsbridge and conversing 'courteously on the subject of certain myths current about the Irish nation'.[52] After their colloquy is briefly interrupted by two autograph-hunters (the column is silent on the issue, but one suspects they were seeking Behan's autograph rather than his companion's), they proceed to blame the 'slanders heaped upon the Irish race' on clichéd Hollywood depictions. However, rather than populist localism, Myles and Behan's platform is decidedly anti-nativist. A few of the more egregious mischaracterisations disseminated on the silver screen, as agreed upon by Myles and 'Dr Behan', include the charges that the Irish are 'open-handed', 'generous', 'honest', 'patriotic', and 'devout'; that they 'respect women' and 'dislike intoxicants'; and that they 'have a considerable literary talent' and 'a lively sense of humour'.

These various dynamics come together in Myles' last rally for himself and Behan before the 17 June 1959 presidential election. Myles had withheld his comment from the public debate over the Irish ban of Behan's *Borstal Boy* in 1958, but stepped in quickly when the small student magazine *You Who* was banned in May 1959 by UCD president Dr Michael Tierney, for including 'a sensible and amusing article by Mr Brendan Behan, laughing somewhat at the pretences of U.C.D. to be a university at all'.[53] While the success of Behan's novel was perhaps a delicate point for the columnist, Behan's censorship by his alma mater was a personal issue, given O'Nolan's own youthful controversy-courting with the 1930s UCD student magazine *Comhthrom Féinne*; Myles avers 'an articulate organ of student opinion' is 'an essential of university life, however brash its opinions'.[54] Once again, Myles draws himself into the issue in order both to ally himself with Behan and to assert his own more radical credentials: 'the editorial board went farther, apparently faring worse, by inviting myself to write for the next issue'.

Having employed Behan's literary celebrity to shine a light on a rather more local political point (namely, that the university is funded by taxpayers and thus abuses its authority by shutting down free speech and debate), Myles proceeds to blur the lines between national and international censorship by implicating Behan in the ongoing Siobhán McKenna BBC controversy. The broadcaster had pulled the second half of *Small World*, a documentary featuring McKenna, for 'alleged anti-British remarks'[55] she had made when she 'questioned Stormont's legitimacy and stated her unambiguous support for "the idealistic young men of the IRA"'.[56] In his column, Myles disseminates 'rumours' that McKenna had not, in fact, made the reported remarks but rather 'the pronouncement was made by Mr Brendan Behan, disguised as Miss McKenna'. Myles takes the opportunity presented by this conceit (in which Behan is confused with someone other than himself, for a change) for his usual jibes at Behan's versatility, manhood and international success ('It has also been said that Mr Behan is appearing in the role of Saint Joan in an important Berlin theatre'). In a characteristic move, Myles mischievously discounts as 'Pure fancy' stories that he himself is 'behind this screen of rumour' and dismisses outright 'the fable that [he has] given official benediction to the presidential candidature of Mr Edward de Valera of Brooklyn, New York, on the grounds that he is a son of [his]'. Thus, Myles establishes himself as both the main advocate against and potential hoaxer behind multiple ongoing reports of censorship in the paper and ridicules de Valera's localist politics by foregrounding his non-native birth and referring to him by his original English name, Edward.

The column closes with an anecdote about Myles' encounter with then prime minister of Northern Ireland, Lord Brookeborough, with whom he had allegedly shared the restaurant car of a northbound train four years previously. While the transition seems like a non sequitur, as with many *Cruiskeen Lawn* columns there is a deep structural cohesion between the column's parts, as it was Brookeborough himself who had sent a delegation to London to insist upon the 'punitive banning' of the second instalment of *Small World* as a result of McKenna's quotes.[57] Myles tricks the PM into believing that he is conversing with a lord, with the upshot that Brookeborough assumes Myles to be 'Lord Moyne'. This new case of mistaken identity carries three relevant connotations. First, the unlikely confusion of Myles with the First Lord Moyne, Walter Edward Guinness (who had been assassinated by Zionist Lehi paramilitaries in Cairo on 6 November 1944), implicating him as a conservative Dublin character with political nous and potentially self-endangering international political views. Secondly, the more probable confusion of Myles with the still living Second Lord Moyne, Bryan Guinness, who, in stark contrast to his father's political career, had been a member of the 'Bright young things' group of 1920s London socialites, an organiser of the 1929 'Bruno Hat' hoax art exhibition and, after the war, a poet, playwright, novelist and trustee of the National Gallery of Ireland. The association ostensibly aligns Myles and his clique (at this stage, slowly whittling down to predominantly himself and Behan) with aristocratic bohemian artistry and hoaxes.[58] Thirdly, and most likely, Brookeborough is having a dig at Myles' drinking problems, given Bryan Guinness' position as vice-chairman of the board of the Guinness Corporation. This is the association Myles chooses to pick up on in the column's closing lines:

'Please see', [Lord Brookeborough] said, 'that Lord Moyne gets every courtesy on his trip to Derry'.
I got that, and apparently virtual ownership of Guinness beside. I am thinking of asking Behan to join me on that Board.

When de Valera resigned as party leader in the aftermath of the June elections and was replaced as taoiseach by Seán Lemass, Myles refocused his faux campaign to leverage political as well as cultural power for himself and Behan (or, perhaps, himself through Behan). As *Cruiskeen Lawn* reports the hot story that Lemass had been 'fined 5s. for being drunk in a public place in London', Myles is informed that he 'had become confused and mixed up Mr Sean Lemas [sic], the Taoiseach, and Mr Brendan Behan'.[59]

I inquired what was the difference.
'One of them is a Prime Minister'.
'Yes – but which?'
'The decent man that brought the country through the trouble in the last war'.
'I don't remember the last war because I was locked up most of the time. Why ISN'T Behan Taoiseach or whatever you call your local Mr McWonder? Who has kept him out of this job?'

Myles proceeds to disqualify Lemass for the position: while Behan looks like Julius Caesar or Nero, Lemass looks like 'that American creation, the tired businessman'; unlike Behan, Lemass 'drinks not at all' and to make matters worse, 'has never written a play (heavens almighty, I have done that myself!)'. The 'trend of [Myles'] dissertation [...] is clear enough': Lemass should step down to the role of 'Assistant President' and elevate Behan to prime minister. And then Behan should appoint Myles 'privy counsellor and general factotum, with uninhibited command of the purse strings. Taoiseach Behan? It sounds all right. As likely a phrase as any predecessor's.'

LIBATIONS AND LAUDATIONS

The dynamic between Behan and Myles that is sketched throughout the column examines diverse points of intersection between public rivalry (literary careers and mock campaigns for political office) and personal intimacy (drinking, of course, but also domestic gatherings, wallpapering, birthdays)[60]. Yet, in its declining years *Cruiskeen Lawn* embraces a franker depiction of the complex interplay between private and public performance that shapes and delimits Irish masculinity and male companionship in O'Nolan and Behan's milieu.

On 3 September 1959, Myles dedicates his entire column to a detailed description of a day he and Behan had spent together. Waiting at a Donnybrook bus stop 'about 11 a.m.', Myles relates:

A large car came to a screaming halt and from the interior there was directed at me a torrent of what I must describe as ebullience, loud vulgar shouting and – let me be honest for once – plain bad language. This bus stop is just outside the police station and I did not want what the newspapers call an altercation. I advanced in genteel gait to this raucous taxi and said in a courteous undertone:
—Good morning, Brendan.

In reply to this greeting Mr Behan used words I cannot print because, as our beloved late editor Bertie Smyllie had to point out to me more than once, this is a family newspaper. [...]
—Come into this dangerous rattle-trap, Mr Behan said. Will ya come with me to the Brazen Head?

—Sairtintly, I answered as I got in.

A weak answer, craven behaviour, you will say? Well, perhaps. But what else could I do? I wasn't armed.

—There is only one thing, I added, I want to go via Meredith's pawnshop in Cuffe street. I want to redeem my watch.[61]

As their mutual friend Anthony Cronin observes, 'The pawning of a watch was rather untypical behaviour for Brian O'Nolan; and in the event its redemption is accompanied by much roaring and blathering to the passers-by during which the narrator's innate sense of respectability is contrasted, probably quite accurately, with Behan's general exhibitionism'.[62]

On leaving the shop, [Behan] looked at a group of bystanders and loafers and then let fly a stentorian roar:

MYLES NA GOPALEEN IS AFTER GETTING HIS WATCH OUT OF PAWN!

I am sure all the girls in Jacobs' biscuit factory heard it. Probably it spoiled a batch ready for baking.

After this embarrassing detour and public humiliation (which indexes the changed dynamic of their relationship through the call-back to the Jacobs' biscuits of the earlier column) the suggestion of Myles' maligned reputation again brings Robert Emmet to mind. When Myles admits his ignorance that the 'crudely filled in holes' on the façade of St Catherine's church are traces of Emmet's scaffold, Behan shouts:

—Course ya didn't know that [...]. How could a ——— from Antrim know a thing like that?

I said nothing. Clearly he was temporarily confusing me with Roger Casement.

Following this latest confusion of identity, they arrive at the Brazen Head, where their conversation turns to other matters of male intimacy (Myles, 'using a courtly if somewhat supercilious undertone, Behan roaring'). Myles boasts that he 'had not once been shaved by another person':

Mr Behan listened to this in silence and wearing an expression which gave me the idea that he was impressed.

—It's aisy seen, he said at last, that you were never in prison.

I escaped about 1 p.m., with my life.

The relationship between Behan and Myles as documented in *Cruiskeen Lawn* begins in 1954, the same year in which *Waiting for Godot* established a late-modernist aesthetic of male friendship in which, as Cole notes, 'wholly intertwined and wildly dysfunctional pairs of men populate a beleaguered world'.[63] Per Cole, Beckett's play 'allies its atmosphere of desiccated absurdity with the relational field of male intimacy' in a way that 'stages the simultaneous impoverishment and plenitude of' that intimacy in a modern trajectory that moves towards 'depletion'.[64] The peculiar narrative of Behan and Myles traced in the pages of *Cruiskeen Lawn* performs a similar function for post-war Dublin. In their characterisation of the alienated (and alienating) communion of Dublin's literary pub culture, these sketches reveal the contours of a crumbling nationalist myth of camaraderie amid the competitiveness of the exclusive and exclusionary male networks of the Dublin literary marketplace. The scene of Myles' pawned watch emphasises the extent to which the bonds produced by these cultural codes are characterised by competitive humiliation and one-upmanship. Yet, amid the variations of camaraderie and alienation, rivalry and self-destruction, absurdity and dysfunction into which they set Myles and Behan, these columns also articulate a subtle *esprit de corps* – even as their protagonists' work and lives become overshadowed by the myths and stark realities that would ultimately subsume their legacies. This plight is captured most pointedly in the 29 January 1962 column 'This Dublin'.[65] Wandering the streets of the city one morning before its citizens have risen from their beds, and already 'full of excoriating turpenteen' having shared a naggin of whiskey with 'a friend' in the Port of Dublin, Myles finds himself alone on O'Connell Street.[66] In his early morning inebriation, Myles confesses to gazing upon the thoroughfare 'with a new vision, the sort of view that can be conferred only by loneliness'. In this vision, he asserts that Nelson's Pillar 'must be removed' and replaced with a more fitting effigy:

Politics would be bound to creep into the choice and the best idea might be to settle at the outset for the two uncommitted in Western Europe. I mean a statue of myself and Brendan Behan, each with a manuscript in the left hand and a pint in the right, two right segocias personifying the spirit of their age [...]. Think about it, citizens.

In his February 1963 profile of O'Nolan for *Scene* magazine, Michael Wale recounts his meeting with the author 'perched on a bar stool in a Dublin suburban bar acting as a foil to the witticisms of Brendan Behan'.[67] The profile, titled 'Dublin's Neglected Genius', plays up the narrative of O'Nolan's tragic obscurity, despite the recent successful revival of his debut novel, by relating that 'The first drink that day was brief, on account of the publican proclaiming that Mr Nolan [sic] had been barred for using abusive language the previous week'. O'Nolan points out that 'a large blow up of one of his columns' from *Cruiskeen Lawn* adorns the bar wall and that, rather than being barred, his drinks should be on the house. However, 'far from being acclaimed the local hero, Mr Nolan's departure was ordered to be as quick as possible. The barman flatly refused to believe that he was the same man who wrote the column.' The ignominy O'Nolan suffers is acute, given that while Behan may be confused for Myles for using 'abusive language' in such a setting, his own testimony that he *is* Myles is dismissed out of hand. Nevertheless, Wale observes, 'Behan and he are great friends.'[68]

This fact is confirmed by the March 1964 obituary that O'Nolan wrote for Behan in *The Sunday Telegraph*. Perhaps in dialogue with Behan's review of *At Swim-Two-Birds*, the eulogy, titled 'Behan Master of Language', is published under the by-line 'Flann O'Brien', who is identified by the paper as '*A personal friend of Brendan Behan, who died on Friday*'.[69] While it ultimately plays up the personal angle foregrounded in this paratextual note, the obituary displays many of the complex attitudes towards Behan's work and reputation that had been advanced in *Cruiskeen Lawn*. At the outset, O'Brien assumes the role of Behan's critic, deeming his playwriting 'in parts both crude and offensive as well as entertaining'. This casual critique sets up the piece's central argument that Behan's true greatness lay not in his writing, but in the lived, everyday performances of his 'peculiarly complicated personality'. 'He was, in fact,' O'Brien asserts, 'much more a player than a playwright', and it is 'this sense of ebullience, zest and exuberance that will remain to tell of Brendan Behan, not his plays'. As becomes clear, this prioritisation of Behan's life over his writing is neither flippant nor back-handed praise from O'Brien, who condemns the 'superb gaucherie' of other obituaries that rush to situate Behan among the ranks of Joyce or even O'Casey. Behan was, to O'Brien, 'something better' than a 'literary practitioner'; he was 'a delightful rowdy, a wit, a man of action in many dangerous undertakings where he thought his duty lay, a reckless drinker, a fearsome denouncer of humbug and pretence, and sole proprietor of the biggest heart that has beaten in Ireland in the last 40 years'. While the wider world remembers him, initially at least, as an internationally renowned playwright and raconteur who 'excelled in language', in O'Brien's final assessment Behan's achievement is irreducibly local. It is only his 'personal associates' who 'will sorrowfully cherish the memory' of his true skill as 'a total master of *bad* language' – a talent that 'must remain unknown to the world at large', but which, when yielded, was 'something unique and occasionally frightening'. This reframing of Behan's real artistry and accomplishment as an insider secret, known only to a small circle of Dubliners, also works to enhance the value of the *Cruiskeen Lawn* columns that had documented his 'enchanting' performances of 'glittering scurrilities' in their own unique way. The piece closes with unusually straightforward, sincere, warm praise, in a poignant register seldom encountered throughout O'Nolan's writing: 'How does Dublin take his tragic departure? I know it is only foolishness in my own head, but the streets seem strangely silent. Their noisy one-time son has gone home, this time for good.'

The importance of O'Nolan's relationship with Behan to his creative output in his waning years is demonstrated, complementarily, in his own obituary, written by Seamus Kelly for the *Irish Times*, a mere two years later, in April 1966. Kelly observes that 'perhaps the most memorable of [O'Nolan's] occasional writings in his last years was the obituary which he wrote for an English Sunday paper of his friend, Brendan Behan. There will be nobody to write so well of him'.[70] To the extent that this is true, it is the series of sometimes ironic, sometimes wildly fanciful and sometimes intimate and painful insights into (and obfuscations of) O'Nolan and Behan's personal friendship and profess-ional rivalry in *Cruiskeen Lawn* that constitutes the 'Secret Scripture' of these kindred spirits in their time and place. Throughout its run, O'Nolan's column featured a number of alternatingly intimate and awkward male encounters and relationships, most famously those of Keats and Chapman, the Brother and his unwilling interlocutor: to these I suggest we add Behan and Myles.

11

BEHAN'S GRAVEYARD OF RADICAL POSSIBILITY: *RICHARD'S CORK LEG* AND THE (IRISH-) AMERICAN DREAM

MICHAEL PIERSE

Brendan Behan commenced work on his final, unfinished play *Richard's Cork Leg* as early as March 1960, with most of what remains of its fragmented, meandering drafts written between December that year and June 1961. These years, before the by-then transatlantically famous Irish writer's death in 1964, were marred by poor health and crippling alcoholism, afflictions that suffocated his still relatively young talent, scuppering efforts to bring this last, faltering project to fruition. The later Behan's writings indicate 'exhaustion and aridity', as John Brannigan observes, and when finally staged in March 1972, at the Peacock Theatre, Dublin, in a posthumous version rescued and reconstituted by producer Alan Simpson, *Richard's Cork Leg* failed to meet the expectations that Behan's earlier stage successes might have aroused (*Brannigan*, 153). If this production enjoyed relative commercial success, transferring later that year to other Irish theatres and eventually to London's Royal Court, it has largely and understandably been characterised since as an undisputed failure – 'entertainment of the least demanding sort'.[1] Bawdy, irreverent, but undoubtedly often trying, Simpson's version of the play was no match for the brio and originality of Behan's *The Quare Fellow* and *The*

Hostage. A two-act bricolage of ideas and scenarios that occurred to Behan sporadically over an extended period of poor productivity, it yielded seemingly little to its would-be adapter and Simpson clearly struggled to mould the manuscript's disorganised mélange. Undoubtedly, the extant drafts of *Richard's Cork Leg*, or *Lá Breagh san Roilg* as it was titled in Irish, afford less than one might hope in terms of a satisfying dramatic formula, fewer of the climactic moments of poignant tragedy – leavened with crisp comedy – that distinguish Behan's earlier plays. Simpson was forced to create a somewhat ineffective ending, and while his revisions clearly had an eye for the comic and slapstick, they were less sensitive to the deeper levels of meaning embedded within the text. Simpson, as the original director of *The Quare Fellow*, had been instrumental in Behan's early success, but his work here proved less fruitful. If there was some justification to his claim to have 'produced the same result as would have been arrived at had the author lived to see it staged' (*CP*, 9) – Behan had left sufficient material to guide the kind of re-working that Joan Littlewood had applied to *The Hostage* – there is much of the 1972 play that also indicates a very unoriginal manoeuvre, a crude replication of formerly successful Behan formulae that were by now clichéd and might have been, in places, judiciously tempered or reduced. As this chapter will show, surviving drafts make clear that this last Behan work had, despite obvious flaws, more to offer. Its range of fascinating analogies, dramatic contrasts and compelling motifs indeed illustrate his residual iconoclastic brilliance, suggesting how tantalisingly close he was to creating something of the order of his earlier work.

This is not to say that Littlewood was overhasty when, during her February 1961 visit to Behan's Ballsbridge home, she suggested that *Richard's Cork Leg* was not yet stageable. Behan's sketchy pitch and recent record of unreliable behaviour would hardly have inspired confidence.[2] We also do not know how much he had on this occasion of the manuscripts that survive. This aside, his loose plot suggests the kind of scenario that Littlewood might have happily work-shopped in the previous decade. Indeed, a play revolving around a graveyard confrontation between various contending ideologies – fascism and socialism, the Rabelaisian and the puritanical – was surely grist to the socialist Littlewood's mill. The seemingly eclectic and often incongruous range of personalities in *Richard's Cork Leg* also evokes the sort of 'glocal' formula that had contributed to *The Hostage*'s success: an aging Spanish Civil War veteran, the Hero Hogan, most likely based on the Irish communist Ambrose Victor

Martin, has enlisted a mercenary young helper, the 'Leper' Cronin, most likely based on Behan, in his plans to sabotage a meeting of the fascist Blueshirts.[3] The meeting has been scheduled for this 'lá breagh' (great day) at a Dublin cemetery, and disguised as blind beggars, the squabbling, O'Caseyesque duo happen there upon two 'whores' who are visiting the grave of a murdered fellow prostitute, Crystal Clear. Clear's martyrdom of sorts – that of a poor woman murdered by affluent men who never face justice for their crime – acts as a foil for the more 'political' (and patriarchal) martyrdom ordinarily venerated by Irish political sects traversing graveyards. Developments of a more international hue also irrupt into the text when an African-American mortician arrives, but his interests in the graveyard are financial rather than political or personal; 'Bonnie Prince Charlie', we learn, has been buying up, revamping and re-styling Irish graveyards, developing new business prospects on behalf of the notorious American graveyards company Forest Lawn. If, in Patrick Pearse's oft-quoted rationalisation of patriotic martyrdom – which must have been ringing in Behan's ears – 'life springs from death; and from the graves of patriot men and women spring living nations', here we discover, as Michel Foucault would discern in the late 1970s, how more and more of life (and even here, uproariously, death) in late capitalism is being commodified; money, not life, or freedom, will spring from these graves and anything else that Forest Lawn can get its hands on.[4] As the play progresses, this unlikely gathering is joined by Hogan's cousin, the puritanical Mrs Mallarkey, who broaches another matter of topical political interest, the 1960s Irish peacekeeping campaign in the Congo. Mallarkey, visiting to disperse the ashes of her dead brother, a Belgian count (Behan, bawdily as ever, relishing the suggestive phonetics), has also brought along her attractive daughter Deirdre, whom Cronin proceeds to seduce. In Act II, the Blueshirts march into the cemetery and Hogan interrupts their meeting with a fiery rebuttal from his 'portable pulpit' (*CP*, 289). When the fascists turn violent, Hogan shoots a Blueshirt and all flee to Mallarkey's home for a typically Behanesque vaudeville of dancing, comedy, parody and song. Mallarkey, we learn, is a sermonising Evangelical Christian leader, who risibly rehearses an impending speech to the 'Anti-Dancing Committee of the Female Prevention Society' to her cavorting audience (*CP*, 295). Her conservative zeal and its laughable obliviousness to the increasingly liberal and changing world about it, as personified by her daughter, takes on a more serious aspect when the coercive forces of conservatism arrive; the party is discovered by the Blueshirts, now tellingly dressed as gardaí, and Cronin is shot dead as he scrambles through a window.[5] In the final tableau, however, he is depicted, like Leslie in *The Hostage*, as a sacrilegious Christ-like apparition, hovering above his own corpse.

BITING SATIRE OR 'GOOFY INCONTINENCE'?

As with other Behan plays, vaudeville is integral to *Richard's Cork Leg*, and much of the play's comedy rests on a music-hall miscellany of witty juxtapositions and bawdy double entendre. This formula mimics, and sometimes blatantly repeats, stock gags and scenarios from Behan's earlier work, with mixed results. On the one hand, Behan develops striking contrasts that insightfully highlight contradictions within religious and political ideologies of various hues. On the other, his repeated digressions and tiresome vulgarity risk blunting his message; here, more than anywhere else in his oeuvre, Behan struggles to meet his stated aesthetic objective, 'to amuse people and any time they get bored divert them with a song or a dance [...] while they were laughing their heads off, you could be up to any bloody thing behind their backs' (*BBI*, 17). Laboured, didactic exchanges are often contrived and only poorly integrated. Excessive vulgarity, unsubtle satire and ad nauseam wordplay – what one critic has termed the play's 'tone of goofy incontinence' – undoubtedly render what might have been funny in smaller doses quite simply overcooked in Simpson's hands.[6] This is the misfortune of his production, but we must allow that Behan's drafts, surfeited as they are with gags, were a brainstormed smorgasbord of potential ideas rather than a finished play. Beneath their bubbling froth, the manuscripts nonetheless suggest how Behan was still a theoretically nuanced thinker and gifted conjurer of dramatic antinomies. At a deeper, subtextual level, *Richard's Cork Leg* furnishes both a tragic and impressive sense of what Behan was still attempting to do behind our backs. His commentaries on Irish establishment hypocrisies and American late-capitalist absurdities produce flashes of brilliance through which this flawed final play might have been retrieved.

At the heart of *Richard's Cork Leg* lies a reflexive contradiction between its author's ostensible embrace of the late-capitalist, Anglo-American culture in which he was by now a celebrity, and his deep distrust of that culture's role in the production and dispersal of ideology. In this, it is evident that Behan, as a former political activist and still radical leftist, chimes with the general trajectory of Western Marxism during his lifetime, with its shift, as Andrew J. Milner notes, 'from an initial celebration of the emancipatory potential of culture as human self-activity, to a subsequent recognition of the debilitating and disabling power of culture as "ideology"'.[7] The play indeed suggests key elements of Gramscian and Adornoesque thinking: the sense in the former that intellectual and moral leadership, or hegemony, was producing a capitalist 'common sense', manufacturing consent; the sense in the latter that the 'culture industry', its commodification of mass and popular culture, was sapping humanity of its intellectual vigour, producing, as Theodor Adorno and Max Horkheimer put it, a 'deception of the masses' and 'infecting everything with sameness'.[8] What better place to express such pessimism about modern popular culture – its standardisation, sameness and avarice – than a graveyard where death is newly monetised by an American corporation? Humanity here is subject to reification, 'the substitution for human relations of thing-like ones (money, the "cash nexus")', as Fredric Jameson characterises it; in this case, ancient ritual becomes modern retail, death an opportunity for consumption rather than redemption.[9]

The Dublin writer's recent, whirlwind immersion in the home of the culture industry – in America's burgeoning post-war discourses of celebrity and opportunity – had both bewildered and captivated him. He was also influenced, as I will show, by a 1948 novel by Evelyn Waugh, *The Loved One: An Anglo-American tragedy*, in which Forest Lawn (thinly disguised as 'Whispering Glades') becomes a node for criticisms of Hollywood's culture industries. Reified relationships and the rapid commercialisation of all aspects of human life are key features of late-capitalist society, which both Behan and Waugh convey. This is not to suggest that Behan was not also entranced by his American experience; indeed, as Dave Hannigan attests, the Irishman 'was drunk on [New York], actually intoxicated by the sheer excitement and the irresistible glamour and the non-stop action of it all'.[10] It was, to him, 'a sort of Lourdes' (*O'Connor*, 264). But if the mayhem-inclined Behan's attraction to America has been depicted as something as visceral and fatal as that of a moth to a flame, he also illustrates an acute awareness of the dangers of a society in which so much of human life was being commercialised and fetishised as never before. The leitmotif of *Richard's Cork Leg*, its fundamental, philosophically profound parallel between capitalism and forms of 'death', produces a satire that strikes at the very essence of the American Dream.

'A PHILOSOPHY OF FUTILITY'

Behan casts late capitalism as a machine-like monster relentlessly substituting corporate values for humanist ones. As a real-life commercial cemetery that trades on the conspicuous consumption of death, Forest Lawn symbolises this displacement of life into the capitalist 'machine'. For celebrities, the company's Californian base was a fashionable final resting place; for Behan, of course, it was ripe with comic possibilities. If the theoretical joy of conspicuous consumption is, as Thorstein Veblen famously argued, luxuriating in the public flaunting of one's social status – one's 'evidence of wealth' and 'reputability' – then the very fact that the subject of this projected joy is, in this instance, deceased, creates a deliciously wry contradiction.[11] Waugh deployed this satirical potential in *The Loved One* and the fact that Behan mentions Waugh several times in *Richard's Cork Leg* suggests his familiarity with this novel. The American company that both writers lampooned is essentially selling snobbery in death, social and cultural capital (ostentatious locations, grandiose encomiums, ornate tombs) *for* the dead. In this process, conspicuous (or posthumous) consumption seeks to replace the traditional role of the afterlife, and in doing so confers a quasi-religious aura onto a newly fetishised service. By way of this kind of 'debasement of culture', 'amusement itself becomes an ideal, taking the place of the higher values it eradicates from the masses'.[12] The transformation in human relations and thinking illustrated by such processes showed, in Paul Nystrom's words, that:

At the present time, not a few people in western nations have departed from old-time standards of religion and philosophy, and having failed to develop forceful views to take their places, hold to something that may be called, for want of a better name, a philosophy of futility. [...] This lack of purpose in life has an effect on consumption [...] concentrating human attention on the more superficial things in which fashion reigns.[13]

For a former IRA volunteer, who, in the late 1930s chose a dangerous, politically committed life that would result in several spells of imprisonment, this 'philosophy of futility' and its suffusion throughout American mid-century society must have seemed both fascinating and absurd. Yet Behan would also know that Forest Lawn was serious business. As profiled in the pages of *Life* magazine, for instance, in January 1944, the company, whose employees are risibly 'expected to be […] above all, cheerful', is allegedly planning '"the most unique cathedral in the world" with room for 76,000 more tombs in its buttresses and a skyscraper columbarium'; 'also on the books is a helicopter field for flying funerals'.[14] This lavish investment in death must have struck Behan, when he ambled through its Los Angeles opulence seventeen years later, as both surreal and philosophically profound. If he was 'enchanted with [this] Disneyland', he also lampooned its breathtaking arrogance, joking that 'the Americans have banished death' (*O'Connor*, 283). Here the afterlife was conjured, in a marketing sleight of hand, as yet another occasion for luxury, a form of consumable 'life'; as Adorno and Horkheimer might put it, 'the culture industry perpetually cheats its consumers of what it perpetually promises'.[15] In the play, Bonnie Prince repeats verbatim some of Forest Lawn's more garish marketing effluvia – the gushing joy over death, the euphemistic lingo of 'Loved Ones' and 'Waiting Ones', the 'Beauty and Happiness such as the earth cannot give' – which provide for so much mirth in Waugh's *The Loved One*.[16] 'Property' here is 'the American [word] for grave', Behan explains, 'like Loved One is the American for corpse, and passing is the American for dying'.[17] There is a macabre exaggeration of Guy Debord's 'society of the spectacle' here, his identification of the modern 'degradation of being into *having*' and '*having* to *appearing*' in that historical conjuncture 'in which social life has become completely dominated by the accumulated productions of the economy'.[18] The language of American late capitalism is euphemism, its purpose evasion – and, moreover, profit.

It is noteworthy here that Behan very briefly remarks on contemporary American funeral practices in the last lines of his risqué short story 'After the Wake' (1950), in which the gay narrator embarks on a 'campaign' to seduce his male neighbour, notwithstanding the revelation of that neighbour's wife's terminal illness (*Wake*, 48). When the suffering woman dies, the narrator can't help but exploit the occasion to realise his sexual fantasies; even as they wake the dead woman, his homoerotic removal of the exhausted husband's clothing as he lies in bed – his 'pants and shirt, from the supply muscled thighs' – clashes grotesquely with the ugliness of the woman's dead but eerily watchful visage nearby, her nostrils 'plugged with cotton-wool', her mouth that 'hadn't closed properly'; 'All in all she looked no better than the corpse of her granny' (*Wake*, 51). When the narrator fancies 'her face looking up from the open coffin on the Americans who, having imported wakes from us, invented morticians themselves', Behan suggests a sense of unnerving surveillance, that she may be 'disgusted', as is earlier suggested, at the narrator's scheming (*Wake*, 52). But that the dead woman looks 'on the Americans' is an odd coda; their 'invention' of morticians indeed seems to suggest that the adornment of the dead shares something with the narrator's hiding of the truth. In the story the narrator, and, by extension, Behan, exposes his homosexuality, and much like the climactic act of undressing, this disclosure provides a taboo thrill that contrasts with the dead woman and with the tradition of exposing corpses before burial. Irish society, Behan suggests, is more eager to expose the dead, the physically ugly, than to tolerate the beautiful and the alive, the man's living body and his narrator's taboo attraction to him. America is not much better; by contrast it seeks to dress up the dead, to glamorise that which is lifeless and dull. Behan's narrator does not seek to covet his neighbour's wife (as her husband actually suspects earlier on), but rather to covet her husband, and moreover to challenge the homophobia and religiosity that is metaphorically 'dead'. Here he echoes Waugh's focus on the ugliness of death and the duplicity of those who dress it up.[19] But for Behan the fixation on death, not life, on both sides of the ocean, acts as a metaphor for the wrongheaded in both the traditional *and* the modern, the conservative *and* the capitalist; whereas Waugh, in his disdain for the 'materialistic, mechanised' modern, turned for succour towards Catholic traditionalism, Behan pointedly seeks something else.[20]

'UN-IRISH AMERICAN ACTIVITIES'

If Waugh ridiculed the English who were increasingly in thrall to American culture, Behan did likewise with his own compatriots. At the time of writing *Richard's Cork Leg* and, significantly, a month after his presentation of the early drafts to Littlewood, Behan's disenchantment with Irish America was particularly acute, after his being banned from New York's 1961 St Patrick's Day parade for being 'a common drunk' unwelcome at this 'semi-religious, almost sacred' event in the city's calendar.[21] An emigré 'among the underdogs' – as Waugh describes his pet-cemetery worker protagonist, Barlow – Behan was no longer welcome among Irish expatriates; Barlow's apparently un-English job makes him an embarrassment to the Hollywood English, just as Behan had become an embarrassment to the East Coast Irish.[22] In both cases, the immigrant community's imperative is to keep up appearances. Behan thought the personal slight of his removal from New York's annual celebration of Irishness an indictment of diasporic myth-making *about* Irishness. That his involvement was blocked by a Justice of the Court of Special Sessions in New York, James J. Comerford, who, born in Waterford, ironically shared with Behan a revolutionary past in the IRA, heightened the sense of hypocrisy; 'the former teenage rebel somehow became synonymous with the stern and rigorous dispatch of justice from the bench in his adopted city', as Hannigan marvels.[23] An incensed Behan ranted at Irish Americans 'hanging shamrocks round your ears', conjuring 'leprechauns' and 'magic mists', spouting 'blather about Glocca Maura': 'I now have a theory on what happened to the snakes when St. Patrick drove them out of Ireland,' he wrote. 'They came to New York and became judges.'[24] This 'snake', Behan thought, was denying his history (and Ireland's) in his drive for respectability, and in the play, Behan thus associates Irish-American myth-making with the discursive silencing of inconvenient Irish histories. We are told that Forest Lawn tellingly avoided extending its business operations to Dublin's Glasnevin Cemetery when it discovered that the place was 'full of revolutionaries'; 'they came to Jim Larkin's tomb' but were concerned when 'they found out he was in Sing Sing', on the opposite side of American law to Comerford (*CP*, 244–5). Larkin, a Liverpool-Irish trade unionist and radical socialist – venerated in Dublin for his role in the 1913 Lockout – was jailed in America for 'un-Irish American activities', we are told, that is, for being an antagonist of capitalism.[25] That Behan was himself a revolutionary, that he had once written a poetic eulogy to Larkin, that he had become firm friends in New York with famed Irish-American labour activist the 'Rebel Girl' Elizabeth Gurley Flynn, and that the play stresses, in its parodies of classic Irish-American songs, the sanitised version of Ireland proliferated by its diaspora, all suggest a contrast between the phoney and authentic, between Ireland's radical histories and its emigrants' expedient accommodations.

The unseemly Ireland of Larkin is replaced with a voguish and vitiated quasi-Gaelic ideal, much as in Waugh's novel the 'Lake Isle' graveyard venue – named and styled after Yeats' poem and complete with mechanically produced bee sounds – is Whispering Glades' most expensive burial place precisely because it accords with this fashionable and, Waugh suggests, artificial version of Irishness:[26] 'Once they had bees, too, but folks was always getting stung so now it's done mechanical and scientific; no sore fannies and plenty of poetry.'[27] Hollywood's superficial culture takes the 'sting' out of history, requires the cultivation of reductive, bland stereotypes that facilitate the culture industry's market-driven commodification. Irishness, or indeed Englishness, must be reducible to stock images, simplified characteristics, and Waugh's Englishmen thrive by colluding in the fiction: 'You never find an Englishman among the underdogs – except in England of course. That's understood out here, thanks to the example we've set. There are jobs that an Englishman just doesn't take.'[28] Indeed, so concerned is the doyen of the Hollywood-English tribe, Sir Ambrose, with Barlow's 'irreparable harm' to their reputation, that he secures funds from the cricket club to have the offending emigré sent home.[29] Invoking Waugh, Behan is of course identifying the same sleeven cynicism with Irish America. Like Barlow's, *his* compatriots might be more than happy to see him sent home. In Behan's play, Ireland enjoys a cultural capital that relies on the mythic and remote, sections of Forest Lawn's Irish cemetery suggestively branded in the familiar myth-making of hackneyed Irish-American blarney, as 'the Ould Sod' and 'Tear No Noge'.[30] If Rose mistakenly thinks that Sing Sing is in Hollywood, Behan would seem to suggest that America has had too much of the Hollywood version of Ireland. Like Forest Lawn's appropriation of the graveyard, the American appropriation of Irishness amounts to an evasion of grimmer and more complicated realities. This fabrication in turn reflects America's own dominant ideologies, its concentration on surface glamour, its aversion to alternative politics, to nuance and the complications of historical specificity.

If, in the society of the spectacle, the commodity transforms social life, then Behan suggests how it bends that life to its purposes by effacing elements doggedly resistant to its logic. Bonnie Prince stuffs his corpses and, like Shelley's Victor Frankenstein, returns them to a reconditioned 'life', but only one that reflects his (and in this case, American hegemonic) interests. In Simpson's version of the play, this comic alchemy is rendered through the appearance of a robotic corpse – very literally a false consciousness – which is resurrected by technological means. Yet, in this Simpson revision, the more slapstick rendering is also less compelling than in Behan's original, where revealing recordings of the dead made during their lifetimes are played for mourners grieving over their loved ones' remains. One of Behan's particularly revealing voices from the dead – which Simpson unfortunately elides from his adaptation – is tellingly subjected to summary censorship when his inconvenient history conflicts with post-McCarthyite American hegemony. Bonnie Prince 'switches [the recording] off hurriedly' when the American, who died in December 1942, hopes that 'the Red Army is still holding those Nazi s.o.b's at Stalingrad. Aren't those Russian boys just the greatest.'[31] Referencing the 'First Red Scare' (Larkin), and the second (post-Second World War), Behan suggests how history is both cyclical and contrived. Bonnie Prince's role as mortician, revamping corpses, entails the transmutation of history, censoring their views. In a related move, the Irish traditional air, 'cornphíopa an Lann dubh', with which *Lá Breagh san Roilg* commences, is notably brought to a halt when 'Striapach 1', Maria Concepta, jarringly produces a Japanese transistor.[32] In another of Behan's manuscripts, the funeral dirge is interrupted by Maynard Ferguson's jazz.[33] In the published version, the image of weeping 'veiled figures' on either side of a Celtic cross is turned to levity when they are revealed as 'Dublin brassers in working gear' (*CP*, 243–4). Each opening scene raises contradictions; tradition jars with modernity, the monocultural with the multicultural, the sacred with the profane. We are reminded that history is being subsumed into the 'machine'. Moreover, in this reflexive foregrounding of his own eclectic borrowing from ancient history, modern jazz, political discourse, traditional balladry and international popular culture – the typical heteroglossia of a Behan text – a confluence of cultures refuses the monologic, the ideological tyranny that, like Bonnie Prince (as capitalist), or indeed the Catholic Waugh (as religious campaigner), forecloses on unwanted or inconvenient perspectives. Yet paradoxically, if his juxtapositions of the old and the new signal a dialogic principle, his symbolism of the modern and technological (jazz, the transistor) eclipsing the ancient and organic (the Celtic cross, the voice) also suggests how mass and popular cultures are replacing and effacing important, older human values. In this way, Behan explores both the generative possibilities and the degenerative reductivism of late-capitalist culture.

'TO REGARD CO-EXISTENCE WITH FAVOUR'

But if Behan sounds an eschatological note of alarm – a portent of humanity's decline, of Debordian 'being' into 'appearing' in modern American life – Ireland's narrow and sclerotic society is no alternative, and this is where he pointedly departs from Waugh's alternative of old-fashioned 'moral and social standards'.[34] When Rose absentmindedly mentions the exoticised and notionally Turkish custom of 'sex among the tombstones' to Deirdre, the latter, having just secretly had sex with Cronin on a tombstone, retorts that she 'wouldn't know' and she is 'going home' to her mother, a woman who rails against the 'sex excitement' of 'modern dance' (*CP*, 288, 295, 296). If capitalist America advertises diversity but produces ideological uniformity, conservative Ireland advertises chastity but produces sexual hypocrisy. The Blueshirts, men who 'shot and bayoneted for the love of Jesus', are curiously well known to the prostitutes, such luminaries as 'Rape Ryan' and 'Nature O'Neill' having encountered them in unstated (but we presume scandalous) circumstances in the past (*CP*, 289). Both Ireland and America are keen to suppress such contradictions. After Seán Lemass' Ireland of the late 1950s and 1960s embarked upon programmes of economic modernisation and internationalisation, American president John F. Kennedy could commend the Irish, on an official visit in 1963, for having 'modernised your economy [...] diversified your industry, liberalised your trade [...] and improved the living standards of your people'.[35] Ireland, inferentially, was moving closer to America, as glowingly confirmed by its most beloved diasporic son. The American takeover of Behan's Dublin graveyard allegorises this historic conjuncture; adopting the appellation of the Jacobite pretender, the Bonnie Prince suggests that he (and by extension, capitalism) is Ireland's latter-day saviour. But Behan implies that the new, more capitalist Ireland will require a Forest Lawn-style makeover, the collision of these mutually alien spheres (traditional Ireland/ the graveyard; modern America/Forest Lawn) providing much comedy in the play. Capitalism's central ethical totem, the concept of private property, is the new sacrosanct, and Bonnie Prince is tellingly perturbed when Mrs Mallarkey casts her cremated brother's ashes without 'permission from the proprietors of this property': 'the air may be free but the ground under it is certainly not', he admonishes; 'I think it's not ethical when you haven't made even a small deposit' (*CP*, 263, 266). A similar message inheres in Behan's reference to the famous

German passion plays at Obberammergau, into which, he notes, 'thousands of people from all over the world […] *pay*' (*CP*, 273; emphasis mine). As Cronin recalls, his uncle, the risibly named 'Socrates' (here again Behan invokes queer history), even planned to commercialise these biblical dramas as 'matinees for convents and colleges', envisaging, uproariously, an advertisement for 'Willie Rourke, the Baker' that would appear on the production's 'Fire Curtain' along with an endorsement line for Christ in the Last Supper scene: 'Take this and eat – it's Rourke's bread, fresh and crusty' (*CP*, 274).[36] Behan again recalls Waugh's Barlow, his plans to make money by becoming a pastor, and the magical 'dream' of Whispering Glades' founder Wilbur Kenworthy, who, in a moment of apparent revelation, discovered his (lucrative) vocation: 'I heard a voice say: "Do this." And behold I awoke and in the Light and Promise of my DREAM I made WHISPERING GLADES.'[37] In Waugh's novel and Behan's play, the profit motive suffuses formerly sacred spheres. But in Behan, again, the principal concern is with the human rather than the celestial, with how human concerns are marginalised by the cupidity invading every aspect of social life: 'To regard co-existence with favour', or 'To want more return for less labour, / Fatter fish, cheaper chips, better beer', as one of Behan's lyrics from the play asserts, becomes a 'crime' (*CP*, 285). This new 'Gospel', as Bonnie Prince characterises it – one the post-revolutionary, post-de Valera Ireland was speedily adopting – would require a different version of Christ, and a different version of Ireland too (*CP*, 285). It is comically significant though that Cronin, as 'Leper' – personifying the Ireland that needs to be cured and saved – is incorrigibly lazy and licentious, refusing Bonnie Prince's corrective role.

In place of late capitalism's fixation on surfaces, its shallow philosophy of futility, Behan insists on depth, on what Jameson would characterise as the Lacanian 'real'; the playwright's relentlessly knowing irony insists on a mediatory dialectics that places all that is seemingly resistant to the historical emphatically back within its ambit. With Jameson, Behan seeks to 'make connections among the seemingly disparate phenomena of social life generally'.[38] Capitalism's duplicity and mercurial adaptability, its focus on 'appearing', occludes the harsh realities of political oppression, Behan suggests. Bonnie Prince, for instance, revealingly shape-shifts through various guises that deny his situatedness as an oppressed black American. Like Waugh's also ironically named mortician, Mr Joyboy, his role is to put a nice 'face' on things, to erase the traces of the idiosyncratic and the authentic; indeed, he questions the possibility of any fixed subjectivity at all, replicating a sort of imagined, endless 'choice' between identities as commodities. However, as one of Waugh's characters puts it, 'Once you start changing a name, you see, there's no reason ever to stop. One always hears one that sounds better.'[39] Behan's plummy 'Prince', who might be Ireland's saviour, an 'Indian potentialtate', the 'Aga Khan', or perhaps an American basketball player, is characterised by pronounced plasticity (*CP*, 254). Tailoring his identity to his various sales pitches, he slips with ease from 'an Oxford or a Trinity or a Yale accent' to an East Coast African-American vernacular; he is Scottish here, he is a 'fully integrated' 'ordinary American' there, later also 'a Britisher', part of the imperial mission that apparently 'civilised' Ireland, his skin colour seemingly – and of course erroneously – no bar to his full participation in the imagined, 'integrated' America of the early 1960s (*CP*, 260, 285). Never is this African American (as his comic accentual slips reveal) a black man in a racist, segregated society, in which the student sit-ins at Greensboro in 1960 and the 'freedom riders' of the American South in 1961 preceded the historic Civil Rights marches that followed throughout the decade. This 'real' has no place in this context – it is conspicuously absent, beyond the stage – but Bonnie Prince's absurd aversion to manifest history surely motions us back towards Behan's meta-commentary, his knowing critique of discursive silencing processes. Like the Harlem Globetrotters, that most marketed of basketball teams, whose brand is printed 'in bright orange-gold' lettering across the back of his gown, Bonnie Prince represents a deceptively 'bonny' mid-century America, the kind critiqued in the television drama series *Mad Men* (2007–15), which illustrates how racial inequalities are effaced in the evasions of 1950s and 1960s advertising and branding.[40] As David K. Wiggins and Patrick B. Miller note, the Globetrotter phenomenon's emphasis on clownish performances, as opposed to sporting competition, meant that 'athleticism shared the court with minstrelsy'. Thus the team's 'repertory reflected the racial stereotypes so deeply embedded in American culture', players performing white America's 'stereotypical notion of black men as lazy and comedic fools'.[41] Black Americans are incorporated into the symbolic matrix of an imagined, inclusive community of American norms, while the country's social and economic practices simultaneously exclude them through othering processes. Bonnie Prince personifies this paradoxical tension between representation and reality. As with the American graveyard, in

American society supposedly everyone can find a place anywhere they *choose*, once they can afford it and are white.[42]

'EPIPHANIC DISCOURSE'

Brannigan identifies in the later Behan what he terms an 'epiphanic discourse' which 'repeatedly return[s] to representations of memory, subjectivity, and morbidity', important themes in *Richard's Cork Leg* (*Brannigan*, 153). On a more provincial level, Behan's reference to the saintly Dublin worker Matt Talbot as a tool in the propaganda of capitalism suggests how the dominant forces of the modern world reconstitute the past in their own image. Talbot, a famed religious martyr, is recalled by Mrs Cronin as a man for whom Dublin's timber merchants sought beatification 'because he refused to take money for overtime' (*CP*, 262). He is rendered similarly in Thomas Kilroy's 1973 play *Talbot's Box*, where Talbot's martyrdom sanctifies working-class subservience; he is a 'model' to 'all Christian workers', a man who 'never complained'.[43] In Behan's play, the 'dead stuffed Yank' on display at the cemetery, whom the prostitutes comically identify as American because he has 'no smell – only soap', suggests how death and by extension the past more generally is de-realised, sanitised and perfumed (*CP*, 254). If history here is a blue-rinsed corpse in a glass case, and if Forest Lawn's calculus is thus a synecdoche for capitalism's attempts to control that (real) history, the only partly colonised Irish graveyard nonetheless tellingly frustrates those designs. Here Behan stresses the stubborn intractability of subterranean, dissident histories as a reservoir of counter-hegemonic resilience and how the cultural alterity of Dublin's working class, in the words of one sociologist, 'asserts itself as a pole of differentiation in Irish society'.[44] The topography that Forest Lawn seeks to control is paradoxically also an emancipatory site of resistance, even a sort of anti-shrine that is impervious to both the pieties of the religious and the profiteering of the rich.

The American feminist writer and activist bell hooks writes of society's margins as potentially powerful sites of resistance. Those living 'on the edge' develop 'a particular way of seeing reality', a 'sense of [society's] wholeness', which yields 'an oppositional world view – a mode of seeing unknown to most of our oppressors'. By way of this sense of alterity and its implicitly dialectical, 'whole' worldview, the margins can paradoxically become enriching, 'much more than a site of deprivation. In fact [...] just the opposite: that is also the site of radical possibility, a space of resistance.'[45] In Behan's play, as one of Crystal Clear's devotees remarks, the graveyard is one of the few places that the Irish authorities 'won't bar us out of', and his subversion of the Irish Catholic's characteristic devotional emphasis on the Virgin Mary (Lourdes, site of the Marian apparitions, is specifically mentioned) in his prostitutes' counter-pilgrimage to Crystal Clear is a powerfully symbolic and iconoclastic affirmation of this emphasis on the margins as an alternative site of revelation (*CP*, 254).[46] Radical history, personified by the socialist Hogan and his struggle against the Blueshirts, is still ironically alive amongst the tombstones, though a new Ireland, in concert with modern America, is keen to keep it underground. Hogan, like Monsewer in *The Hostage*, albeit politically more red than green, may be quixotic in his delusional, ersatz version of republican 'active service', dashing after old enemies in a graveyard (*CP*, 280), but if this somewhat outmoded politics places a barrier between Hogan and the various marginalised figures in the play, his 'red' politics nonetheless represent something both more authentic than the American ideologies of Bonnie Prince and more humane than the totalitarianism of the Blueshirts. Not unlike Behan himself, Cronin, Hogan's shaky ally, 'used to be a follower of Karl Marx' but now admits to have 'no politics except women, drink and a smoke'.[47] He also professes to 'detest' communists on a personal level. However, again like his creator, Cronin has sympathies with the Communist Party 'because it's the only one that all the big shots are terrified of. All the big-bellied bastards that I hate, hate the reds' (*CP*, 252). Hogan is, after all, a 'Hero' of the Spanish republican struggle, a war in which Behan (anticipating the quixotic antics of his characters) would reputedly have enlisted had his bike not suffered a flat tyre as he made his way to join the International Brigade (*O'Sullivan*, 33). Hogan's graveyard confrontation with the Blueshirts also recalls Behan's real confrontation with weapon-wielding Irish Francoists in St Stephen's Green, Dublin, in 1936, when the then thirteen-year-old defiantly waved a gun at fascists who threatened republican protesters.[48] If Behan clearly identifies with Cronin's fecklessness, he also motions, if somewhat mirthfully and self-deprecatingly, towards the notionally leftist politics that they share. The past and its struggles are still important, Behan stresses, as he rails against an anti-intellectual culture, which, Cronin claims, unites Irish hegemony with that of the Anglo-American world:

The English and Americans dislike only *some* Irish – the same Irish that the Irish themselves detest, Irish writers – the ones that *think*. But then they hate their own people who think. I just like to think, and in this city I'm hated and despised. (*CP*, 280)

Behan claims that there is little room in Ireland for what he terms the 'lay contemplative', the person who dares to 'meditate', who bridges the gap between furtive thought and forbidden expression. Ireland bridles at its taboos, bristles at those who articulate them. Cronin, a raconteur like his creator, must therefore check what he says:

They give me beer, because I can say things that I remember from my thoughts – not everything, because, by Jesus, they'd crucify you, and you have to remember that when you're drunk, but some things, enough to flatter them. (*CP*, 280)

The focus on historiographical silencing invoked here recurs in the play's pattern of missing links and hinted silences, the things that did not, or cannot, make the stage.

As Michel-Rolph Trouillot observes, historical silencing is 'an active and transitive process: one "silences" a fact or an individual as a silencer silences a gun'.[49] Trouillot's image is evocative and intriguing: the 'gun' of history is just as potent, perhaps more so if its discursive devices are 'silent'; and the discursive device and its process – the silencer more than silenced fact – is where our focus ought to be. This is the 'most elusive domain', as Slavoj Žižek terms it, 'the "spontaneous" ideology at the heart of social "reality" itself'.[50] After Cronin explains Hogan's activities against Francoism, Maria relates her own father's violent rejection of fascism, yet her 'spontaneous' confusion of alignments and ideologies allegorises her generation's disconnection from the increasingly forgotten idealism of Ireland's revolutionary past. 'My poor father that was in Dartmoor with Mr De Valera hit a Blueshirt with a hammer,' she recalls:

Split him open. (*Sighs.*) That was my poor father for you – to God and Ireland true! Faith and Fatherland. We have the hammer at home, on the cabinet beside the bottle of Lourdes water, and a picture of Blessed Evelyn Waugh. (*CP*, 250)

The subtext of course is Maria's disconnection from history; she has confused (along with the personage of Evelyn Waugh) what her father fought for, falsifying his anti-fascist past in the forgetful present, much as de Valera's profile as 'a social conservative of a profoundly Catholic complexion, despite his revolutionary past' cast him for critics as a falsification of the ideals of the revolutionary period.[51] The Irish language version of Behan's play is particularly caustic in this regard:

'Agus breathnaigh ar De Valera anois. Fiche agus dhá mhíla punt sa mbliain aige agus pálás suas i bPáirc an Fhíonn Uisce.'

'And look at De Valera now. Twenty-two thousand pounds a year and a palace up in the Phoenix Park.'[52]

Maria can travesty her father's assault on a Blueshirt as the story of a man fighting with, rather than against, the Catholic Church, just as the Republic can travesty the ideals of its founders by treating its republican president to a 'palace'. Equally, Mrs Mallarkey's devotion to her brother, who died in the Congo and whose ashes she spreads on the graveyard, evokes a social process of forgetfulness about the legacy of imperialism in both Africa and Ireland, Behan's song about 'Belgian Black and Tans' suggesting the hypocrisy of those Irish who fail to grasp the postcolonial parallels (*CP*, 266). His reference to the Congo and Belgium's historically controversial role there came in the wake of the deaths of Irish peacekeeper soldiers at the hands of Baluba tribesmen in 1960, which caused 'a wave of sadness, mingled with pride, to sweep the country', as Joseph Lee recalls.[53] Behan would undoubtedly have noted with some concern the 'Congolese denunciations of Irish troops as being inherently partial to the interests of other Europeans', claims which, as Ben Tonra notes, were 'wounding' for postcolonial Ireland, and here Behan clearly despairs at Irish forgetfulness.[54] Indeed, Cronin even thinks that Irish republican hero Roger Casement's explosive report on Belgian imperialism was concerned with how 'the Belgian showed great bravery in going to civilize the Congo' (*CP*, 266). For Behan the distortion attendant on such travesties relates back to this 'elusive domain' of ideology, the 'silencer' that facilitates the epistemic and actual violence of power, and which also explains Irish hypocrisy and myopia in the immediate aftermath of the soldier deaths:

BAWD II. What did they murder him for?

MRS MALLARKEY. Because he was trying to civilize them. He'd only set fire to two villages when his supersonic jet had to make a forced landing. The natives killed him and the others with their spears.

CRONIN. What? No ground to air missiles? Primitive heathens! They had no weapons of civilized war. Poor man he was a gentleman. (*CP*, 265)

Mallarkey, who eulogises her brother, the 'Belgian Count's' exploits, fails to display any knowledge of Belgium's slaughter of millions of Congolese (*CP*, 266). The act of casting his ashes to the wind thus presents a metaphor for the disintegration of history (or *his* story), the dispersal of truth into myth. That these ashes are accidentally flung in Hogan's face also suggests Behan's view on how those Irish who fought fascism in Spain are now dishonoured at home. When Cronin makes deprecatory remarks on the behaviour of drunken Belgians, it is notable that Mallarkey can't hear him: 'I'm a little deaf,' she explains (*CP*, 266).[55] Deafness and blindness are recurring motifs in the play, symbolising the ignorance that Behan felt debilitated so many, for as he once opined, 'I think the proper aim of all arts is the abolition of the village idiot.'[56] Ireland is 'a little deaf' when it comes to uncomfortable truths; it is a 'psychiatric state', Behan's graveyard representing the repressed yet lively realm of its unconscious, its marginal histories, which repeatedly return troubling ideas (*CP*, 287).

In one of the more bawdy sections of Behan's manuscript, which Alan Simpson again chose to excise from his version of the play, Rose tells the story of a gardener who, for propriety's sake, cuts the penis off a dead donkey and throws it away, only to find that it has landed in 'the nuns' garden' (*CP*, 313). The more the abomination is jettisoned from the surface of Irish life, the more it crops up where it is not wanted. That little is said in the play about the murdered prostitute Crystal Clear, whose grave Maria and Rose are visiting, emphasises Behan's reflexive stress on historiographical silencing, on how certain, less palatable aspects of Irish society are 'cut off', yet made all the more conspicuous in the process. Even the name 'Crystal Clear' indicates how the dead woman's story has literally come to be unseen. Clear's death references the real-life, notorious 1925 murder in the Dublin Mountains of prostitute Lizzy O'Neill, also known as Honor Bright, whose memory is marked by a still-visible plaque on the city's Ticknock Road, and whose story could have admittedly been harnessed to greater effect in Behan's play, as it had 'unlimited potential in the hands of the man who had written *The Quare Fellow*', as Colbert Kearney remarked (*Kearney*, 141). O'Neill spanned two worlds in a small city, her death emblematic of an Ireland sharply divided by class, in which the wealthy and well-connected enjoyed a privileged relationship with the law:

> O'Neill, a country girl who, it is said, having become pregnant on coming to Dublin, turned to the oldest profession in order to support her illegitimate son. [...] Her body was found near the Lamb Doyle pub, at Ticknock in the Dublin Mountains, on 9 June 1925. She had been shot through the heart. Two men were charged with her murder on 1 February 1926. They were Garda Superintendent Leopold Dillon and Dr Patrick Purcell.[57]

Neither man was convicted of any involvement, nor was anyone else.[58] Like the makeshift cross anonymously etched on a stone at the spot where O'Neill's body was found, Maria Concepta and Rose of Lima's annual journey up the mountains to 'say a prayer and sing a hymn' for Clear thus takes the form of a protest as well as a pilgrimage, a ritual refusal to forget those who, in Cronin's words (cut from Simpson's production), 'didn't matter' (*CP*, 314). The wreaths they lay for her—sent from 'the queers' and 'the Protestant Prostitutes of the Donegal Pass'—suggest a non-sectarian unity amongst Ireland's marginalised, a defiant, hookean dissidence from those who, in Cronin's words, 'don't fall into any officially approved category of pityees' (*CP*, 268, 276).[59]

'THE MEASURE OF OUR FUTURE'

Behan's hinted, often oblique analogies and subterranean histories open out and pluralise the possible layers of meaning within (and beyond) the text, suggesting its unfinalisable multiplicity, the limited nature of what can or cannot be staged, and thus also the processes of selection and silencing with which historical narrative is inscribed. He draws our attention to the distortions attendant on Irish national and American global hegemonies. He assails two ostensibly very different societies: an insular, conservative Ireland and an outward-looking, consumerist America. These two – one busy refashioning its radical past to suit a stiflingly conformist present, the other promoting the apparently liberating yet ultimately illusory optimism of the American Dream – converge in Forest Lawn and its 'happy Eternal life', which proffers heaven purchasable in hard cash, which promises to make everything subservient to the monologic of profit (*CP*, 261). Both cultures 'sell' forms of 'death', their evasions and revisions, their epistemological trickery, proffering a barren vision of the present. In different ways then, they are both also grotesquely necrophiliac, as the theme of sex in graveyards, which Brannigan associates with the musings of Joyce's Leopold Bloom, suggests (*Brannigan*, 156). (Notably, the Hero character in the Irish version of Behan's play is called Leopold.) In this mix of themes that revolve around his key preoccupation with history's processes of silencing, Behan is struggling to respond to the diminishing purchase of the human in both late-capitalist America and post-Lemass Ireland. Teeming with life amongst headstones, *Richard's Cork Leg* seems to say, with Raymond Williams, that

> There are ideas, and ways of thinking, with the seeds of life in them, and there are others, perhaps deep in our minds, with the seeds of a general death. Our measure of success in recognizing these kinds, and in naming them making possible their common recognition, may be literally the measure of our future.[60]

Behan's play finds the 'seeds of life' on the margins, in the still resonant power of narratives of struggle and oppression, the peripheral but powerful in those histories as a site of radical potential. In this reading, *Richard's Cork Leg*, in its various forms, provides an insightful commentary on mid-century Ireland and America, which has yet more to offer than many critics have heretofore recognised, and a good deal more too for those who might seek to think again about the theatrical possibilities of this last of Behan's plays.

NOTES AND REFERENCES

Introduction

1. Brendan Behan to Sindbad Vail, June 1951 (*Letters*, 45).

2. For a discussion of Behan's alcoholism see Claire Lynch, 'The Drinker with the Writing Problem: Brendan Behan's anecdotal alcoholism', *Irish University Review*, vol. 44, no. 1, May 2014, pp. 165–81.

3. John Jordan, 'More about Brendan' (originally published in *Hibernia*, 4 February 1977), in Hugh McFadden (ed.), *Crystal Clear: The selected prose of John Jordan* (Dublin: The Lilliput Press, 2006), p. 170.

4. Augustine Martin, 'Brendan Behan', *Threshold*, no. 18, 1963, p. 22.

5. Joan Littlewood in conversation with Donal Foley, RTÉ radio, 1974, http://www.rte.ie/archives/exhibitions/925-brendan-behan/317556-brendan-behan-the-writer-the-rebel-and-the-rollicking-boy/ [accessed 22 January 2019].

6. Kenneth Tynan, 'The End of the Noose', *The Observer*, 27 May 1956, https://www.theguardian.com/theguardian/from-the-archive-blog/2014/mar/20/from-the-archive-brendan-behan/ [accessed 22 January 2019].

7. Irving Wardle, 'The Sad Death of Brendan Behan', *The Observer*, 22 March 1964, http://www.theguardian.com/news/2014/mar/23/observer-archive-sad-death-brendan-behan/ [accessed 22 January 2019].

8. The Druid production was directed by Jim Sheridan. *The Hostage* was also produced by Wonderland productions at the Pearse Centre, Dublin in 2009.

9. See also Maeve Murphy, 'Releasing the Hostage', *Theatre Ireland*, No. 13 (1987), 34–38.

10. Myles na Gopaleen, 'Cross Here', *CL*, 3 October 1957, p. 8.

11. This claim is further boosted by the notes, drafts, and typescripts for and of *Richard's Cork Leg* which were recently sold as part of 'The literary and personal archive of Brendan Behan', p. 208.

1 Brendan Behan's *Borstal Boy*

1. Maurice Richardson, 'Young Prisoners', in E.H. Mikhail (ed.), *The Art of Brendan Behan* (London: Vision, 1979), pp. 80ff.

2. See Seán McMahon (ed.), *The Best from The Bell: Great Irish writing* (Dublin: The O'Brien Press, 1978), pp. 83ff.

3. Seán Ó Faoláin, 'This Is Your Magazine' in McMahon (ed.), *The Best from The Bell*, p. 16.

4. I will use 'Brendan' to distinguish between the character in the text and 'Behan' the author.

5. See Maurice Sheridan, 'Within the Gates', in Mikhail (ed.), *The Art of Brendan Behan*, pp. 84ff.

6. Frank O'Connor in Mikhail (ed.), *The Art of Brendan Behan*, p. 90.

7. W.B. Yeats, *Essays and Introductions* (London: Macmillan, 1961), p. 526.

8. Frank O'Connor, 'The Future of Irish Literature', in David Pierce (ed.), *Irish Writing in the Twentieth Century: A reader* (Cork: Cork University Press, 2000), p. 502.

9. Ibid., p. 503.

10. Seán Ó Faoláin, 'Ah, Wisha! The Irish Novel', *Virginia Quarterly Review*, vol. 17, no. 2, Spring 1941, pp. 265–74.

11. See Clair Wills, *That Neutral Island: A cultural history of Ireland during the Second World War*, (London: Faber & Faber, 2007), pp. 290ff.

12. See for example Joe Cleary in *Outrageous Fortune: Capital and culture in modern Ireland* (Dublin: Field Day Publications, 2007).

13. See Aibhlín McCrann (ed.), *Memories, Milestones and New Horizons: Reflections on the regeneration of Ballymun* (Belfast: Blackstaff Press, 2008).

14. See Eamonn Hughes, '"The Fact of Me-ness": Autobiographical writing in the Revival period', in Margaret Kelleher (ed.), *Irish University Review: special issue, New Perspectives on the Irish Literary Revival*, vol. 33, no. 1, Spring/Summer 2003, pp. 28–45.

15. See Corey Phelps, 'Borstal Revisited' and Colbert Kearney 'Borstal Boy: A Portrait of the Artist as a Young Prisoner' in E.H. Mikhai (ed.), *The Art of Brendan Behan*, pp. 108ff.

16. See Richard Brown, '*Borstal Boy*: Structure and meaning' *Colby Quarterly*, vol. 21, no. 4, December 1985, pp. 188–97.

17. Edward Said, *Orientalism* (London: Penguin Books, 1978).

18. Fintan O'Toole, 'Culture Shock: Brendan Behan – playwright, novelist, terrorist', *Irish Times*, 6 September 2014, p. 9.

19. Patrick Colm Hogan, 'Brendan Behan on the Politics of Identity: Nation, culture, class, and human empathy in *Borstal Boy*', *Colby Quarterly*, vol. 35, no. 3, September 1999, pp. 163–4.

20. See Sylvère Lotringer, 'The Thin Man: An interview with Brendan Behan', *Field Day Review*, vol. 1, 2005, pp. 3–28.

2 Lessons of Detention

1. Oscar Wilde, *The Annotated Oscar Wild*, ed. H Montgomery Hyde (London: Orbis, 1982), p. 463.

2. The sentence that reads: 'It was a cold raw evening, and the light leaving the sky, wondering how it ever got into it' (*BB*, 30), provides ample evidence of Behan's talent for serious mimicry of Chandleresque description.

3. Virginia Woolf, *Orlando*, ed. Maria DiBattista (New York: Harcourt, Inc., 2006), p. 47.

4. Wilde, *The Annotated Oscar Wilde*, p. 463.

3 Bohemian Behan

1. Brendan Behan, 'Secret Scripture', *Irish Times*, 30 July 1960, p. 6.

2. Anthony Cronin, *No Laughing Matter: The life and times of Flann O'Brien* (New York: Fromm, 1989), pp. 90, 99.

3. Walter Benjamin, *Charles Baudelaire: A Lyric Poet in the Era of High Capitalism*, trans. Harry Zohn (London: Verso, 1997), pp. 35–66.

4. Peter Brooker, *Bohemia in London: The Social Scene of Early Modernism* (Basingstoke: Palgrave, Macmillan, 2004), p. viii.

5. Tyrus Miller, *Late Modernism: Politics, fiction, and the arts between the world wars* (Berkeley: University of California Press, 1999), p. 20.

6. Tim Pat Coogan, *The IRA* (Basingstoke: Palgrave Macmillan, 2005), pp. 128–9; J. Bowyer Bell, *The Secret Army: The IRA* (New Brunswick, NJ: Transaction, 1997), pp. 147–50.

7. Brian Hanley, '"Oh here's to Adolph Hitler": The IRA and the Nazis', *History Ireland*, vol. 13, no. 3, May/June 2005, pp. 31–35. https://www.historyireland.com/20th-century-contemporary-history/oh-heres-to-adolph-hitler-the-ira-and-the-nazis/

8. Brendan Behan, 'The Family Was in the Rising', *The Dubbalin Man* (Dublin: A & A Farmar, 1997), pp. 75–8.

9. Ibid., p. 75.

10. Brendan Behan, 'Letter to Seán Furlong', Intercepted 27 September 1942; Brendan Behan PF729326/V1, National Archives KV2/3181.

11. Seán Furlong, 'Letter to Fred May', Intercepted 27 September 1942; Brendan Behan PF729326/V1, National Archives KV2/3181.

12. Ibid., pp. 136, 92.

13. 'Letter to Seamus de Burca, 15 June 1943', in E.H. Mikhail (ed.), *The Letters of Brendan Behan* (London: Macmillan, 1992), p. 21.

14. Frederick May, *Sunlight and Shadow*, RTÉ National Symphony Orchestra, Cond. Robert Houlihan, RTÉ Lyric FM CD Recording, 2004.

15. Philip Graydon, 'Frederick May', in Harry White and Barra Boydell (eds) *Encyclopaedia of Music in Ireland* (Dublin: UCD Press, 2014), pp. 638–9. The work was not performed in Ireland until after the war, in the Phoenix Hall on 22 December 1946.

16. Harry White, *The Keeper's Recital: Music and cultural history in Ireland, 1770–1970* (Cork: Cork University Press in association with Field Day, 1998), p. 136.

17. Mark Fitzgerald, 'Inventing Identities: The case of Frederick May', in Mark Fitzgerald and John O'Flynn (eds), *Music and Identity in Ireland and Beyond* (Farnham: Ashgate, 2014), p. 100.

18. Ibid.

19. W.H. Auden, 'In Memory of Ernst Toller', in Edward Mendelson (ed.), *Collected Auden* (London: Faber, 2004), p. 249.

20. Fred May, 'Letter to Seán Furlong', Intercepted 27 September 1942; Brendan Behan PF729326/V1, National Archives KV2/3181.

21. Seán Furlong, 'Letter to Brendan Behan', Intercepted 27 September 1942; Brendan Behan PF729326/V1, National Archives KV2/3181.

22. Fred May, 'Letter to Seán Furlong', Intercepted 27 September 1942; Brendan Behan PF729326/V1, National Archives KV2/3181; *O'Sullivan*, p. 96.

23. *The Landlady*, MS, Mountjoy *c.*1943; Brendan Behan Estate.

24. 'Letter to Seamus de Burca, 16 August 1943', *Letters*, p. 24.

25. Ibid.

26. Seán Ó Briain, 'In Jail with Brendan Behan', in E.H. Mikhail (ed.), *Brendan Behan: Interviews and recollections*, vol. 1 (Dublin: Gill & Macmillan, 1982), pp. 16–18.

27. Ibid., p. 94.

28. Ó Briain, 'In Jail with Brendan Behan', p. 17.

29. Breandán Ó Beacháin, 'Jackeen ag Caoineadh na mBlascaod', *Comhar*, vol. 7, no. 10, October 1948, p. 10.

30. See Andrew McNeillie, 'The Dublin End: Anecdotes of Brendan Behan on Árainn', *Irish University Review*, vol. 44, no. 1, Spring/Summer 2014, pp. 59–77; Brendan Behan, 'Heart Turns West at Christmas', *Irish Press*, 24 December 1954, p. 4.

31. Brendan Behan, 'Oscar Wilde', trans. Donagh MacDonagh, *Irish Times,* 20 September 1952, p. 6.

32. Frank Harris, *Oscar Wilde* (London: Constable, 1938), p. viii.

33. Thomas O'Grady, 'Thanks Be to Joyce: Brendan Behan à Paris', in Martha C. Carpentier (ed.), *Joycean Legacies* (Basingstoke: Palgrave Macmillan, 2015), pp. 33–53.

34. Stephen Watt, 'Love and Death: A reconsideration of Behan and Genet', in Stephen Watt, Eileen Morgan and Shakir Mustafa (eds), *A Century of Irish Drama* (Bloomington: Indiana University Press, 2000), pp. 130–45.

35. Brendan Behan, *Poems and a Play in Irish*, ed. Proinsias Ní Dhorchaí (Dublin: The Gallery Press, 1981) p. 19.

36. Hannah Arendt, 'French Existentialism', in Susannah Young-Ah Gottlieb (ed.), *Reflections on Literature and Culture* (Stanford, CA: Stanford University Press, 2007), pp. 115–16.

37. Brendan Behan, 'After the Wake', *Points*, no. 8, December 1950/January 1951, pp. 52–6.

38. Ibid., p. 56.

39. Ibid., p. 52.

40. Brendan Behan, 'Bridewell Revisited', *Points*, nos. 11–12, Winter 1951–2, pp. 11–21.

41. Ibid., p. 15.

42. Ibid., p. 20–1.

43. Brendan Behan, 'Confessions of an Irish Rebel', Unpublished MS, Proscenium Press Archives, University of Delaware Library Special Collections, File 313, Series I, F7.

44. Anthony Roche, *Contemporary Irish Drama: From Beckett to McGuinness* (Basingstoke, Palgrave Macmillan, 2009), pp. 13–41.

45. Anthony Roche, *Contemporary Irish Drama: From Beckett to McGuinness* (Dublin: Gill & Macmillan, 1994), p. 23.

46. Alan Simpson, *Beckett and Behan and a Theatre in Dublin* (London: Routledge & Kegan Paul, 1962), p. 9.

47. Ibid., p. 8.

48. Ibid., p. 57.

49. John Ryan's magazine *Envoy* followed a similar pattern, publishing Behan and Beckett in its second issue, followed in later issues with work by Nathalie Sarraute, Martin Heidegger and an essay about Camus.

50. Deirdre McMahon's essay in this volume explores in more detail the grounds for aesthetic comparison between the work of Behan and Beckett, and situates Behan firmly within a European modernist tradition.

51. Theodor Adorno, *Aesthetic Theory*, trans. Robert Hullot-Kentor (London: Bloomsbury, 2013), p. 1.

4 Modernist Writer

1. 'The Disputed Authorship of Brendan Behan's *The Hostage*', Conference Paper, EGS Seminar Series, University College Dublin, 2012. The conference paper is derived from Chapter Two of Dr Clare's earlier PhD thesis, entitled 'The Stage Englishman in Irish Literature', which is held in UCD's James Joyce Library.

2. Stephen Watt, 'Love and Death: A reconsideration of Behan and Genet', in Stephen Watt, Eileen Morgan and Shakir Mustafa (eds), *A Century of Irish Drama* (Bloomington: Indiana University Press, 2000), pp. 130-45, at pp. 130-1.

3. Séamus de Búrca, *Brendan Behan: A Memoir* (Dublin: Proscenium Press, 1993), p. 12.

4. For discussion of Behan's early engagement with European modernism in the Dublin of his youth, and the formal and thematic similarities between Behan's *The Quare Fellow* and Eugene O'Neill's early expressionist play *The Hairy Ape*, see Deirdre McMahon, 'Hairy Apes and Quare Fellows: The legacy of Eugene O'Neill in the work of Brendan Behan', *The Eugene O'Neill Review Special Issue,* Audrey McNamara and Nelson O'Ceallaigh Ritschel (eds), vol. 39, no. 1, 2018, pp. 72–94.

5. Margaretta D'Arcy, *Loose Theatre: Memoirs of a guerrilla theatre activist* (Crewe: Trafford, 2005), p. 180. Cf. 'Hairy Apes and Quare Fellows', pp. 75–6.

6. I am grateful to Margaretta D'Arcy for this information.

7. Carolyn Swift, *Stage by Stage* (Dublin: Poolbeg Press, 1985), p. 138.

8. Lucy Collins (ed.), *Poetry by Women in Ireland: A critical anthology 1870–1970* (Liverpool: Liverpool University Press, 2012), pp. 44–6.

9. The original note is held in the Brendan Behan Papers (C1596), Manuscripts Division, Department of Rare Books and Special Collections, Princeton University Library. Sindbad Vail lived at the address noted from 1946–57.

10. 'After the Wake' was published in Vail's literary magazine *Points* (no. 8) in December 1950 and then by Denis Cotter in *Brendan Behan: Poems and stories* (Dublin: The Liffey Press, 1978).

11. See Anthony Roche, 'Beckett and Behan: Waiting for your man', in *Contemporary Irish Drama* (Basingstoke: Palgrave Macmillan, 2009), pp. 14, 19; John Brannigan, *Brendan Behan: Cultural nationalism and the revisionist writer* (Dublin: Four Courts Press, 2014), p. 62; Seán Ó Briain, 'In Jail with Brendan Behan', in E.H. Mikhail, *Brendan Behan: Interviews and recollections*, vol. 1 (Dublin: Gill and Macmillan, 1982), p. 17.

12. Colbert Kearney, 'Borstal Boy: A portrait of the artist as a young prisoner' *Ariel: a review of international English literature*, vol. 7, no. 2, 1976, p. 48.

13. For a discussion of modernism and memory theatre, see Jeanette R. Malkin, *Memory-Theater and Postmodern Drama* (Ann Arbor: University of Michigan Press, 1999), pp. 5–7.

14. Sylvère Lotringer, 'The Thin Man: An interview with Brendan Behan', *Field Day Review*, no.1, 2005, p. 25.

15. Quoted in ibid.

16. Ibid., p. 5.

17. Jean-Philippe Hentz, 'Brendan Behan's France: Encounters in Saint-Germain-de-Prés': *Journal of Franco-Irish Studies*, no. 1, 2008: 43–61, at pp. 49–51.

18. Anthony Roche, 'The "Irish" Translation of Samuel Beckett's *En Attendant Godot*', in S.E. Gontarski (ed.), *The Edinburgh Companion to Samuel Beckett and the Arts* (Edinburgh: Edinburgh University Press, 2014), pp. 199–208.

19. Alan Simpson, *Beckett and Behan and a Theatre in Dublin* (London: Routledge & Kegan Paul, 1962), pp. 8, 19, 20, 57.

20. Behan is paraphrasing from Eliot's letter to Ezra Pound, published in *The Townsman*, no. 1, July, 1938, entitled '"Five Points on Dramatic Writing" by T.S. Eliot', a copy of which is held at Exeter University Special Collections, MS 397/648.

21. Gerard Whelan with Carolyn Swift, *Spiked: Church-State Intrigue* and *The Rose Tattoo* (Dublin: New Island, 2002), pp. 37, 310.

22. Ian R. Walsh, *Experimental Irish Theatre after W.B. Yeats* (Basingstoke: Palgrave Macmillan, 2012), p. 171.

23. Ibid., p. 15; Desmond E.S. Maxwell, *A Critical History of Modern Irish Drama 1891–1980* (Cambridge: Cambridge University Press, 1984), p. 140.

24. Christopher Morash, *A History of Irish Theatre 1601–2000*, (Cambridge: Cambridge University Press, 2002) p. 186. Morash discusses the climate of censorship preceding these years, and the introduction of the 1929 Censorship of Publications Act.

25. Commenced in 1941 (*O'Sullivan*, p. 94), Behan's early draft of the opening pages of *Borstal Boy*, 'I Become A Borstal Boy', was published in *The Bell* in 1942. The finished autobiographical novel was published in 1958.

26. Anthony Roche, 'Beckett and Behan', pp. 17–18.

27. John Calder, *The Garden of Eros: The Story of the Paris Expatriates and the Post-War Literary Scene* (London: Calder Publications, 2013), pp. 50, 53, 77. *Merlin* editor Richard Seaver

quotes Behan as saying he had never heard of Beckett and was prompted to seek him out upon reading Seaver's 1952 essay on Beckett for *Merlin*: "Read your piece in *Merlin*", [Behan] was saying, "about this man Beckett. I'd never heard of him. If he's half as good as you make him out, I have to meet him': *The Tender Hour of Twilight: Paris in the '50s, New York in the '60s* (ed.) Jeannette Seaver (New York: Farrar, Straus & Giroux, 2012), p. 141. Given accounts of Behan having previously met Beckett, his widely documented friendship with Beckett's cousin John, and the fact that Beckett was already a published author raises questions around Seaver's account and suggests a healthy dose of irony on Behan's part.

28. The original of this letter is kept in the Pike Theatre Archive, MS 10813, TCD Manuscripts and Archives Research Library (Pike 10813/395/114).

29. Anthony Roche, 'Beckett and Behan', p. 18.

30. Anthony Roche rightly notes the overly negative tone that Beckett's biographer Deirdre Bair lends to Ulick O'Connor's original account of Beckett's visit to Behan. See Roche, *Contemporary Irish Drama* (2009), p. 18, Bair, *Samuel Beckett* (1990), pp. 591–2, *O'Connor*, p. 311.

31. In *Theater heute*, no. 5, May 1964, p. 57. Cf. George Craig et al., *The Letters of Samuel Beckett*, volume III (Cambridge: Cambridge University Press, 2014), p. 587.

32. Patrick Bixby, 'Narrating the No Man's Land: Deterritorializing Ireland and postcolonial identity in the trilogy', in *Samuel Beckett and the Postcolonial Novel* (Cambridge: Cambridge University Press, 2009), p. 160.

33. Ibid.

34. See discussion by Audrey Wasser on the novel genre and its ties to interiority, and the relation of that to Beckett's writing: 'From Figure to Fissure: Beckett's *Molloy, Malone Dies*, and *The Unamable*', *Modern Philology*, no. 109, 2011, pp. 248–9.

35. Stephen Watt, 'Love and Death', p. 135.

36. Ibid., p. 139.

37. Bernice Schrank, 'Brendan Behan's *Borstal Boy*: Politics in the vernaculars', *Brendan Behan: Irish University Review Special Issue*, vol. 44, no. 1, 2014, ed. John Brannigan, pp. 129–148, at p. 138.

38. Kearney, 'Borstal Boy: A Portrait of the Artist as a Young Prisoner', p. 48.

39. Samuel Beckett, *Molloy* (London: Faber & Faber, 2009), p. 9.

40. Ibid., p. 143.

41. Ibid., p. 4.

42. Brendan's approach into Dublin Bay invokes Woolf's *Orlando*, specifically the title character's 'raging and conflicting emotions' upon sighting the cliffs of England and 'The Tower of London [. . .]; Westminster Abbey [and] The Houses of Parliament', Virginia Woolf, *Orlando*, ed. Maria DiBattista (New York: Harcourt, 2006), pp. 120–2).

43. Beckett, *Molloy*, p. 5.

44. Ibid., p. 29.

45. In his translation of the ancient Irish verse, Ferguson writes: 'A PLENTEOUS place is Ireland for hospitable cheer, / Uileacán dubh O! / Where the wholesome fruit is bursting

from the yellow barley ear; / Uileacán dubh O! [and] Large and profitable are the stacks upon the ground, / Uileacán dubh O! / The butter and the cream do wondrously abound; / Uileacán dubh O!' Ferguson's insertion of the lament of 'Alas' (trans. Rev. Patrick S. Dinneen, *Foclóir Gaedhilge agus Béarla* (Dublin: Educational Company of Ireland, 1927), p. 1292) after each line suggests it is the 'Curled [...] ringleted, and plaited [...] captain[s] who come [...] sailing across the Irish sea' who will strip Ireland of its riches. Samuel Ferguson, 'The Fair Hills of Holy Ireland' in Padraic Colum (ed.) *An Anthology of Irish Verse*, (New York: Liveright Publishing Corporation, 1948), pp. 182–3.

46. John Mitchel, *Jail Journal; or, Five Years in British Prisons* (New York: *The Citizen*, 1854), p. 55.

47. Ibid., p. 57.

48. Ibid., p. 56.

49. Ibid., p. 85.

50. Colin Graham, *Deconstructing Ireland* (Edinburgh: Edinburgh University Press, 2001), p. 4.

51. Ibid.

52. Ibid., p. 3.

53. Dan Head was an IRA member who was killed in the War of Independence during the attack on the Customs House: Seán McCann *The World of Brendan Behan* (New York: Twayne Publishers, 1966), p. 32.

54. Graham, *Deconstructing Ireland*, p. 3.

55. Ibid.

56. Ibid., p. 4.

57. Qtd. in ibid.

58. For a comparison between *Waiting for Godot* and *The Quare Fellow*, see Roche 'Beckett and Behan', p. 22; Frank McGuinness, 'Saint Behan' in *Brendan Behan: Irish University Review Special Issue*, vol. 44, no. 1, 2014, ed. John Brannigan, p. 78.

59. Walsh, *Experimental Irish Theatre after W.B. Yeats*, p. 172.

60. Beckett, *Molloy*, p. 4.

61. For the significance of the fact that the identity cards outside each prisoner's cell are, effectively, blank from the point of view of a theatre audience, see Roche, 'Beckett and Behan', p. 27. Cf. Frank McGuinness, 'Saint Behan', p. 79.

62. John Brannigan, 'Belated Behan: Brendan Behan and the cultural politics of memory', *Éire-Ireland*, no. 37, 2002, pp. 39–52, at pp. 48–9.

63. Robert Hogan and Michael J. O'Neill (eds), *Joseph Holloway's Abbey Theatre: A selection from his unpublished journal, Impressions of a Dublin Playgoer* (Carbondale: Southern Illinois University Press, 1967), p. 274, n. 1, and *O'Sullivan*, p. 176.

64. Swift, *Stage by Stage*, p. 105.

65. Roche, 'Beckett and Behan', p. 16.

66. Swift, *Stage by Stage*, p. 105.

67. Lawrence J. McCaffrey, 'Seán Ó Faoláin and Irish Identity', *New Hibernia Review*, no. 9, 2005, p. 145.

68. Watt, 'Brendan Behan, Borscht Belt Comedian', Brannigan (ed.), *Special Issue*, pp. 149–64.

69. Stephen Watt, 'Love and Death', p. 134.

70. Qtd. in Walsh, *Experimental Irish Theatre after W.B. Yeats*, p. 167.

71. Watt, 'Love and Death', p. 134.

72. Ian R. Walsh, p. 174.

73. Anthony Roche, 'Beckett and Behan', p.21.

5 Eros And Liberation

1. Oscar Wilde, *The Annotated Oscar Wilde*, ed. H Montgomery Hyde (London: Orbis, 1982), pp. 424–63.

2. Georg Lukács, *The Historical Novel*, trans. Hannah and Stanley Mitchell (London: Merlin Press, 1962), p. 266.

3. Jean Genet, *Miracle of the Rose*, trans. Bernard Frechtman (London: Faber, 1973).

4. Alan Sinfield, *On Sexuality and Power* (New York: Columbia University Press, 2004), p. 54.

5. Kadji Amin, 'Anachronizing the Penitentiary, Queering the History of Sexuality', *GLQ: A Journal of Lesbian and Gay Studies*, vol. 19, no. 3, 2013, pp. 301–40 at p. 303.

6. Ibid. p. 307.

7. Ibid. p. 305.

8. Heather Love, *Feeling Backward: Loss and the politics of queer history* (Cambridge, MA: Harvard University Press, 2007), p. 29.

9. Cited in *Kearney*, p. 84–5. The manuscript, entitled *The Courteous Borstal*, is held in the Morris Library at Southern Illinois University. In a very useful response to the version of this essay presented at the Brendan Behan conference held in Rome, John Brannigan pointed out that this section of the manuscript is heavily marked and over-written with multiple revisions, a typographical symptom, perhaps, of Behan's intellectual and emotional unease with the rigidities of sexual definition he was invoking.

10. Eve Kosofsky Sedgwick, *The Epistemology of the Closet* (New York: Penguin, 1990), pp. 1–22.

11. Alan Sinfield, *The Wilde Century* (London: Cassell, 1995), p. 3.

12. Cited in Rosemary Hennessy, *Profit and Pleasure: Sexual identities in late capitalism* (London: Routledge, 2000), p. 215.

13. Herbert Marcuse, *Eros and Civilisation* (New York: Vintage, 1962), p. 187.

14. Ibid., p. 184.

15. Frantz Fanon, *The Wretched of the Earth*, trans. Constance Farrington (London: Penguin, 1991), pp. 119–49.

16. Alan Sinfield, *The Wilde Century*, pp. 1–3.

17. Herbert Marcuse, *Eros and Civilisation*, p. 159.

18. Ibid., pp. 157–79; Fanon, *The Wretched of the Earth*, pp. 166–99.

19. Bernice Shrank, 'Brendan Behan's *Borstal Boy*: Politics in the vernaculars', *Irish University Review*, vol. 44, no. 1, Summer 2014, pp. 129–48 at p. 129.

20. *Kearney*, p. 95.

6 Brendan Behan's Irish-Language Poetry

1. See Colbert Kearney, 'Filíocht Bhreandáin Uí Bheacháin', *Scríobh*, no. 3, 1978, pp. 44–57 and Colbert Kearney, *The Writings of Brendan Behan*, (Dublin: Gill &Macmillan, 1977). Ten poems were published in *Comhar* between 1946 and 1952. Nine were reprinted in the April edition of *Comhar*, 1964. *Poems and a Play in Irish*, edited by Proinsias Ní Dhorchaí (Dublin: Gallery Press, 1981), contains thirteen short lyrics in total.

2. Máirtín Ó Cadhain, *As an nGéibheann: Litreacha chuig Tomás Bairéad* (Dublin: Sairséal & Dill, 1973), p. 201.

3. Seán Ó Tuama, *Nuabhéarsaíocht 1939–1949* (Dublin: Sairséal & Dill, 1950), p. 10.

4. Kearney, 'Filíocht Bhreandáin Uí Bheacháin', pp. 46–9.

5. Richard Rankin Russell, 'Brendan Behan's Lament for Gaelic Ireland: "The Quare Fellow"', *New Hibernia Review/Iris Éireannach Nua*, vol. 6, no. 1, 2001, pp. 73–93.

6. Seán Ó Briain, 'I Knew Brendan Behan', *Kerryman*, 23 May 1964, pp. 6–7.

7. Kearney, 'Filíocht Bhreandáin Uí Bheacháin', p. 48.

8. Risteárd Ó Foghludha (ed.), *Ar Bruach na Coille Muaire: Liam Dall Ó hIfearnáin agus a shaothar fileata* (Dublin: Oifig an tSoláthair, 1939), p. 58. As a published translation of this poem in its entirety is not available, the current author has made a literal translation of this verse for illustrative purposes.

9. Ibid., p. 100.

10. Breandán Ó Buachalla, *Aisling Ghéar: Na Stíobhartaigh agus an t-aos léinn, 1603–1788* (Dublin: An Clóchomhar, 1996), pp. 442–4.

11. Brendan Behan, 'Aithríghe', *Comhar*, vol. 6, no. 10, 1945, p. 5.

12. Niall Murphy, '"Social Sinn Féin and Hard Labour": The journalism of W.P. Ryan and Jim Larkin 1907–14', *Irish Studies Review*, vol. 22, no. 1, 2014, pp. 43–52.

13. Valentin Iremonger, *Horan's Field: and Other Reservations* (Dublin: Dolmen Press, 1972).

14. Donagh McDonagh, 'A Jackeen's Lament for the Blaskets', Noel Duffy and Theo Dorgan (eds), *Watching the River Flow: A century in Irish poetry* (Dublin: Poetry Ireland, 1999), p. 131.

15. Mark Quigley, 'Modernity's Edge: Speaking silence on the Blasket Islands', *Interventions: International journal of postcolonial studies*, vol. 5, no. 3, 2003, pp. 382–406

16. Kearney discusses the connotations of the words 'rannaire' and 'file' and the lack of English-language equivalents 'to differentiate between the poetical practitioner and the poet' (*Kearney*, p. 57).

17. Patrick Pearse, 'About Literature', *An Claidheamh Soluis*, 26 Bealtaine 1906, p. 6.

18. Ibid., p. 7.

19. Ulick O'Connor's translation of this line of the poem is more literal: 'If a poet came to stir these embers' (*O'Connor*, p. 130).

20. Louis de Paor, 'Modern Poetry in Irish 1939–2000', in Philip O'Leary and Margaret Kelleher (eds), *The Cambridge History of Irish Literature, Vol. II*, (Cambridge: Cambridge University Press, 2006), p. 326.

21. Barry McCrea, *Languages of the Night: Minor languages and the imagination in twentieth-century Ireland and Europe* (New Haven and London: Yale University Press, 2015), pp. 64–9.

22. Lillis Ó Laoire, 'Dearg Dobhogtha Cháin/The Indelible Mark of Cain: Sexual dissidence in the poetry of Cathal Ó Searcaigh', in Éibhear Walshe (ed.) *Sex, Nation and Dissent in Irish Writing* (Cork: Cork University Press, 1997), pp. 226–7.

23. For an excellent discussion of Ó Searcaigh's transgressive reimagining of traditional sources see Ó Laoire, 'Dearg Dobhogtha Cháin'.

24. Originally published as 'Do Sheán Ó Súilleabháin' ('To Seán Ó Suilleabháin') in *Comhar* in August 1949 with the following explanatory note: 'Oscar Wilde, Poète et Dramaturge, né à Dublin le 15 octobre, 1856, est mort dans cette maison le 30 novembre, 1900' (Behan, *Comhar*, vol. 8, Lúnasa, 1949, p. 14).

25. de Paor, 'Modern Poetry in Irish 1939–2000', p. 325.

26. McCrea, *Languages of the Night*, p. 67.

27. Geraldine Meaney, Mary O'Dowd and Bernadette Whelan, *Reading the Irish Woman: Studies in cultural encounter and exchange 1714–1960* (Liverpool: Liverpool University Press, 2013), pp. 130–75.

28. J.J. Lee, *Ireland 1912–1985: Politics and society* (Cambridge: Cambridge University Press, 1989), pp. 314–15.

29. See Seán Ó Tuama, *An Grá in Amhráin na nDaoine: Léiriú téamúil* (Dublin: An Clóchomhar, 1960), p. 31.

30. Ó Briain, 'I Knew Brendan Behan', pp. 6–7.

31. Julia Carlson, *Banned in Ireland: Censorship and the Irish writer* (London: Routledge, 1990), pp. 151-7.

32. Brendan Behan, 'The Language', *Irish Times*, 17 January 1961, p. 5.

33. Gogan, a lexicographer as well as a poet, was reported to have declared 'Tabharfaidh mise an Ghaeilge cheart ar "existentialism" daoibh … Bithiúnachas!' quoted in Tomás Mac Síomóin, 'Stoirm Scéine agus Dún Uí Dhireáin', in Caoimhín Mac Giolla Léith (ed.), *Cime mar Chách: Aistí ar Mháirtín Ó Direáin* (Dublin: Coiscéim, 1993) p. 29.

34. Gan ainm, 'Scrúdú Coinsiais', *Comhar*, vol. 11, no. 3, 1952, pp. 12–13.

35. Cian Ó hÉigeartaigh and A. Nic Gearailt, *Sáirséal agus Dill 1947–1981: Scéal foilsitheora* (Indreabhán: Chó Iar-Chonnacht, 2014), pp. 116–26.

36. Riobard Mac Góráin, 'Breandán Ó Beacháin: "Nach bhfuilimse in ann Gaeilge a scríobh?"', *Comhar*, vol. 43, no. 3, 1984, pp. 10–12.

37. Brian Fitch, *Beckett and Babel: An investigation into the status of bilingual work* (Toronto: University of Toronto Press, 1988), p. 156.

7 Brendan Behan's *The Hostage*

1. See Declan Kiberd, 'Introduction' to *Poems and a Play in Irish* (*PPI*, pp. 9–11). See also Ríona Ní Fhrighil, 'Brendan Behan's Irish Language Poetry' and Deirdre McMahon, 'Brendan Behan: Modernist writer', in this volume.

2. Richard Wall, '*An Giall* and *The Hostage* Compared', *Modern Drama*, no. 18, 1975, pp. 165–72.

3. See Lawrence Venuti, *The Translator's Invisibility: A history of translation* (Abingdon: Routledge, 2008 [2005]).

4. See for instance Susan Bassnett and André Lefevere, *Constructing Cultures: Essays on Literary Translation* (Cleveton, Toronto, Sydney and Johannesburg: Multilingual Matters, 1998).

5. See Phyllis Zatlin, *Theatrical Translation and Film Adaptation: A practitioner's approach* (Cleveton, Buffalo and Toronto: Multilingual Matters, 2005).

6. See for instance J.W. Hokenson and M. Munson, *The Bilingual Text: History and theory of literary self-translation* (Manchester and Kinderhook: St. Jerome Publishing, 2007); or P. López López-Gay, *(Auto)traducción y (re)creación: 'Un pájaro quemado vivo' de Agustín Gómez Arcos* (Almeria: Instituto de Estudios Almerienses, 2005); or the more recent A. Ferraro and R. Grutman (dir.), *L'autotraduction littéraire: Perspectives théoriques* (Paris: Garnier, 2016). The topic has also been the subject of a seminar curated by the ITEM (Institut des Textes et Manuscrits Modernes) in association with the ENS and the CNRS in Paris: http://www.item. ens.fr/sem-multilinguisme-2017-2018 [accessed 24 January 2019].

7. George Steiner, *After Babel: Aspects of language and translation* (Oxford: Oxford University Press, 1992 [1975]), pp 124–8.

8. Paul Ricoeur, *La mémoire, l'histoire, l'oubli* (Paris: Seuil, 2000). Translated into English as *Memory, History Forgetting*, trans. Kathleen Blamey and David Pellauer (Chicago: University of Chicago Press, 2004).

9. Declan Kiberd, 'Introduction', in *PPI*, pp. 9–11, at p. 11.

10. Susan Bassnett, 'Translation and Creativity', in Susan Bassnet and Peter Bush, *The Translator as Writer* (London: Continuum, 2006), p. 180.

11. Kiki Gounardidou, 'Introductory Remarks: The visibility of theatre translation', *Metamorphoses: A journal of literary translation*, vol. 9, no. 1, Spring 2001, pp. 10–14.

12. Nadine Holdsworth, *Joan Littlewood's Theatre* (Cambridge: Cambridge University Press, 2011).

13. Antoine Berman, *L'épreuve de l'étranger* (Paris: Gallimard, 1984).

14. Clifford Landers, *Literary Translation: A practical guide* (Cleveton, Buffalo and Toronto: Multilingual Matters, 2001), p. 104.

15. For conditions in the Damer see Breandán Ó hEithir's *Féach* report which dates from 1969. The webpage highlights the physical state of the building: 'Cé go bhfuil an amharclann fuar agus na soilse go dona, "tá croí éigin san áit". An fadhb is mó atá acu ná daoine a mhealladh isteach.' [Although the theatre is cold and the lighting bad there is a certain heart in the place]. https://www.rte.ie/archives/2014/1006/650380-inside-the-damer-theatre-1969/ [accessed 9 January 2018].

16. Oxford English Dictionary online, http://www.oed.com.ezproxy.univ-paris3.fr/view/ Entry/204844?redirectedFrom=translation&, viewed 12 September 2018.

17. Seamus Heaney and Robert Hass, *Sounding Lines: The Art of Translating Poetry*, http:// townsendcenter.berkeley.edu/sites/default/files/publications/OP20_Sounding_Lines.pdf [accessed 9 January 2018].

18. Christine Raguet, *De la lettre à l'esprit: traduction ou adaptation?* (Paris: Presses de la Sorbonne Nouvelle, Revue Palimpsestes, n°16, 2004), p. 10.

19. André Lefevere, *Translation, Rewriting, and the Manipulation of Literary Fame* (London and New York: Routledge, 1992), p. 9.

20. Rainier Grutman, 'Self-translation', in Mona Baker and Gabriela Saldanha (eds), *Routledge Encyclopedia of Translation Studies* (London and New York: Routledge, 2011), pp. 257–60, at p. 257.

21. Valeria Sperti, 'L'autotraduction littéraire: enjeux et problématiques', *Revue Italienne d'Etudes françaises*, http://journals.openedition.org/rief/1573#ftn13 [accessed 12 January 2018].

22. Barnes, Clive, 'Theatrical Curiosity of Behan's "Hostage": Timely Theme in Eve Untimely Fashion Ironic Tone Pervades Tragedy About I.R.A.', *New York Times*, 11 Oct 1972, p.50.

23. Anthony Cordingly and C. Frigau-Manning, *Collaborative Translation: From the Renaissance to the digital age* (London and NewYork: Bloomsbury, 2017).

24. Anthony Cordingly and C. Frigau-Manning, 'What Is Collaborative Translation?', in *Collaborative Translation*, electronic edition, loc 279–366.

25. Michel Foucault, 'Qu'est-ce qu'un auteur?', *Bulletin de la Société Française de Philosophie*, vol. 63, no. 3, 1969, pp. 73–104.

26. Cordingly, and Frigau-Manning, 'What Is Collaborative Translation?', loc 376.

27. Busáras was built between 1947 and 1953 by Michael Scott in the style of Le Corbusier. It won the RIAI gold medal for architecture for 1953–5. http://www.irisharchitectureawards.ie/ gold-medal/winner/busaras [accessed 13 February 2018].

28. See foclóir.ie, http://www.teanglann.ie/ga/fgb/abú [accessed 27 January 2018].

29. Here I am using a distinction made by Valeria Sperti, see note 21.

30. Pascale Casanova makes this distinction in *La langue mondiale* (Paris: Le Seuil, 2015).

31. See the Irish-language poet Biddy Jenkinson's refusal to have her work translated into English in Ireland.

32. Paul Ricoeur, *L'écriture de l'histoire et la représentation du passé*, Conférence Marc Bloch, 13 Juin 2000, *Annales HSS*, Juillet-Août 2000.

33. Paul Ricoeur, *Philosophie de la volonté II: Finitude et culpabilté* (Paris: Aubier 1988 [1960]), p. 64.

8 Brendan Behan and Elie Wiesel

1. Cian Ó hÉigeartaigh agus Aoileann Nic Gearailt, *Sáirséal agus Dill 1947–1981: Scéal foilsitheora* (Conamara: Cló Iar-Chonnacht, 2014), p. 115.

2. Máire Ní Chinnéide, *An Damer: Stair amharclainne* (Baile Átha Cliath: Gael Linn, 2008), p. 27.

3. Ibid.

4. Behan is quoted in Richard Wall, 'Introduction', in Richard Wall (ed.), *An Giall/The Hostage* (Washington, DC: Catholic University of America Press, 1987), pp. 20–1.

5. Ibid., p. 19.

6. Ibid., p. 106.

7. Ibid., p. 125.

8. Elie Wiesel, 'An Interview Unlike any Other', in *A Jew Today* (New York: Random House, 1978), pp. 21–2.

9. Ibid., p. 22.

10. Ibid., pp. 22–3.

11. Elie Wiesel, *Night*, Trans. Marion Wiesel, (New York: Hill & Wang, 2006), pp. 13–14.

12. See Robert Franciosi, 'Introduction', in Robert Franciosi (ed.), *Elie Wiesel: Conversations*, (Jackson: University Press of Mississippi, 2002) pp. ix–x.

13. François Mauriac, 'Foreword', in Wiesel, *Night*, pp. 20–4.

14. Ellen S. Fine, *The Legacy of Night: The literary universe of Elie Wiesel* (Albany: State University of New York Press, 1982), p. 10.

15. Harry Cargas, *Conversations with Elie Wiesel* (South Bend IN: Justice Books, 1992), p. 86.

16. Elie Wiesel, *Dawn* (New York: Fontana Books, 1973), p. 22.

17. Ibid., p. 30.

18. Ibid., pp. 31, 33–4.

19. Ibid., p. 11.

20. Ibid., pp. 11–12.

21. Ibid., pp. 12–13.

22. Ibid., p. 7.

23. Ibid., p. 58.

24. Ibid., pp. 67.

25. Ibid., p. 77.

26. Ibid., p. 81.

27. Ibid., p. 92.

28. Ibid., p. 96.

29. Ibid. pp. 9–10.

30. Ibid., p. 96.

31. Robert McAfee Brown, *Elie Wiesel: Messenger to All Humanity* (Notre Dame: University of Notre Dame Press, 1983), pp. 63–4.

32. One French critic, Luc Estang, envisaged the possibility of *Dawn* being staged in the form of a trial that took place over the course of one long night. See Fine, *The Legacy of Night*, p. 38.

33. Eddie Golden is quoted in *O'Connor*, p. 294.

34. Behan, *Poems and a Play in Irish*, p. 64.

35. Brendan Behan, *An Giall and The Hostage*, ed. Richard Wall (Washington: Catholic University of America Press, 1987), p. 62.

36. O'Toole, 'Culture Shock: Brendan Behan – playwright, novelist, terrorist'.

9 'Not Exactly Patterned in the Same Mould'

1. Declan Kiberd, *Inventing Ireland: The literature of the modern nation* (London: Vintage Books, 1995), p. 161.

2. Enrico Terrinoni, 'Humour in the Prison: Brendan Behan confesses', *epiphany*, Online Journal of the Faculty of Arts and Social Sciences, vol. 1, no. 1, Fall 2008, pp. 62–79, at p. 66.

3. Brendan Behan, 'Brendan Behan on Joyce'. A lecture delivered before the James Joyce Society at the Gotham Book Mart in New York City, 1962, (All quotes in this article are taken from the published transcript of this lecture, which is not paginated. The numerous misspellings have not been corrected.) Here he was echoing what Frank Budgen reported were Joyce's words:

> I enquired about *Ulysses*. Was it progressing?
> 'I have been working hard on it all day,' said Joyce.
> 'Does that mean that you have written a great deal?' I said.
> 'Two sentences,' said Joyce.
> I looked sideways but Joyce was not smiling. I thought of Flaubert.
> 'You have been seeking the mot juste?' I said.
> 'No,' said Joyce. 'I have the words already. What I am seeking is the perfect order of words in the sentence. There is an order in every way appropriate. I think I have it.'

Frank Budgen, *James Joyce and the Making of 'Ulysses' and Other Writings* (London: Oxford University Press, 1972), p. 20.

4. Colbert Kearney, 'Borstal Boy: A Portrait of the Artist as a Young Prisoner', *Ariel: A review of international English literature* (Calgary, Alberta), vol. 2, no. 2, April 1976, pp. 47–62. Later

republished in E.H. Mikhail (ed.), *The Art of Brendan Behan* (New York: Barnes & Noble, 1979), pp. 108–22.

5. Terrinoni, 'Humour in the Prison: Brendan Behan Confesses', p.70.

6. Bart Moore-Gilbert, *Postcolonial Life-writing: Culture, politics and self-representation* (New York: Routledge, 2009), p. 28.

7. Ibid., p. 29.

8. Desmond Ryan, 'Still Remembering Sion', *University Review*, vol. 5. no. 2, Summer 1968, 245–52, at p. 245.

9. The text of Behan's lecture is riddled with misspellings. In this brief extract we find 'Beech' for 'Beach', Theatre de Louvre for 'Théatre de l'Oeuvre', 'Boulevard Cliché' should be 'Rue de Clichy'.

10. 'An Irishman's Diary', *Irish Times*, 4 July 1960, p. 4.

11. Sylvia Beach, *Shakespeare and Company* (Lincoln NE: University of Nebraska Press, 1991), p. 164.

12. James Joyce, *A Portrait of the Artist as a Young Man* (London: Paladin, 1999), p. 55.

13. See Anthony MacDonnell, 'Two Dublin Tragedies', *Evening Herald*, 26 November 1967, p. 6.

14. Myles na Gopaleen, *Cruiskeen Lawn*, *Irish Times*, 3 January 1959, p. 9.

15. Breandán Ó Beacháin, 'Buíochas le Joyce', *Comhar*, vol. 8, uimh 8, Lúnasa 1949, p. 14. Behan published the poem under the title 'Buíochas do James Joyce' in his *Brendan Behan's Island* (*BBI*, p. 179).

16. Declan Kiberd, 'Review of *The Art of Brendan Behan*', *Review of English Studies*, New Series, vol. 33, no. 130, May 1982, p. 238.

17. Thomas O'Grady, 'Thanks Be To Joyce: Brendan Behan à Paris', in Martha C. Carpentier (ed.), *Joycean Legacies* (London: Palgrave, 2015), pp. 33–54, at p. 48.

18. Ibid., p. 38.

19. Ibid., p. 48.

20. Joyce, *A Portrait*, p. 33.

21. In a 1957 letter, Behan writes: 'I was excommunicated from the Catholic Church when I was arrested and refused to disavow the Irish Republican Army in prison, and I think the book tells of my loneliness in exile from the only church I had ever known, or taken seriously, the church of my people, of my ancestors hunted in the mountains, and of my bitterness about this' (*Letters*, p. 114).

22. As he put it in a letter dated 10 January 1960 to the *Sunday Times*: 'The Catholic Herald and The Tablet recognise my work as that of a Catholic. Which I am, though a bad one. I could not write as I do if I were not some kind of a one' (*Letters*, p. 174).

23. Bryan McMahon, 'Brendan Behan: A vital human being. A memoir' in E.H. Mikhail (ed.), *Brendan Behan: interviews and recollections*, Volume 2 (Dublin: Gill & Macmillan, 1982), pp. 249–54, at p. 252.

24. Joyce is quoted in Patricia Hutchins, *James Joyce's World* (London: Methuen, 1957), p. 139.

10 Secret Scriptures

1. Ruben Borg, Paul Fagan and Werner Huber, 'Editors' Introduction', in Ruben Borg, Paul Fagan and Werner Huber (eds), *Flann O'Brien: Contesting Legacies* (Cork: Cork University Press, 2014), p. 3.

2. Brendan Behan, 'Secret Scripture', *Irish Times*, 30 July 1960, p. 6.

3. Carol Taaffe, *Ireland Through the Looking-Glass: Flann O'Brien, Myles na gCopaleen and Irish cultural debate* (Cork: Cork University Press, 2008), p. 127; in reference to the sentiment's earlier articulation in Anthony Cronin, *No Laughing Matter: The life and times of Flann O'Brien* (London: Grafton, 1989), p. vii.

4. Hugh Kenner, *A Colder Eye: The modern Irish writers* (New York: Knopf, 1983), p. 255.

5. 'The Quare Fellow', *Irish Times*, 20 March 2014, p. 15.

6. Declan Kiberd, *The Irish Writer and the World* (Cambridge: Cambridge University Press, 2005), p. 38.

7. Kiberd promotes Behan and O'Nolan as 'exemplary exponents' of the twentieth-century bilingual tradition in Irish writing that 'rejected the stark choice [of writing in Irish or English] as a constricting and unnecessary decision' (ibid., p. 67). Elsewhere, John Brannigan compares them as writers who contest the cultural nationalism of their 'precursors and patrons' through anti-romantic modes. John Brannigan, *Brendan Behan, Cultural Nationalism and the Revisionist Writer* (Dublin: Four Courts Press, 2002), p. 55.

8. Joseph Brooker has called for cultural contextual analyses that 'pursue a more intensive, historically informed understanding of O'Nolan' in 'juxtaposition with his peers' such as Denis Devlin, Brian Coffey, Niall Sheridan, Niall Montgomery, R.M. Smyllie, Patrick Kavanagh and Brendan Behan. Joseph Brooker, 'Ploughmen without Land: Flann O'Brien and Patrick Kavanagh', in Julian Murphet, Rónán McDonald and Sascha Morrell (eds), *Flann O'Brien & Modernism* (New York: Bloomsbury, 2014), pp. 93–4.

9. A complementary approach, which is beyond the scope of the present essay, might also consider the contrary case of the images of Brian O'Nolan, 'Myles na Gopaleen' and 'Flann O'Brien' that are constructed in Behan's column writing for the *Irish Press* and elsewhere. Such an inquiry might take Behan's suggestive catechism at the close of his 1960 review as a point of departure:

> Q. Who is Flann O'Brien?
> A. Brian Nolan.
> Q. Who is Brian Nolan?
> A. Myles na Gopaleen.
> Q. What did these three men do?
> A. They wrote three books called 'At Swim-Two-Birds'. (Behan, 'Secret Scripture', p. 6)

10. Acknowledging standard critical caveats about not confusing the intentions and motivations of literary figures with their creators, throughout this essay I refer to 'Myles' rather than O'Nolan for those stances, attitudes and poses struck by that persona in the *Cruiskeen Lawn* columns, even in those instances in which the distinction appears to be minimal (as it was increasingly for 'Myles' and O'Nolan throughout the 1950s and '60s).

11. John Ryan, *Remembering How We Stood: Bohemian Dublin at the mid-century* (New York: Taplinger, 1975), p. xiv.

12. 'Refused to Leave Restaurant', *Irish Times*, 3 April 1954, p. 9.

13. They were early stablemates at Seán Ó Faoláin's *The Bell*, which published a series of 'Flann O'Brien' essays from 1940–1941 as well as Behan's first notable literary work, 'I Become a Borstal Boy' in June 1942. After his prison release in 1946, Behan 'began to socialise in more bohemian circles, forming a kind of loose coterie with Anthony Cronin, John Ryan, Flann O'Brien, Alan Simpson, Carolyn Swift, Seán O'Sullivan and (briefly, before they quarrelled) Patrick Kavanagh, in the emerging literary pubs of Dublin' (*Brannigan*, p. 31). They were both published by Ryan's *Envoy* in 1950; *Comhar*, the Irish-language magazine where O'Nolan's brother Caoimhín also published, was Behan's 'main source of patronage in 1951'; and by 1952 Myles' editor at the *Irish Times* Robert (Bertie) Smyllie, 'had taken a great liking' to Behan, and began to give him writing assignments (*O'Sullivan*, pp. 160, 168).

14. Matthew Brown, 'The Trials of Patrick Kavanagh', *New Hibernia Review*, vol. 15, no. 1, p. 36.

15. G.A. Olden, 'More Irish Comedies Wanted on R.E.', Radio Review, *Irish Times*, 1 April 1954, p. 4.

16. Myles na Gopaleen, 'Faustus', *Cruiskeen Lawn*, *Irish Times*, 3 April 1954, p. 10 [Hereafter *Cruiskeen Lawn*, *Irish Times* abbreviated as *CL*].

17. Myles na Gopaleen, 'A Square Root', *CL*, 6 October 1954, p. 4.

18. Sarah Cole, *Modernism, Male Friendship, and the First World War* (Cambridge: Cambridge University Press, 2003), p. 3.

19. Anthony Cronin, *No Laughing Matter*, p. 206. Cronin notes that after the deaths in 1956 of his mother and his close friend Dickie McManus (one of his 'few real human contacts'), O'Nolan 'had begun at this point to see a good deal of Brendan Behan'. Ibid., pp. 205–6.

20. Myles na Gopaleen, 'Behanism', *CL*, 23 July 1956, p. 6.

21. *The Irish Times* announcement of Behan's Radio Éireann broadcasts introduces him as 'a house-painter by trade and a poet by inclination' (qtd. in *O'Sullivan*, p. 162). Even the paper's report on his marriage rehearses this motif: 'Brendan is a painter, too, of course, though his work has been seen more often on the shop-fronts of the city and in the residential flats of Ballsbridge'. Quidnunc, 'An Irishman's Diary', *Irish Times*, 19 February 1955, p. 8.

22. Carol Taaffe, *Ireland Through the Looking-Glass*, pp. 141, 142.

23. Flann O'Brien, *The Complete Novels* (New York: Everyman's Library, 2007), p. 116. Behan seems to have approved of the poem, as he quotes it in full in *Brendan Behan's Island* in a section about Guinness: 'A friend of mine, Flann O'Brien, who wrote the brilliant novel, *At Swim-Two-Birds*, has a little poem about it in that book; it's called "The Workman's Friend"' (p. 32).

24. Maebh Long, *Assembling Flann O'Brien* (London: Bloomsbury, 2014), p. 43.

25. Paul Fagan and Ruben Borg, '*The Parish Review*: Founders' Note', *The Parish Review: Journal of Flann O'Brien studies*, vol. 1, no. 1, Summer 2012, p. 5.

26. O'Nolan had been profiled, for example, in 'Eire's Columnist', *TIME Magazine*, vol. 42, no. 8, 23 August 1943, pp. 30–1.

27. Myles na Gopaleen, 'A Liquid Acid', *CL*, 18 May 1957, p. 8.

28. Myles na Gopaleen, 'Brendan Being', *CL*, 4 September 1957, p. 6.

29. Behan proclaimed the opening night of the Royal Court Theatre's 1958 double bill of *Krapp's Last Tape* and *Endgame* 'very funny; the more truthful because it's the more funny, and the more funny because it's the more truthful. Noel Coward could have done this if he'd gone to T.C.D.' 'London Letter', *Irish Times*, 30 October 1958, p. 6. For an account of Behan and Beckett's encounters in Paris in 1952, see *O'Sullivan*, p. 148.

30. Brendan Behan, 'Secret Scripture', p. 6.

31. The *Irish Times* Paris correspondent reports on the Behans as celebrities: 'Brendan Behan and his wife, Beatrice, were looking wonderfully well on Monday, after their holidays on Ibiza, during which he finished his recently commissioned Gaelic play. He stopped off in Paris to discuss the [adaptation of the *Quare Fellow* to be] produced here in October.' Desmond F. Ryan, 'Letter from Paris: Blood, tears and ballet', *Irish Times*, 14 April 1958, p. 6.

32. Myles na Gopaleen, 'Cross Here', *CL*, 3 October 1957, p. 8.

33. Myles na Gopaleen, 'Last Friday', *CL*, 11 May 1960, p. 8.

34. Myles na Gopaleen, 'The Author Diets', *CL*, 14 August 1959, p. 8.

35. Myles na Gopaleen, 'Rate for the Job?', *CL*, 30 March 1959, p. 8.

36. Brown, 'The Trials of Patrick Kavanagh', p. 17.

37. Myles na Gopaleen, 'Tell of Vision', *CL*, 14 November 1957, p. 8.

38. The irony, which he could not have known at this point, is that O'Nolan would be a pioneering contributor to Teilifís Éireann, writing two television series for the station: *The Ideas of O'Dea* (1963–4) and *Th'Oul Lad of Kilsalaher* (1965).

39. Myles na Gopaleen, 'Nice Mistakes', *CL*, 17 February 1959, p. 6.

40. Myles na Gopaleen, 'Pro Pat Pati', *CL*, 18 March 1958, p. 6.

41. Myles na Gopaleen, 'TV or Not TV', *CL*, 28 June 1958, p. 10.

42. 'To Switch on Illuminations', *Irish Times*, 2 December 1958, p. 7.

43. Quidnunc, 'An Irishman's Diary', *Irish Times*, 4 December 1958, p. 8.

44. Myles na Gopaleen, 'Above in the Park', *CL*, 4 December 1958, p. 8.

45. Ibid.

46. Myles na Gopaleen, 'Old Youth', *CL*, 27 January 1959, p. 6.

47. John Philpot Curran, *Forensic Eloquence: Sketches of trials in Ireland for high treason, etc.* 3rd edn (New York: Brisban & Brannan, 1806), p. 352.

48. Myles na Gopaleen, 'The Real Man–II', *CL*, 26 February 1959, p. 6.

49. Myles na Gopaleen, 'The Real Man–IV', *CL*, 2 March 1959, p. 6.

50. Na Gopaleen, 'Old Youth'.

51. Ibid. Myles regularly teases Behan by comparing him to mythical Irish figures, as when he jokes that he detects 'a mystical thaumaturgic affinity between Saint Patrick and Brendan Behan, for history has it that the Irish brigand Nial Niogiallach first brought Patrick to Ireland as a HOSTAGE'. Myles na Gopaleen, 'Getting Things Pat', *CL*, 14 September 1958, p. 6.

52. Myles na Gopaleen, 'Ourselves Alone', *CL*, 6 March 1959, p. 6.

53. 'U.C.D. Newspaper Banned', *Irish Times*, 6 May 1959, p. 1. This was the second occasion on which Myles had intervened when Behan had been censored by his alma mater. In 1956, a ban on Behan's advertised attendance at the university to chair a debate on the motion 'That this country needs a revolution' solicited a blunt but frank evaluation from Myles: 'Mr Behan is a man of ability and distinction and the "authorities" thus offer him public insult.' Myles na Gopaleen, 'Nuirology', *CL*, 27 October 1956, p. 8.

54. Myles na Gopaleen, 'Current Events', *CL*, 9 May 1959, p. 8.

55. 'Siobhan McKenna Ban: B.B.C. criticised by British newspapers', *Irish Times*, 2 May 1959, p. 9.

56. Lionel Pilkington, *Theatre and the State in Twentieth-Century Ireland: Cultivating the people* (London: Routledge, 2002), p. 178.

57. Ibid.

58. Myles makes numerous cracks at Bryan Guinness for exactly these artistic pretensions, as when he rejects the idea of leaving the *Irish Times* to 'get a job driving a lorry for Guinness's', as this would 'entail chatting with Lord Moyne in the sheds, between runs, about *poetry*! I don't know – I'm bad enough where I am.' Myles na gCopaleen, *CL*, 8 January 1951, p. 4.

59. Myles na Gopaleen, 'B.B. or S.L.?', *CL*, 18 July 1959, p. 8.

60. Myles on one occasion bizarrely mistakes the overnight sprouting of mushrooms on his lawn as eggs that Behan had left there for the columnist's birthday. Myles na Gopaleen, 'Stool Pigeon', *CL*, 11 October 1960, p. 8.

61. Myles na Gopaleen, 'That Human Behan', *CL*, 3 September 1959, p. 9.

62. Anthony Cronin, *No Laughing Matter*, pp. 206–7.

63. Sarah Cole, *Modernism, Male Friendship, and the First World War*, p. 1.

64. Ibid.

65. Other casual references to Behan can be found through this period in Myles na Gopaleen, 'Toasts & Palaeographs', *CL*, 14 February 1961, p. 6; 'Ars Gratia Sartre', *CL*, 25 February 1961, p. 10; 'Some Squawks', *CL*, 13 April 1961, p. 9; and 'Ucidicity III', *CL*, 7 April 1962, p. 8.

66. Myles na Gopaleen, 'This Dublin', *CL*, 29 January 1962, p. 8.

67. Michael Wale, 'Dublin's Neglected Genius', *Scene*, 23 February 1963, p. 29. I'm extremely grateful to Maebh Long for bringing this article to my attention.

68. Wale alludes to the fact that 'Often Behan would appear anonymously in the daily column which would be a reprint, somewhat gilded, of the past day's bar conversation' – hinting at the existence of any number of obscured appearances of Behan in *Cruiskeen Lawn* not covered in the present article.

69. Flann O'Brien, 'Behan, Master of Language', the *Sunday Telegraph*, 22 March 1964. I am extremely grateful to Catherine Ahearn and Tobias Harris for helping to track down the original copy of the obituary, which has never been republished in full.

70. Seamus Kelly (Quidnunc), 'Brian O'Nolan Dies: Scholar, satirist, and wit', *Irish Times*, 2 April 1966, p. 1.

11 Behan's Graveyard of Radical Possibility

1. Noeleen Dowling, 'Behan's touch was missing', *Cork Examiner*, 17 March 1972, p. 13. It also opened in the Irish Arts Centre, New York, on 11 March 1983, with Jim Sheridan directing (see also *O'Connor*, pp. 270–2).

2. See Joan Littlewood, *Joan's Book: Joan Littlewood's peculiar history as she tells it* (London: Minerva, 1994), p. 561 and *O'Sullivan*, pp. 271–4.

3. The events at the graveyard bear striking resemblance to a 1936 protest Behan attended in which Martin spoke against fascism; see Dave Hannigan, *Behan in the USA: The rise and fall of the most famous Irishman in New York* (Wicklow: Ballpoint Press, 2014), pp. 88–9. In the Irish version, there are brief appearances of a man selling the news-sheet '*Aiséirí*', along with a news poster reading 'ABAIR ÁR NATHAIR IN AGHAIDH AN TEORANN' ('say an Our Father against the border'). The newspaper, in fact spelled '*Aiséirghe*', was an organ of the fascist party, Ailtirí na hAiséirghe (Architects of the Resurrection); Breandán Ó Beacháin, *Lá Breá sa Roilig*, mss: Dublin, National Library of Ireland, MS G 1,296, p. 3.

4. Cited in Joost Augusteijn, *Patrick Pearse: The making of a revolutionary* (London: Palgrave, 2010), p. 269; see Michel Foucault, *The Birth of Biopolitics: Lectures at the Collège de France, 1978–1979*, trans. Graham Burchell (New York: Palgrave Macmillan, 2008).

5. Simpson's finale was written with reference to a note that Behan left about his own intentions for the play.

6. Robert Brustein qtd. in E.H. Mikhail (ed.), *The Art of Brendan Behan* (London: Vision, 1979), p. 181.

7. Andrew J. Milner, *Contemporary Cultural Theory* (London: UCL Press, 1994), p. 82.

8. Theodor W. Adorno and Max Horkheimer, *Dialectic of Enlightenment*, trans. Edmund Jephcott (Standford: Stanford University Press, 2002), pp. 34, 94.

9. Fredric Jameson, *Late Marxism: Adorno, or, the persistence of the dialectic* (London: Verso, 1990), p. 180.

10. Hannigan, *Behan in the USA*, p. 26.

11. Thorstein Veblen, *The Theory of the Leisure Class* (London: Macmillan, 1915 [1899], pp. 74, 75.

12. Adorno and Horkheimer, *Dialectic of Englightenment*, pp. 114, 115.

13. Cited in Jackson Lears, *Fables of Abundance: a cultural history of advertising in America* (New York: Basic Books, 1994) p. 232; Paul Nystrom, *Economics of Fashion* (New York: The Ronald Press, 1928).

14. Anon., 'Forest Lawn', *Life*, 3 January 1944, pp. 65–76 at p. 74.

15. Max Horkheimer and Theodor Adorno, 'The Culture Industry: Enlightenment as mass deception', in Chris Jenks (ed.) *Culture: Critical concepts in sociology*, Vol. 2 (London: Routledge, 2003), pp. 146–80], at p. 160.

16. Evelyn Waugh, *The Loved One: An Anglo-American tragedy* (London: Penguin Modern Classics, 2000), Amazon Kindle e-book, p. 39.

17. Brendan Behan, *Richard's Cork Leg*, mss. Dublin, National Library of Ireland, MS29, 086, p. 30.

18. Guy Debord, *The Society of the Spectacle*, trans. Ken Knabb (Canberra: Hobgoblin, 2002), p. 9; emphasis in original.

19. For instance, Dennis Barlow, after several pages of absurd discussions about the appropriate location at Whispering Glades for his dead suicide-victim friend, meditates briefly on the horrific appearance of 'the sack of body suspended and the face above it with eyes red and horribly staring from their sockets', before the graveyard salesperson assures him 'our cosmeticians […] have never failed'. The dead man will, in turn, become another item on Whispering Glades' conveyor belt of corpses, 'the strangulated Loved One', as Aimée Thanatogeos clinically describes him; he will be 'prepared' and made over, after the American fashion, whereas on the other side of the Atlantic, and as a suicide victim, he might be hidden and taboo, we may infer. Evelyn Waugh, *The Loved One*, pp. 45–6, 65.

20. Qtd. in Joseph Pearce, *Catholic Literary Giants: A field guide to the Catholic literary landscape* (San Francisco: Ignatius Press, 2014), p. 211.

21. This is how parade organising committee member James J. Comerford described both Behan and the parade; Hannigan, *Behan in the USA*, p. 104.

22. Waugh, *The Loved One*, p. 11.

23. Hannigan, *Behan in the USA*, p. 105.

24. Cited in ibid., p. 107.

25. Ibid.; Larkin was jailed in 1920, during the First Red Scare, on a charge of 'criminal anarchy', for his activities in support of communism in the USA. Seán O'Casey would subsequently act as secretary of the Release Larkin Campaign.

26. See W.B. Yeats, 'The Lake Isle of Innisfree', in Richard J. Finneran (ed.), *The Collected Works of W.B. Yeats. Vol. 1: The Poems* (New York: Scribner, 1997), p. 35.

27. Waugh, *The Loved One*, p. 82.

28. Ibid., p. 11.

29. Ibid., p. 12.

30. Brendan Behan, *Richard's Cork Leg*, mss. Dublin, National Library of Ireland, MS29, 086, p. 31.

31. Ibid., p. 30.

32. Breandán Ó Beacháin, *Lá Breá sa Roilig*, op. cit. p. 1; Brendan Behan, *Richard's Cork Leg*, mss. Dublin, National Library of Ireland, MS29, 085, p. 3.

33. Brendan Behan, *Richard's Cork Leg*, mss. Dublin, National Library of Ireland, MS29, 086, p. 1.

34. Waugh qtd. in Michael G. Brennan, *Evelyn Waugh: Fictions, faith and family* (London: Bloomsbury, 2013), p. 37.

35. Qtd. in James Lydon, *The Making of Ireland: From ancient times to present* (London: Routledge, 1998), p. 391.

36. Socrates, along with Shakespeare and Marlowe, are cited as possibly gay figures from history in 'After the Wake' (*Wake*, p. 48). Interestingly, a replica of Leonardo da Vinci's

Last Supper painting, which apparently took seven years to render in stained glass, was commissioned for Forest Lawn in the 1940s. Behan may well have been hinting at this particular commercialisation of Christian iconography. Anon., 'Forest Lawn', p. 68.

37. Waugh, *The Loved One*, p. 39.

38. Fredric Jameson, *The Political Unconscious: Narrative as a socially symbolic act* (London: Routledge, 2002), p. 25.

39. Waugh, *The Loved One*, p. 90.

40. In *Mad Men* this advertising gloss on African American reality is crystallised in the hypocrisy of a late 1950s-early 1960s advertising agency that is commercially eager to embrace the African American market yet also politically wary of the contemporary agitation for black civil rights. See Clarence Lang, 'Representing the *Mad* Margins of the Early 1960s: Northern civil rights and blues idiom', in Lauren M.E. Goodlad, Lilya Kaganovsky and Robert A. Rushing (eds), *Mad Men, Mad World: Sex politics, style & the 1960s* (Durham and London: Duke University Press, 2013), pp. 73–91.

41. David K. Wiggins and Patrick B. Miller, *The Unlevel Playing Field: A documentary history of the African American experience in sport* (Chicago: University of Illinois Press, 2003), p. 230.

42. The issue of graveyard racial segregation produced particular controversy in the United States of the 1950s and '60s as 'the Korean and the Vietnam wars brought home, with the bodies of soldiers killed in action, the realization that people good enough to die for their country were not good enough to be buried in a place of their choice'; Angelika Krüger-Kahloula, 'On the Wrong Side of the Fence: Racial segregation in American cemeteries', in Geneviève Fabre and Robert O'Meally (eds), *History & Memory in African American Culture* (New York: Oxford University Press, 1994), pp. 130–49, at p. 130.

43. Thomas Kilroy, *Talbot's Box* (Dublin: Gallery Press, 1979), pp. 30–1.

44. Michel Peillon, *Contemporary Irish Society: An introduction* (Dublin: Gill & Macmillan, 1982), p. 35.

45. bell hooks, 'Marginality as Site of Resistance', in Russell Ferguson, Martha Gever, Trinh T. Minh-ha, Cornel West (eds), *Out There: Marginalization and contemporary cultures* (Cambridge, MA: MIT Press, 1990), pp. 341–3.

46. In *The Hostage* this focus on the margins as a place of counter-hegemonic openness is refracted through sexual dissidence. In short stories such as 'A Woman of No Standing' (1950) and 'The Catacombs' (1981), marginal figures are also used by Behan to challenge normative attitudes (to extra-marital relationships and abortion, for instance).

47. Brendan Behan, *Richard's Cork Leg*, mss. Dublin, National Library of Ireland, MS29, 086, pp. 27, 10.

48. See Hannigan, *Behan in the USA*, pp. 88–9.

49. Michel-Rolph Trouillot, *Silencing the Past: Power and the production of history* (Boston: Beacon, 1995), p. 48.

50. Slavoj Žižek, *Mapping Ideology* (London: Verso, 1994), p. 9.

51. Terence Brown, *The Irish Times: 150 years of influence* (Croydon: Bloomsbury, 2015), p. 134.

52. Ó Beacháin, *Lá Breá sa Roilig,* p. 4; the current author's translation.

53. J.J. Lee, *Ireland, 1912-1985: Politics and society* (Cambridge: Cambridge University Press, 1989), p. 370. Ireland lost 26 soldiers over the course of the campaign.

54. Ben Tonra, *Global Citizen and European Republic: Irish foreign policy in transition* (Manchester: Manchester University Press, 2006), p. 46. The Algerian War, in which the French were, in Behan's words, 'led by madmen, gangsters and collaborators' 'murdering Algerians', no doubt in his view provided a corollary for the actions of the Belgians (Hannigan, *Behan in the USA*, p. 95). Behan also hints at how the violent suppression of African insurgency is accompanied by a global conspiracy of silence: the Bonnie Prince relates that Forest Lawn offers a service to the UN to bury African dignitaries who 'succumb' – he slips – 'I mean pass on from the New York climate and the rival hospitalities of the Americans and the Russians' (*CP*, p. 266).

55. Although, in Behan's earlier manuscript, it is notable that Hogan has his own variety of deafness, he knows nothing about 'them Hungryarians' – Behan appears to be hinting at recent Soviet aggression. Brendan Behan, *Richard's Cork Leg*, mss. Dublin, National Library of Ireland, MS29, 086, p. 12.

56. Dave Hannigan, op. cit., p. 82.

57. Tim Pat Coogan, *Ireland in the Twentieth Century* (London: Arrow, 2003), p. 708.

58. Behan may well have heard the perhaps apocryphal story that O'Neill had named the son she left behind after the Irish rebel hero Kevin Barry. Sam McGrath, 'Ramble of January' (22 January 2014) <http://comeheretome.com/2014/01/22/ramble-of-january-2014/, [accessed 16 May 2015] (para. 12 of 35).

59. Behan also cites the coast of a leafy Dublin suburb, Killiney, as the place where one of his prostitutes, Rose of Lima, was first 'had be a man', a 'prefect in charge of the Working Girls' Protection Society'. That this sturdy upholder of public morality 'said he'd show what I wasn't to let the boys do to me' points to the hidden underside of Irish public piety and the role of the religious in unspeakable sexual abuse, and a divinity student's dalliance with Rose is mentioned some time later. In light of similar stories in *The Hostage*, however, they seem hackneyed and lose their capacity to shock. None of her affluent clients were ever convicted of O'Neill's murder, and the treatment of her own class in criminal matters is markedly different, Behan implies: as Maria Concepta notes of Hogan's beard, 'if a young unemployed fellow from the flats went 'round like that he'd be arrested' (*CP*, p. 251). As he had done in earlier plays, Behan engages a motif common to working-class writers, such as A.P. Wilson, Patrick MacGill, Seán O'Casey and James Plunkett, whereby the prostitute becomes the paradoxical accuser of an unethical society, its moral dysfunction upbraided by one condemned in its own moralising terms.

60. Raymond Williams, *Culture & Society: 1780-1950* (New York: Anchor, 1960), pp. 357–8.

BIBLIOGRAPHY

Primary

Behan, Brendan, 'Aithrighe', *Comhar,* vol. 6, uimh. 10, 1947, p. 5

—— 'After the Wake', *Points*, no. 8, December 1950/January 1951, pp. 52–6

—— 'Bridewell Revisited', *Points*, no. 11–12, Winter 1951–2, pp. 11–21

—— 'Oscar Wilde', trans. Donagh MacDonagh, *Irish Times,* 20 September 1952, p. 6

—— 'Heart Turns West at Christmas', *Irish Press*, 24 December 1954, p. 4

—— 'Secret Scripture', *Irish Times*, 30 July 1960, p. 6

—— 'The Language', *Irish Times*, 17 January 1961, p. 5

—— 'Brendan Behan on Joyce'. A lecture delivered before the James Joyce Society at the Gotham Book Mart in New York City, 1962. Folkways Records FL9826.

—— 'Confessions of an Irish Rebel', Unpublished MS, Proscenium Press Archives, University of Delaware Library Special Collections, File 313, Series I, F7

—— *Brendan Behan's Island: An Irish sketch-book*, with drawings by Paul Hogarth (London: Hutchinson, 1962)

—— *Brendan Behan: Poems and stories*, ed. Denis Cotter (Dublin: The Liffey Press, 1978)

—— *After the Wake: Twenty-one Prose works including previously unpublished material.* ed. Peter Fallon (Dublin: O'Brien Press, 1981)

—— *Poems and a Play in Irish*, ed. Proinsias Ní Dhorchaí with an Introduction by Declan Kiberd (Dublin: Gallery Press, 1981)

—— *An Giall and The Hostage*, ed., Richard Wall (Washington: Catholic University of America Press, 1987)

—— *Borstal Boy* (London: Arrow, 1990)

—— *Confessions of an Irish Rebel* (London: Arena, 1990)

—— *The Letters of Brendan Behan*, ed. E.H. Mikhail (London: Macmillan, 1992)

—— 'The Family Was in the Rising' in *The Dubbalin Man* (Dublin: A. & A. Farmar, 1997), pp. 75–8

—— 'A Jackeen's Lament for the Blaskets', trans. Donagh MacDonagh in *Watching the River Flow: A century in Irish poetry*, eds, Noel Duffy and Theo Dorgan (Dublin: Poetry Ireland, 1999)

—— *The Complete Plays*, introduced by Alan Simpson (London: Methuen, 2000)

Ó Beachain, Breandán, 'Jackeen ag Caoineadh na mBlascaod', *Comhar*, vol. 7, uimh. 10, (October 1948), p. 10

—— 'Buíochas le Joyce', Do Sheán Ó Súilleabháin, *Comhar*, vol. 8, uimh. 8, Lúnasa, 1949, p. 14

—— *Lá Breá sa Roilig,* Dublin, National Library of Ireland, MS G 1, 296

Secondary

Adorno, Theodor, *Aesthetic Theory*, trans. Robert Hullot-Kentor (London: Bloomsbury, 2013)

—— and Max Horkheimer, *Dialectic of Enlightenment*, trans. Edmund Jephcott (Standford: Stanford University Press, 2002)

Amin, Kadji, 'Anachronizing the Penitentiary, Queering the History of Sexuality', *GLQ: A Journal of Lesbian and Gay Studies*, vol. 19, no. 3, 2013, pp. 301–40

Anon., 'Forest Lawn', *Life*, 3 January 1944, pp. 65–76

Arendt, Hannah, 'French Existentialism', in Susannah Young-Ah Gottlieb (ed.), *Reflections on Literature and Culture* (Stanford, CA: Stanford University Press, 2007), pp. 115–16

Auden, W.H., ed. Edward Mendelson, *Collected Auden* (London: Faber, 2004)

Augusteijn, Joost, *Patrick Pearse: The Making of a Revolutionary* (London: Palgrave, 2010)

Bair, Deirdre, *Samuel Beckett: A Biography* (London: Vintage, 1990)

Barnes, Clive, 'Theatrical Curiosity of Behan's "Hostage": Timely Theme in Eve Untimely Fashion Ironic Tone Pervades Tragedy About I.R.A.', *New York Times*, 11 October 1972, p.50

Bassnett, Susan, and André Lefevere, *Constructing Cultures: Essays on Literary Translation* (Cleveton, Toronto, Sydney and Johannesburg: Multilingual Matters, 1998)

—— and Peter Bush (eds), *The Translator as Writer* (London: Continuum, 2006)

Beach, Sylvia, *Shakespeare and Company* (Lincoln, NE: University of Nebraska Press, 1991)

Beckett, Samuel, n.t., 'A Tribute to Brendan Behan', 10 April 1964, Theatre heute, 5, (May 1964), 57

—— *Molloy* (London: Faber & Faber, 2009)

—— *The Letters of Samuel Beckett*, volume III, ed. George Craig et al. (Cambridge: Cambridge University Press, 2014)

Benjamin, Walter, *Charles Baudelaire: A Lyric Poet in the Era of High Capitalism*, trans. Harry Zohn (London: Verso, 1997)

Berman, Antoine, *L'épreuve de l'étranger* (Paris: Gallimard, 1984)

Bixby, Patrick, *Samuel Beckett and the Postcolonial Novel* (Cambridge: Cambridge University Press, 2009)

Borg, Ruben, Paul Fagan and Werner Huber (eds), *Flann O'Brien: Contesting Legacies* (Cork: Cork University Press, 2014)

Bowyer Bell, J., *The Secret Army: The IRA* (New Brunswick, NJ: Transaction, 1997)

Brannigan, John, 'Belated Behan: Brendan Behan and the cultural politics of memory', *Éire-Ireland*, no. 37, 2002, pp. 39–52

—— *Brendan Behan: Cultural nationalism and the revisionist writer* (Dublin: Four Courts Press, 2002)

Brennan, Michael G., *Evelyn Waugh: Fictions, Faith and Family* (London: Bloomsbury, 2013)

Brooker, Joseph, 'Ploughmen without Land: Flann O'Brien and Patrick Kavanagh', in Julian Murphet, Rónán McDonald and Sascha Morrell (eds), *Flann O'Brien & Modernism* (New York: Bloomsbury, 2014), pp. 93–106

Brooker, Peter, *Bohemia in London: The Social Scene of Early Modernism* (Basingstoke: Palgrave, 2004)

Brown, Matthew, 'The Trials of Patrick Kavanagh', *New Hibernia Review*, vol. 15, no. 1, 2011, p. 36

Brown, Richard, '*Borstal Boy*: Structure and meaning', *Colby Quarterly*, vol. 21, no. 4, December 1985, p.p. 188–97

Brown, Robert McAfee, *Elie Wiesel: Messenger to All Humanity* (Notre Dame: University of Notre Dame Press, 1983)

Brown, Terence, *The Irish Times: 150 years of Influence* (Croydon: Bloomsbury, 2015)

Budgen, Frank, *James Joyce and the Making of 'Ulysses', and Other Writings* (London: Oxford University Press, 1972)

Calder, John, *The Garden of Eros: The Story of the Paris Expatriates and the Post-War Literary Scene* (London: Calder Publications, 2013)

Cargas, Harry, *Conversations with Elie Wiesel* (South Bend, IN: Justice Books, 1992)

Carlson, Julia (ed.), *Banned in Ireland: Censorship and the Irish Writer* (London: Routledge, 1990)

Casanova, Pascale, *La Langue Mondiale* (Paris: Le Seuil, 2015)

Clare, David, 'The Disputed Authorship of Brendan Behan's *The Hostage*: Conference Paper derived from Chapter Two of 'The stage Englishman in Irish literature', Unpublished PhD thesis, University College Dublin, 2012

Cleary, Joe, *Outrageous Fortune: Capital and Culture in Modern Ireland* (Dublin: Field Day Publications, 2007)

Cole, Sarah, *Modernism, Male Friendship, and the First World War* (Cambridge: Cambridge University Press, 2003)

Collins, Lucy, (ed.), *Poetry by Women in Ireland: A Critical Anthology 1870–1970* (Liverpool: Liverpool University Press, 2012)

Colum, Padraic (ed.), *An Anthology of Irish Verse* (New York: Liveright Publishing Corporation, 1948)

Coogan, Tim Pat, *Ireland in the Twentieth Century* (London: Arrow, 2003)

—— *The IRA* (Basingstoke: Palgrave Macmillan, 2005)

Cordingly, Anthony and C. Frigau-Manning, *Collaborative Translation: From the Renaissance to the Digital Age* (London/NewYork: Bloomsbury, 2017)

Cronin, Anthony, *No Laughing Matter: The Life and Times of Flann O'Brien* (New York: Fromm, 1989)

Curran, John Philpot, *Forensic Eloquence: Sketches of Trials in Ireland for High Treason, etc.* 3rd edn (New York: Brisban & Brannan, 1806)

D'Arcy, Margaretta, *Loose Theatre: Memoirs of a Guerrilla Theatre Activist* (Crewe: Trafford, 2005)

Debord, Guy, *The Society of the Spectacle*, trans. Ken Knabb (Canberra: Hobgoblin, 2002)

de Búrca, Séamus, *Brendan Behan: A Memoir* (Dublin: Proscenium Press, 1993), p.12

de Paor, Louis, 'Modern Poetry in Irish 1939–2000', in *The Cambridge History of Irish Literature, Vol. II,* ed. Philip O'Leary and Margaret Kelleher (Cambridge: Cambridge University Press, 2006), pp. 317–56

Dineen, Rev. Patrick S. Foclóir Gaedhilge agus Béarla (Dublin: Educational Company of Ireland, 1927)

Dowling, Noeleen, 'Behan's touch was Missing', *Cork Examiner*, 17 March 1972, p. 13

Duffy, Noel and Theo Dorgan (eds.), *Watching the River Flow: A Century in Irish Poetry* (Dublin: Poetry Ireland, 1991)

Fagan, Paul and Ruben Borg, '*The Parish Review*: Founders' note', *The Parish Review: Journal of Flann O'Brien studies*, vol. 1, no. 1, Summer 2012, p. 5

Fanon, Frantz, *The Wretched of the Earth*, trans. Constance Farrington (London: Penguin, 1991)

Ferraro, A. and R. Grutman (dir.), *L'autotraduction littéraire. Perspectives théoriques* (Paris: Garnier, 2016)

Fine, Ellen S., *The Legacy of Night: The Literary Universe of Elie Wiesel* (Albany: State University of New York Press, 1982)

Fitch, Brian, *Beckett and Babel: An Investigation into the Status of Bilingual Work* (Toronto: University of Toronto Press, 1988)

Fitzgerald, Mark and John O'Flynn (eds), *Music and Identity in Ireland and Beyond* (Farnham: Ashgate, 2014)

Foucault, Michel, 'Qu'est-ce qu'un auteur?' *Bulletin de la Société française de philosophie* , vol. 63, no. 3, 1969, pp. 73–104

—— *The Birth of Biopolitics: Lectures at the Collège de France, 1978–1979*, trans. Graham Burchell (New York: Palgrave Macmillan, 2008)

Franciosi, Robert, 'Introduction', in *Elie Wiesel: Conversations*, ed. and introduction by Robert Franciosi (Jackson: University Press of Mississippi, 2002)

Furlong, Seán, 'Letter to Fred May', Intercepted 27 September 1942; Brendan Behan PF729326/V1, National Archives KV2/3181

Gan ainm, 'Scrúdú Coinsiais', *Comhar,* vol. 11, uimh. 3, 1952, pp. 12–13.

Genet, Jean, *Miracle of the Rose*, trans. Bernard Frechtman (London: Faber, 1973)

—— *Un Chant d'Amour.* Dir. Jean Genet (n.p.:BFI, 2003)

Gounardidou, Kiki, 'Introductory Remarks: The visibility of theatre translation', *Metamorphoses: A journal of literary translation*, vol. 9, no. 1, Spring 2001, pp. 10–14

Graham, Colin, *Deconstructing Ireland* (Edinburgh: Edinburgh University Press, 2001)

Graydon, Philip, 'Frederick May', in *Encyclopaedia of Music in Ireland*, ed. Harry White and Barra Boydell (Dublin: UCD Press, 2014), pp. 638–9

Grutman, Rainier, 'Self-translation', in Mona Baker and Gabriela Saldanha (eds), *Routledge Encyclopedia of Translation Studies* (London/New York: Routledge, 2011), pp. 257–60

Hanley, Brian, '"Oh here's to Adolph Hitler": The IRA and the Nazis', *History Ireland*, vol. 13, no. 3, May/June 2005), pp. 31–35.

Hannigan, Dave, *Behan in the USA: The Rise and Fall of the Most Famous Irishman in New York* (Wicklow: Ballpoint Press, 2014)

Harris, Frank, *Oscar Wilde* (London: Constable, 1938)

Heaney, Seamus and Robert Hass, *Sounding Lines: The Art of Translating Poetry*, http:// townsendcenter.berkeley.edu/sites/default/files/publications/OP20_Sounding_Lines.pdf [accessed 9 January 2018]

Hennessy, Rosemary, *Profit and Pleasure: Sexual Identities in Late Capitalism* (London: Routledge, 2000)

Hentz, Jean-Philippe, 'Brendan Behan's France: Encounters in Saint-Germain-de-Prés', *Journal of Franco-Irish Studies*, no. 1, 2008, pp. 43–61

Hogan, Patrick Colm, 'Brendan Behan on the Politics of Identity: Nation, culture, class, and human empathy in *Borstal Boy*', *Colby Quarterly*, vol. 35, no. 3, September 1999, pp. 154–72

Hogan, Robert and Michael J. O'Neill, (eds.), *Joseph Holloway's Abbey Theatre: A Selection from his Unpublished Journal, Impressions of a Dublin Playgoer* (Carbondale: Southern Illinois University Press, 1967)

Hokenson, J.W. and M. Munson, *The Bilingual Text: History and Theory of Literary Self-Translation* (Manchester and Kinderhook (NY): St Jerome Publishing, 2007)

Holdsworth, Nadine, *Joan Littlewood's Theatre* (Cambridge: Cambridge University Press, 2011)

hooks, bell 'Marginality as Site of Resistance', in Russell Ferguson, Martha Gever, Trinh T. Minh-ha, Cornel West (eds), *Out There: Marginalization and Contemporary Cultures* (Cambridge, MA: MIT Press, 1990), pp. 341–3.

Horkheimer, Max and Theodor Adorno, 'The Culture Industry: Enlightenment as mass deception', in Chris Jenks (ed.), *Culture: Critical Concepts in Sociology*, vol. 2 (London: Routledge, 2003), pp. 146–80

Hughes, Eamonn, '"The Fact of Me-ness": Autobiographical writing in the Revival period' in Margaret Kelleher (ed.), *Irish University Review: special issue, New Perspectives on the Irish Literary Revival*, vol. 33, no. 1, Spring/Summer 2003, pp. 28–45

Hutchins, Patricia, *James Joyce's World* (London: Methuen, 1957)

Iremonger, Valentin, *Horan's Field and Other Reservations* (Dublin: Dolmen Press, 1972)

Jameson, Fredric, *Late Marxism: Adorno, or, The Persistence of the Dialectic* (London: Verso, 1990)

—— *The Political Unconscious: Narrative as a Socially Symbolic Act* (London: Routledge, 2002)

Jordan, John, 'More about Brendan', in *Crystal Clear: The selected prose of John Jordan*, ed. Hugh McFadden (Dublin: Lilliput Press, 2006), p. 170

Joyce, James, *A Portrait of the Artist as a Young Man* (London: Paladin, 1999)

Kearney, Colbert, 'Borstal Boy: A portrait of the artist as a young prisoner', *Ariel: A review of international English literature*, vol. 7, no. 2, April 1976, pp. 47–62

—— 'Filíocht Bhreandáin Uí Bheacháin', *Scríobh, no.* 3, 1978, pp. 44–57

—— *The Writings of Brendan Behan* (Dublin: Gill & Macmillan, 1977)

Kenner, Hugh, *A Colder Eye: The Modern Irish Writers* (New York: Knopf, 1983)

Kiberd, Declan, 'Review of *The Art of Brendan Behan*', *Review of English Studies*, New Series, vol. 33, no. 130, May 1992

—— *Inventing Ireland: The Literature of the Modern Nation*. (London: Vintage Books, 1995)

—— *The Irish Writer and the World* (Cambridge: Cambridge University Press, 2005)

Kilroy, Thomas, *Talbot's Box* (Dublin: Gallery Press, 1979)

Krüger-Kahloula, Angelika, 'On the Wrong Side of the Fence: Racial segregation in American cemeteries', in Geneviève Fabre and Robert O'Meally (eds), *History & Memory in African American Culture* (New York: Oxford Universary Press, 1994), pp. 130–49

Landers, Clifford, *Literary Translation: A Practical Guide* (Cleveton, Buffalo and Toronto: Multilingual Matters, 2001)

Lang, Clarence, 'Representing the *Mad* Margins of the Early 1960s: Northern civil rights and blues idiom', in Lauren M.E. Goodlad, Lilya Kaganovsky and Robert A. Rushing (eds), *Mad Men, Mad World: Sex politics, style and the 1960s* (Durham and London: Duke University Press, 2013), pp. 73–91

Lears, Jackson, *Fables of Abundance: A Cultural History of Advertising in America* (New York: Basic Books, 1994)

Lee, J.J., *Ireland, 1912–1985: Politics and society* (Cambridge: Cambridge University Press, 1989)

Lefevere, André, *Translation, Rewriting, and the Manipulation of Literary Fame* (London/New York: Routledge, 1992)

Littlewood, Joan, *Joan's Book: Joan Littlewood's Peculiar History as She Tells It* (London: Minerva, 1994)

Long, Maebh, *Assembling Flann O'Brien* (London: Bloomsbury, 2014)

López López-Gay, Patricia, *(Auto)traducción y (re)creación: 'Un pájaro quemado vivo' de Agustín Gómez Arcos* (Almeria: Instituto de Estudios Almerienses, 2005)

Lotringer, Sylvère, 'The Thin Man: An interview with Brendan Behan', *Field Day Review*, vol. 1, 2005, pp. 3–28

Love, Heather, *Feeling Backward: Loss and the Politics of Queer History* (Cambridge, MA: Harvard University Press, 2007)

Lukács, Georg, *The Historical Novel*, trans. Hannah and Stanley Mitchell (London: Merlin Press, 1962)

Lydon, James, *The Making of Ireland: From Ancient Times to Present* (London: Routledge, 1998)

Lynch, Claire, 'The Drinker with the Writing Problem: Brendan Behan's anecdotal alcoholism', in John Brannigan (ed.), *Brendan Behan – Irish University Review*, special issue vol. 44, no. 1, 2014, pp. 165–81

MacDonnell, Anthony, 'Two Dublin Tragedies', *Evening Herald*, 26 November 1967, p. 6

Mac Góráin, Riobard, 'Breandán Ó Beacháin: "Nach bhfuilimse in ann Gaeilge a scríobh?"', *Comhar*, vol. 43, uimh, 3, 1984, pp. 10–12

Malkin, Jeanette R., *Memory-Theater and Postmodern Drama* (Ann Arbor, MI: University of Michigan Press, 1999)

Marcuse, Herbert, *Eros and Civilisation* (New York: Vintage, 1962)

Martin, Augustine, 'Brendan Behan', *Threshold*, no. 18, 1963, p. 22

Maxwell, Desmond E.S., *A Critical History of Modern Irish Drama 1891–1980* (Cambridge: Cambridge University Press, 1984)

May, Frederick, *Sunlight and Shadow*. RTÉ National Symphony Orchestra, Cond. Robert Houlihan. RTÉ Lyric FM CD Recording, 2004

McCaffrey, Lawrence J., 'Seán Ó Faoláin and Irish Identity', *New Hibernia Review*, no. 9, 2005, pp. 144–56

McCann, Seán, *The World of Brendan Behan* (New York: Twayne Publishers, 1966)

McCrann, Aibhlín (ed.), *Memories, Milestones and New Horizons: Reflections on the Regeneration of Ballymun* (Belfast: Blackstaff Press, 2008)

McCrea, Barry, *Languages of the Night: Minor Languages and the Imagination in Twentieth-century Ireland and Europe* (New Haven and London: Yale University Press, 2015)

McGrath, Sam, 'Ramble of January' (22 January 2014), http://comeheretome.com/2014/01/22/ramble-of-january-2014/ [accessed 16 May 2015]

McGuinness, Frank, 'Saint Behan', *Brendan Behan – Irish University Review* special issue, ed. John Brannigan, vol. 44, no. 1, pp. 78–91

McMahon, Deirdre, 'Hairy Apes and Quare Fellows: The legacy of Eugene O'Neill in the work of Brendan Behan', *The Eugene O'Neill Review Special Issue*, ed. Audrey McNamara and Nelson O'Ceallaigh Ritschel, vol. 39, no. 1, 2018, pp. 72–94

McMahon, Seán (ed.), *The Best from The Bell: Great Irish Writing* (Dublin: The O'Brien Press, 1978)

McNeillie, Andrew, 'The Dublin End: Anecdotes of Brendan Behan on Árainn', in John Brannigan (ed.), *Brendan Behan – Irish University Review* special issue, ed. John Brannigan, vol. 44, no. 1, 2014, pp. 59–77

Meaney, Gerardine, Mary O'Dowd and Bernadette Whelan, *Reading the Irish Woman: Studies in Cultural Encounter and Exchange, 1714–1960* (Liverpool: Liverpool University Press, 2013)

Mendelson, Edward (ed.), *Collected Auden* (London: Faber, 2004)

Mikhail E.H. (ed.), *The Art of Brendan Behan* (London: Vision, 1979)

—— *Brendan Behan: Interviews and Recollections*, Vols I and II (Dublin: Gill & Macmillan, 1982)

Miller, Tyrus, *Late Modernism: Politics, Fiction, and the Arts Between the World Wars* (Berkeley: University of California Press, 1999)

Milner, Andrew J., *Contemporary Cultural Theory* (London: UCL Press, 1994)

Mitchel, John, *Jail Journal; or, Five Years in British Prisons* (New York: *The Citizen*, 1854)

Moore-Gilbert, Bart, *Postcolonial Life-Writing: Culture, Politics and Self-Representation* (New York: Routledge, 2009)

Morash, Christopher, *A History of Irish Theatre 1601–2000* (Cambridge: Cambridge University Press, 2002)

Murphy, Nial, '"Social Sinn Féin and Hard Labour": The journalism of W.P. Ryan and Jim Larkin 1907–14', *Irish Studies Review*, vol. 22, no. 1, 2014, pp. 43–52

Ní Chinnéide, Máire, *An Damer: Stair amharclainne* (Baile Átha Cliath: Gael Linn, 2008)

Nystrom, Paul, *Economics of Fashion* (New York: The Ronald Press, 1928)

Ó Briain, Seán, 'I Knew Brendan Behan', *Kerryman*, 23 May 1964, pp. 6–7

O'Brien, Flann, *The Complete Novels* (New York: Everyman's Library, 2007)

Ó Buachalla, Breandán, *Aisling Ghéar: Na Stíobhartaigh agus an t-aos léinn, 1603–1788* (Dublin: An Clóchomhar, 1996)

Ó Cadhain, Máirtín, *As an nGéibheann: Litreacha Chuig Tomás Bairéad* (Dublin: Sairséal & Dill, 1973)

O'Connor, Frank, 'The Future of Irish Literature', in David Pierce (ed.), *Irish Writing in the Twentieth Century: A Reader* (Cork: Cork University Press, 2000), pp. 500–3

O'Connor, Ulick, *Brendan Behan* (London: Abacus, 1993)

Ó Faoláin, Seán, 'Ah, Wisha! The Irish Novel' *Virginia Quarterly Review*, vol. 17, no. 2, Spring 1941, pp. 265–74

—— 'This Is Your Magazine', in Seán McMahon (ed.), *The Best from The Bell: Great Irish Writing* (Dublin: The O'Brien Press, 1978), pp. 16

Ó Foghludha, Risteárd (ed.), *Ar Bruach na Coille Muaire: Liam Dall Ó hIfearnáin agus a Shaothar Fileata* (Dublin: Oifig an tSoláthair, 1939)

O'Grady, Thomas, 'Thanks Be to Joyce: Brendan Behan à Paris', in Martha C. Carpentier (ed.), *Joycean Legacies* (Basingstoke: Palgrave, 2015), pp. 33–53

Ó hÉigeartaigh, Cian agus Aoileann Nic Gearailt, *Sáirséal agus Dill 1947–1981: Scéal foilsitheora* (Conamara: Cló Iar-Chonnacht, 2014)

Ó hÉithir, Breandán, *Féach* https://www.rte.ie/archives/2014/1006/650380-inside-the-damer-theatre-1969/ [accessed 9 January 2018]

Ó Laoire, Lillis, 'Dearg Dobhogtha Cháin/The Indelible Mark of Cain: Sexual dissidence in the poetry of Cathal Ó Searcaigh', in Éibhear Walshe (ed.), *Sex, Nation and Dissent in Irish Writing* (Cork: Cork University Press, 1997), pp. 221–34

Olden, G.A., 'More Irish Comedies Wanted on R.É.', Radio Review, *Irish Times*, 1 April 1954, p. 4

O'Sullivan, Michael, *Brendan Behan: A Life* (Dublin: Blackwater Press, 1997)

O'Toole, Fintan, 'Culture Shock: Brendan Behan – playwright, novelist, terrorist', *Irish Times*, 6 September 2014, http://www.irishtimes.com/culture/culture-shock-brendan-behan-playwright-novelist-terrorist-1.1918967 [accessed 26 January 2019]

Ó Tuama, Seán, *An Grá in Amhráin na nDaoine: Léiriú téamúil* (Dublin: An Clóchomhar, 1960)

—— *Nuabhéarsaíocht 1939–1949* (Dublin: Sairséal & Dill, 1950)

Pearce, Joseph, *Catholic Literary Giants: A Field Guide to the Catholic Literary Landscape* (San Francisco: Ignatius Press, 2014)

Pearse, Patrick, 'About Literature', *An Claidheamh Soluis*, 26 Bealtaine 1906, pp. 6–7

Peillon, Michel, *Contemporary Irish Society: An Introduction* (Dublin: Gill & Macmillan, 1982)

Pilkington, Lionel, *Theatre and State in Twentieth-Century Ireland: Cultivating the People* (London: Routledge, 2001)

Quigley, Mark, 'Modernity's Edge: Speaking silence on the Blasket Islands', *Interventions: International journal of postcolonial studies*, vol. 5, no. 3, 2003, pp. 382–406

Raguet, Christine, *De la lettre à l'esprit: traduction ou adaptation?* (Paris: Presses de la Sorbonne Nouvelle, Revue Palimpsestes, n°16, 2004)

Rankin Russell, Richard, 'Brendan Behan's Lament for Gaelic Ireland: "The Quare Fellow"', *New Hibernia Review/Iris Éireannach Nua*, vol. 6, no. 1, 2001, pp. 73–93

Richardson, Maurice, 'Young Prisoners', in E.H. Mikhail (ed.), *The Art of Brendan Behan* (London: Vison, 1979)

Ricoeur, Paul, *Philosophie de la volonté II: Finitude et culpabilté* (Paris: Aubier, 1988)

—— *L'écriture de l'histoire et la représentation du passé*, conférence Marc Bloch, 13 Juin 2000, *Annales. Histoire, Sciences Sociales*, vol. 55, no. 4, Juillet-Août 2000, pp. 731–47

—— *La mémoire, l'histoire, l'oubli* (Paris: Seuil, 2000)

—— *Memory, History, Forgetting*, trans. Kathleen Blamey and David Pellauer (Chicago: University of Chicago Press, 2004)

Roche, Anthony, *Contemporary Irish Drama: From Beckett to McGuinness* (Dublin: Gill & Macmillan, 1994)

—— *Contemporary Irish Drama: From Beckett to McGuinness* (Basingstoke: Palgrave Macmillan, 2009)

—— 'The "Irish" Translation of Samuel Beckett's *En Attendant Godot*', in *The Edinburgh Companion to Samuel Beckett and the Arts*, (ed.) S.E. Gontarski (Edinburgh: Edinburgh University Press, 2014), 199–208

Ryan, Desmond, 'Still Remembering Sion', *University Review*, Vol. 5. No. 2 (Summer 1968), pp. 245–52

—— 'Letter from Paris: Blood, tears and ballet', *Irish Times*, 14 April 1958, p. 6

Ryan, John, *Remembering How We Stood: Bohemian Dublin at the Mid-Century* (New York: Taplinger, 1975)

Said, Edward, *Orientalism* (London: Penguin Books, 1978)

Seaver, Richard, *The Tender Hour of Twilight: Paris in the '50s, New York in the '60s: A Memoir of Publishing's Golden Age*, (ed.) Jeanette Seaver (New York: Farrar Straus and Giroux, 2012)

Sedgwick, Eve Kosofsky, *The Epistemology of the Closet* (New York: Penguin, 1990)

Schrank, Bernice, 'Brendan Behan's *Borstal Boy*: Politics in the vernaculars' in *Brendan Behan – Irish University Review* special issue, ed. John Brannigan, vol. 44, no. 1, pp. 129–48

Simpson, Alan, *Beckett and Behan and a Theatre in Dublin* (London: Routledge & Kegan Paul, 1962)

Sinfield, Alan, *The Wilde Century* (London: Cassell, 1995)

—— *On Sexuality and Power* (New York: Columbia University Press, 2004)

Sperti, Valeria, 'L'autotraduction littéraire: enjeux et problématiques', *Revue Italienne d'Etudes françaises*, http://journals.openedition.org/rief/1573#ftn13 [accessed 12 January 2018]

Steiner, George, *After Babel: Aspects of language and translation* (Oxford: Oxford University Press, 1992 [1975])

Swift, Carolyn, *Stage by Stage* (Dublin: Poolbeg Press, 1985)

Taaffe, Carol, *Ireland Through the Looking-Glass: Flann O'Brien, Myles na gCopaleen and Irish Cultural Debate* (Cork: Cork University Press, 2008)

Terrinoni, Enrico, 'Humour in the Prison: Brendan Behan confesses', *epiphany*, online Journal of the Faculty of Arts and Social Sciences, vol 1, no. 1, Fall 2008, pp. 62–79

Tonra, Ben, *Global Citizen and European Republic: Irish Foreign Policy in Transition* (Manchester: Manchester University Press, 2006)

Trouillot, Michel-Rolph, *Silencing the Past: Power and the Production of History* (Boston: Beacon, 1995)

Tynan, Kenneth, 'The End of the Noose', *Observer*, 27 May 1956, https://www.theguardian.com/theguardian/from-the-archive-blog/2014/mar/20/from-the-archive-brendan-behan [accessed 22 January 2019]

Veblen, Thorstein, *The Theory of the Leisure Class* (London: Macmillan, 1915 [1899])

Venuti, Lawrence, *The Translator's Invisibility: A History of Translation* (Abingdon: Routledge, 2008)

Walsh, Ian R., *Experimental Irish Theatre after W.B. Yeats* (Basingstoke: Palgrave Macmillan, 2012)

Wall, Richard, '*An Giall* and *The Hostage* Compared', *Modern Drama*, no. 18, 1975, pp. 165–72

Wardle, Irving, 'The Sad Death of Brendan Behan', *Observer*, 22 March 1964, http://www.theguardian.com/news/2014/mar/23/observer-archive-sad-death-brendan-behan [accessed 22 January 2019]

Wasser, Audrey, 'From Figure to Fissure: Beckett's *Molloy*, *Malone Dies*, and *The Unamable*', *Modern Philology*, no. 109, 2011, pp. 245–65

Watt, Stephen, Eileen Morgan and Shakir Mustafa (eds), *A Century of Irish Drama* (Bloomington IN: Indiana University Press, 2000)

—— 'Brendan Behan, Borscht Belt Comedian' in John Brannigan (ed.), *Brendan Behan – Irish University Review* special issue, ed. John Brannigan, vol. 44, no. 1, pp. 149–64

Waugh, Evelyn, *The Loved One: An Anglo-American Tragedy* (London: Penguin Modern Classics, 2000)

Whelan, Gerard with Carolyn Swift, *Spiked: Church-State Intrigue and The Rose Tattoo* (Dublin: New Island, 2002)

White, Harry, *The Keeper's Recital: Music and Cultural History in Ireland, 1770–1970* (Cork: Cork University Press in association with Field Day, 1998)

Wiesel, Elie, *Dawn* (New York: Fontana Books, 1973)

—— 'An Interview Unlike any Other' in *A Jew Today* (New York: Random House, 1978), pp. 21–2

—— *Night*, trans. Marion Wiesel, Foreword by François Mauriac (New York: Hill & Wang, 2006)

Wiggins David K. and Patrick B. Miller, *The Unlevel Playing Field: A Documentary History of the African American Experience in Sport* (Chicago: University of Illinois Press, 2003)

Wilde, Oscar, *The Annotated Oscar Wilde*, ed. H. Montgomery Hyde (London: Orbis, 1982)

Williams, Raymond, *Culture and Society: 1780–1950* (New York: Anchor, 1960)

Wills, Clair, *That Neutral Island: A Cultural History of Ireland During the Second World War* (London: Faber & Faber, 2007)

Woolf, Virginia, *Orlando*, ed. Maria DiBattista (New York: Harcourt, 2006)

Yeats, W.B., *Essays and Introductions* (London: Macmillan, 1961)

—— *The Collected Works of W.B. Yeats, Vol. I: The Poems*, ed. Richard J. Finneran (New York: Scribner, 1997)

Zatlin, Phyllis, *Theatrical Translation and Film Adaptation: A practitioner's approach* (Cleveton, Buffalo and Toronto: Multilingual Matters, 2005)

Žižek, Slavoj, *Mapping Ideology* (London: Verso, 1994)

Archival Sources

Brendan Behan Papers, Manuscripts Division, Department of Rare Books and Special Collections, Princeton University Library

Exeter University Special Collections

Pike Theatre Archive

The Trinity College Dublin Manuscripts and Archives Research Library

The Morris Library at Southern Illinois University

National Archives, Kew

National Library of Ireland

Proscenium Press Archives, University of Delaware Library

RTÉ Archives

INDEX